Design Innovations in Electric and Hybrid Electric Vehicles

SP-1089

GLOBAL MOBILITY DATABASE

All SAE papers, standards, and selected books are abstracted and indexed in the Global Mobility Database.

Published by:
Society of Automotive Engineers, Inc.
400 Commonwealth Drive
Warrendale, PA 15096-0001
USA
Phone: (412) 776-4841
Fax: (412) 776-5760
February 1995

ISBN 1-56091-639-7
SAE/SP-95/1089
Library of Congress Catalog Card Number: 94-74742
Copyright 1995 Society of Automotive Engineers, Inc.

Persons wishing to submit papers to be considered for presentation or publication through SAE should send the manuscript or a 300 word abstract of a proposed manuscript to: Secretary, Engineering Meetings Board, SAE.

Printed in USA

PREFACE

The papers in this SAE special publication, <u>Design Innovations in Electric and Hybrid Electric Vehicles</u> (SP-1089), cover technology for both electric and hybrid electric vehicles. As is well accepted, to have a good hybrid electric vehicle requires first having a good electric vehicle. Major manufacturers have initiated the effort required to take electric vehicle technology from the laboratory through the required development steps to provide an automotive product. This work will provide a foundation for the development of hybrid electric vehicles.

Unique engines, unique operating strategies and unique packaging solutions will all be the hallmark of successful hybrid electric vehicles. Over the past several years, the hybrid-electric vehicle concept has been gaining attention as a possible way to reduce emissions and increase fuel efficiency compared to a conventional vehicle. Hybrid-electric vehicles contain a hybrid power supply system - one that incorporates a minimum of two independent power sources to supply the drivetrain. The main advantage of this concept is it permits flexibility in power system design and power distribution between sources. This versatility enables greater flexibility in designing the powertrain to meet the required performance of the vehicle. The challenge is to combine the different power sources such that the advantages outweigh the increased cost of this configuration. These papers cover some of the latest technical developments related to the engine aspect of hybrid-electric vehicle development. Topics included in this year's session are: development of hybrid-electric vehicle design code; optimization of vehicle and engine control strategies; and novel engines for hybrid-electric vehicles.

Also critical to the automotive products of the future is the engineering talent required to produce the innovative designs. One of the programs aimed at exciting students to the new automotive opportunities is the HEV Challenge. This program is well represented by papers in this book. Experience has shown that the HEV Challenge is not only motivating students, but also surfacing innovative automotive engineering solutions to difficult problems. We are pleased to be able to share some of this excitement through this publication.

All of these subjects and the design methodologies required to achieve them, are covered by papers in this collection. We hope that this year's papers will trigger your imagination and provide the foundation for innovative developments that will help electric and hybrid electric vehicles play an important role in our transportation system.

Bradford Bates
Ford Motor Co.
Chairman, Electric Vehicle Committee

Frank Stodolsky
Argonne National Laboratory

Session Organizers

TABLE OF CONTENTS

950176

Technical Analysis of the 1994 HEV Challenge

**Nicole M. LeBlanc, Michael Duoba, Spencer Quong,
Robert P. Larsen, and Marvin Stithim**
Argonne National Lab.

William Rimkus
Ford Motor Co.

ABSTRACT

The 1994 Hybrid Electric Vehicle Challenge provided the backdrop for collecting data and developing testing procedures for hybrid electric vehicle technology available at colleges and universities across North America. The data collected at the competition was analyzed using the HEV definitions from the draft SAE J1711 guidelines. The energy economy, percentage of electrical to total energy used, and acceleration performance was analyzed for any correlation between the over-the-road data and the commuter-sustaining, commuter-depleting, and reserve-sustaining hybrid vehicles.

The analysis did not provide any direct correlation between over-the-road data and the three hybrid types. The analysis did show that the vehicle configurations provide the best information on vehicle performance. It was also clear that a comprehensive data analysis system along with a well-defined testing procedure would allow for a more complete analysis of the data.

INTRODUCTION

The 1994 Hybrid Electric Vehicle (HEV) Challenge involved 36 universities and colleges. The intent of the Challenge was to have teams design and build hybrid electric vehicles with performance targets similar to that of today's vehicles, while meeting stringent safety requirements. These vehicles provided data on current hybrid electric vehicle technology and were not considered as near-term production vehicles. These vehicles were quite complex and varied in design. This large number of complex vehicles made the analysis of the data difficult.

The HEV Challenge tested these vehicles for acceleration, range, emissions, and energy economy. The HEV Challenge consisted of three distinct classes of vehicles: Escort Conversion Class, Ground-Up Class, and Saturn Conversion Class. Except for the Saturn Conversion Class, there was no limitation on the type of hybrid electric vehicle a team could design. While the

vehicles competed in these three distinct classes, this paper focuses on classifying the hybrids on the basis of performance data and the intent of the vehicle design.

BACKGROUND

The hybrid electric vehicles in the 1994 HEV Challenge consisted of one of three types of hybrids (termed commuter-sustaining, commuter-depleting, and reserve-sustaining). The vehicle control strategies were to be passive, and the battery minimum range was specified for certain vehicle classes. A hybrid electric vehicle type refers to the intent of the vehicle control strategy and the intent of the vehicle design. The vehicle could be an urban vehicle which incorporates an internal combustion engine (ICE) for extended range or high load situations. Another role for a hybrid electric vehicle may require that it operates as an all-purpose vehicle, not limited to designated driving cycles.

The students were required to define use of their HEV. Because the vehicles differed in design and purpose, analyzing the data became difficult. The industry has only recently begun developing formal performance characteristics and design specifications for a hybrid electric vehicle. The Society of Automotive Engineers established a task force to develop a recommended practice for uniform testing of HEVs. This draft procedure is called the *Recommended Practice for Measuring the Electric Energy Consumption, All Electric Range, Fuel Economy, and Exhaust Emissions of Hybrid Electric Vehicles -- SAE J1711* [1]. The structure of this paper follows these guidelines for defining hybrid vehicles.

The basic philosophy of the draft HEV procedure focused on "defining hybrids via the vehicle driving mission (available combination of driving modes) and not concentrating on the vehicle design" (Task Force Draft Minutes 1/24/93[2]). The HEVs involved in the Challenge have not been defined through these test procedure, but by the vehicle driving mission, using the vehicle specifications.

The data analyzed was collected during the Range Event, Emissions Event, and Acceleration Event. The Range Event was limited to 3 hours, and 20 minutes over a 3.54km loop. Vehicles traveled in HEV mode and, because of extreme weather conditions, the teams made stops every 30 minutes for a driver change. Speeds were limited to a top instantaneous speed of 88 km/h and a minimum of 64 km/h with an average of 72 km/h. The terrain consisted of straight-aways and hills with grades close to 8.22% over 4.6m. The amount of liquid fuel, electrical fuel, and distance covered was collected to analyze the energy economy of these vehicles.

The Emission Event for the Ground-Up and Escort Conversion Class consisted of a modified Federal Test Procedure (FTP). Four pollutants, total hydrocarbons (THC), non-methane hydrocarbons (NMHC), carbon monoxide (CO), and nitrogen oxides (NOx), were tested. The vehicles began the test completely charged. The vehicles ran phases 1 and 2 of the FTP (one Urban Driving Schedule (UDS)) in the zero emissions vehicle (ZEV) mode and a typical FTP in HEV mode. The portion of the ZEV emissions test provided the data for state of charge (SOC) adjustments to the hybrid gram per mile values. The vehicles had to attain simultaneous control of all four pollutants to score in this event. Using the results from the HEV Challenge Emissions Event, the hybrids that successfully completed the test could be labeled using the SAE draft guidelines.

The Acceleration Event was held over a 201m straight-away. Vehicles started from rest and accelerated over the complete distance for the fastest times. The Ground-Up and Escort Conversion Class had to run in both ZEV and HEV modes to be eligible for the total points. The Saturn Conversion class ran only in HEV mode.

RESULTS

COMMUTING ELECTRIC RANGE, CHARGE - DEPLETING (CD) HEVS - These HEVs contain a usable all-electric range that is greater than twice the UDS measured from a 100% SOC and at least two Highway Fuel Economy Test (HWFET) cycles. This is the definition for the commuting, all-electric range. The vehicle is considered to have a battery-depleting hybrid mode if the electrical energy originally supplied from an off-board charger is depleted during the same time that the consumable fuel on-board is used [1].

Generally, the vehicle design incorporated an electric motor configuration with a large battery capacity (for a greater electric vehicle (EV) range) combined with a smaller kW powered engine. The vehicles consisted of both parallel or series configuration.

There were three vehicles that tested as CD hybrids from the emissions tests. These vehicles included the ones from Califonia State Polytechnic University, Pomona, University of Tulsa, and University of Alberta. The

remaining HEVs categorized as CDs had control strategies that were battery depleting. Information provided in the team technical reports was used to classify these vehicles. Where information on the control strategy was missing, the description of the intent of the design of the vehicle was used to classify the vehicles. Teams described their vehicle as a CD or described the use of the vehicle for urban commuting with the internal combustion engine (ICE) available for supplemental power for additional range. The vehicle would be used primarily as an EV for urban commuting, but would utilize the ICE for high-power situations or extended range with no battery state of charge sustaining capabilities.

COMMUTING ELECTRIC RANGE, CHARGE-SUSTAINING (CS) HEVS - This HEV contains usable all-electric range requirements of a CD but has a battery-sustaining hybrid mode. Battery-sustaining means these vehicles are able to drive continuous UDS cycles without a net drop in SOC and they are able to drive continuous HWFET cycles without a net drop in SOC [1].

CS hybrids consist of parallel or series configurations. The range performance of the CS hybrid in HEV mode is limited to the amount of liquid fuel available for the ICE.

Three vehicles that successfully completed the emissions testing for the HEV Challenge tested as CS hybrids. These vehicles are from the University of California, Davis, University of Illinois - Urbana, and West Virginia University. The University of Illinois stated in their technical report that their vehicle was designed as a range-extender but they are categorized in this paper as a CS hybrid on the basis of their performance data [3]. Based on the descriptions of the control strategies and hybrid modes, the remaining teams were categorized as CS hybrids.

RESERVE ELECTRIC RANGE, CHARGE-SUSTAINING (RS) HEVS - These HEVs have little or no all-electric range, but are able to drive continuous UDS cycles without a net drop in SOC, and they are able to drive continuous HWFET cycles without a net drop in SOC. Therefore, they are considered battery-sustaining hybrids [1].

The RS hybrid has a minimal electric-only range and operates in a hybrid mode at all times. The strategy of this type of hybrid uses the auxiliary power unit to provide additional power at high-load situations. There was not enough data available from emissions tests that could be used to categorize the Saturn Class hybrids as was done for the Ground-Up and Escort Classes.

The Saturn Conversion Class was structured to have the teams design a power assist hybrid. Analysis of the Saturn Class is based on the assumption that all of these vehicles were designed as RS hybrids.

TECHNOLOGY OVERVIEW - The component selection of the teams ranged from lead-acid batteries to nickel metal hydrides; dc series motors to ac induction motors; and a 570cc Briggs & Stratton engines to Geo 1.0L engines. There was no difference in the component selection due to the type of hybrid vehicle or due to the vehicle configuration (series and parallel).

The size of the electric motor (EM), the ICE, and the total battery energy available are graphed for each type of hybrid (Charts 1 & 2). The CD and CS hybrids were comparable in total battery energy ranges and sizing of the EM and ICE. Each type of hybrid is further broken down in these charts by the parallel configuration and the series configuration. The series configurations for both hybrid types have total battery energy available averaging 11.5kWh (CS) and 13.6kWh (CD) compared to 11.6kWh (CS) and 12.6kWh (CD) for the parallel configurations. The power selection of the electric motor did not vary from the CD to CS hybrids. The power selection range of the

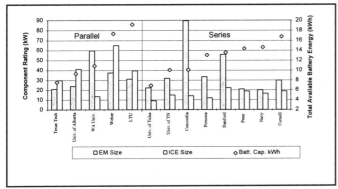

CHART 1. Breakdown of Component Power and Total Available Battery Energy for Commuter-Depleting Hybrids.

EM in the RS hybrids was smaller, ranging from 13.0kW to 53.7kW compared to 8.9kW to 89.5kW for CD and CS hybrids.

Chart 3 shows the component selection for the RS hybrids. The RS hybrids had a smaller total battery energy, as expected for this hybrid type, averaging 5.0 kWh. The ICE power selection was 18% higher for the RS hybrid

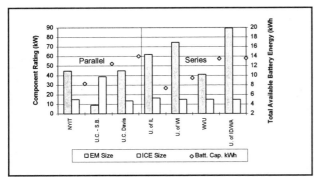

CHART 2. Breakdown of Component Power and Total Available Battery Energy for Commuter-Sustaining Hybrids.

than for the CS and 41% higher than for CD hybrids (averages 18.9kW and 26.1kW, respectively). The lowest ICE power (31.9kW) selection was found in the University of Tulsa's vehicle, a series configuration CD hybrid (9.10kW).

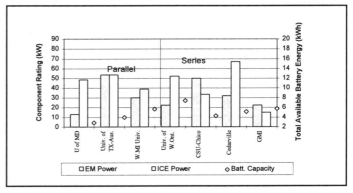

CHART 3. Component Power Rating and Total Available Battery Energy for Reserve-Sustaining Hybrids.

The majority of the control strategies of these vehicles used feedback from the battery pack's SOC to determine the ICE operation schedule. Other systems were manually controlled, on the basis of the power requirements for the current driving conditions. The summaries of a few of the vehicles presented are simplified descriptions the control strategies.

Cal. Poly-Pomona stated that the design of their vehicle emphasized the ZEV operation. There were control switches for ZEV and HEV modes as required from the rules of the HEV Challenge. This series configuration controlled the power output of the ICE to equal the amount of energy used to drive the vehicle. The battery voltage was monitored for any drops below 110 V. There was some on-board charging that was self-regulating [4]. Another series configuration CD hybrid regulated the ICE differently. Stanford operated the ICE at a constant speed. The ICE operated at a constant load while the alternator regulated the power output of the engine. In the team's paper, the control strategy ideally would monitor the battery state of charge (volts and amps), along with the battery temperature and fuel level [5]. Texas Tech a parallel configuration CD hybrid, monitored the ICE operation for constant revolutions per minute (RPM) and torque. The controller matched the output of the electric motor to the ICE drive shaft [6].

The CS hybrids showed up with similar systems. The University of Wisconsin a series CS hybrid, used the battery state of charge as the determining factor in the start-up of their ICE. The power from the ICE was delivered to the batteries, which is a similar setup to Cal. Poly-Pomona [7]. West Virginia's strategy varied slightly from the other series hybrids. The controller of the ICE sent power to the system controller, where the power was distributed to the motor and batteries. The SOC of the battery pack was still monitored to determine the allocation of the power from the

ICE. The ICE output was kept constant [8]--a slightly different twist to the strategy.

University of California, Davis had a parallel, CS hybrid. Unique to this vehicle was the component selection for a parallel configuration. Instead of utilizing the ICE as the primary power source, the electric motor provided the motive power. Similar to a CD series design, the EM provided power for city driving, while the ICE took over at highway speeds. The control strategy involved monitoring the battery pack's SOC to determine remaining range. The EM started the ICE for high-speed starts. The fuel management system disabled the electronic fuel injection until the ICE reached the proper speed. Under high discharge conditions, the ICE provided the cruising power, while the electric motor assisted in high load situations [9].

The University of Maryland, a parallel, RS hybrid had one of the most complicated control systems of these vehicles. The control strategy used inputs from the battery state of charge and the accelerator pedal position, to control the load level of the ICE, which is assisted from the EM. This scheme would operate the ICE at its more efficient range. The second stage of the strategy required the controller to monitor the manifold air pressure to adjust for the necessary power requirements to optimize fuel economy [10].

ENERGY ECONOMY RESULTS - The HEVs from the 1994 HEV Challenge were sorted into the hybrid classes on the basis of the emissions testing performed at the competition and the description of the control strategies in the technical papers. While only seven vehicles had enough complete data to break down into hybrid types, the majority of the vehicles did have data collected from performance events at the competition. These seven vehicles completed the emissions test cycle (FTP) in ZEV and HEV or ICE-on modes. The energy consumption for each vehicle was graphed (see Chart 4) to show the comparison of electrical energy used in the ZEV and HEV modes (or ICE-on mode). The ICE-on mode forced the ICE to be

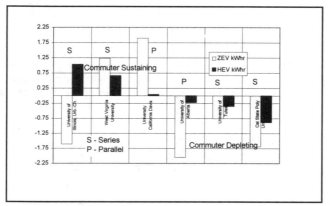

CHART 4. Break down of CD and CS hybrids on the basis of the HEV Challenge Emission Results.

operational. If the vehicle completed the HEV test without depleting the SOC of the battery, then the vehicle was assumed to be a CS hybrid.

The comparison of the HEV electrical to the total HEV energy was made from over-the-road data collected during the Range Event and the Emissions Event. These two events did not use the same cycle. Converting to kilowatt-hours, the percentage of electrical to total energy was calculated for the University of Alberta, West Virginia University, Cal Poly.-Pomona, University of California, Davis, and University of Tulsa. By comparing the amount of electrical energy to the total energy in the hybrid mode, some correlation between the results of the emissions testing and the Range Event can be seen (see Chart 5). The results from the Range Event followed the trend in the Emissions results. It must be pointed out that this analysis

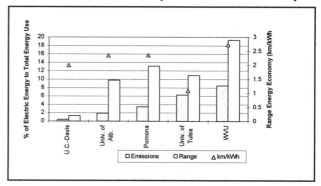

CHART 5. Comparison of the Percentage of Electrical to Total Energy Used in the Hybrid Mode for the Emissions and Range Events.

did not take into account the strategy of the ICE. University of California, Davis used the lowest percentage of electrical energy in both instances, whereas West Virginia University used the largest percentage electrical energy. University of California, Davis was the only one of these vehicles that used the ICE without any input from the EM during their emissions test. Their vehicle would have been battery-depleting if both power sources were invoked.

The percentage of electrical energy increased for vehicles in the Range Event compared to the results from the dynamometer rolls. This increase is due primarily to the variation in the track and change of drivers during the Range Event.

From the Emissions Event, University of California, Davis had the lowest percentage of electrical energy, 0.2%, following a battery-sustaining hybrid strategy. West Virginia University, also a CS hybrid as defined from the Emissions Event, was at the other end of the spectrum, using close to 8.6% of the total energy for electrical power. The management of the energy consumption by the control strategy cannot be determined through this analysis. Analysis of the second-by-second data and a larger data sampling would help support this analysis. Preliminary analysis of these control strategies suggest that they are still in their infancy and require further refinement.

The remaining hybrid vehicles were categorized based on the description of the control strategy stated in the technical papers. Without the battery depletion information from the state of charge, no direct comparison could be made using the guidelines from the draft SAE HEV Emissions Test Procedure. This information is critical to the analysis of the road data and analyzing the effectiveness of the vehicle's hybrid strategy.

The road data collected from the Range Event was used to compare energy economy of the three hybrid types. Chart 6 shows the energy economy (km/kWh) for each vehicle which was categorized as a CD, CS, or RS hybrid. Though there is not a large difference between these vehicles in the lower economy ranges, CS hybrids show a tendency to have slightly higher economies than the other categories. The average energy economy for the CD hybrids was 2.23km/kWh compared to 1.83 and 1.48km/kWh for the CS and RS, respectively. The reserve-sustaining group had the poorest performance of the three. This class, new in 1994, had the least amount of time to optimize their vehicles which would also account for lower energy economy results.

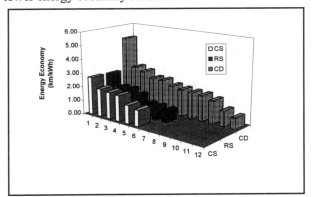

CHART 6. Energy Economy Results for the CS, CD and RS Hybrids.

Breaking down the comparison between the series and parallel configurations, the parallel vehicles demonstrated greater energy economy values (see Chart 7). This correlation supports the higher fuel economy for the CS hybrids, since the majority of the CS hybrids were of parallel configurations.

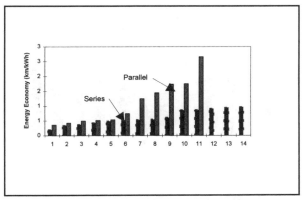

CHART 7. Range Event Energy Economy of All Vehicles by Hybrid Configuration.

ACCELERATION PERFORMANCE RESULTS-The Acceleration Event consisted of a 201m straight-away. The Escort Conversion and Ground-Up Classes were required to make a minimum of two runs, one in HEV mode and the other in ZEV mode. Runs in both modes were required since these classes had to have a minimum 40.2km range in electric-only mode. The Saturn Conversion Class ran only in HEV mode. Only the acceleration runs made in the HEV mode were examined for all vehicles.

To see if there were any performance differences in the acceleration of the hybrid type, a comparison was made of the combined available power for both the CS and CD and the acceleration times. The power ratings for the EM and the ICE were combined for the parallel configurations (see Chart 8), while the series configurations (see Chart 9) showed the power ratings side by side. Parallel hybrids had faster times for the 201m run. Weber State, a CD, split-parallel hybrid, had the fastest time at 12.44 seconds. This vehicle incorporated a 1.0 L Geo engine combined with an Advanced DC series motor (37.3 kW). The slowest time was recorded at 22.63 seconds for the University of Tulsa. This vehicle was a CD series hybrid. The University of Tulsa's hybrid was under-powered, using a 22.39kW Baldor Electric AC Induction motor and a 9.10kW, 359cc Honda engine.

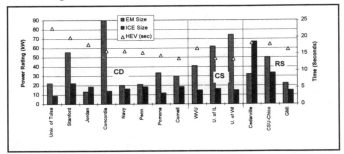

CHART 8. Acceleration Times for CD, CS, and RS Series Configuration Hybrids.

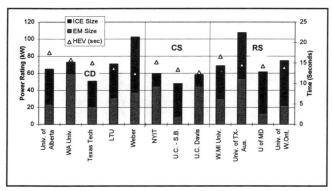

CHART 9. Acceleration Times for CD, CS, and RS Parallel Configuration Hybrids.

While the acceleration times are distributed over a larger range, there does not appear to be any distinct difference in the times for the CS, CD, and RS hybrids. Those vehicles incorporating a large EM had faster acceleration times for the CS and CD hybrids.

DISCUSSION OF RESULTS

The analysis compared energy economy, percent of electrical-to-total energy, and vehicle acceleration for the three hybrid types. By breaking down each hybrid type into the two configurations for hybrids, a comparison was made to try to better understand the vehicles and their control strategy with available performance data.

The CD hybrids demonstrated slightly higher energy economies than the CS and RS hybrids. These hybrids may have fewer losses as a result of the control strategy. There is no need to redirect the power of the ICE to maintain the SOC of the battery pack. Both the RS and CS must continuously provide energy to the battery pack to remain battery-sustaining. There are more losses associated with a system where the energy from the ICE charges the battery pack, which in turn provides energy to the EM to power the vehicle compared to systems that direct energy to power the vehicle. The RS showed the lowest energy economy results. The RS hybrid's strategy utilized the ICE throughout operation of the vehicle to maintain the battery SOC, which would account for some of the lower energy economy results. Another impact on the energy economy was the amount of time available to the students to optimize their design and thoroughly test their vehicles. This class was newest to the 1994 HEV Challenge.

The breakdown of the electrical energy to total energy used in both the Emissions test and the Range Event did not provide any new information on hybrid types. It was apparent from Chart 5 that a larger percentage of the electrical energy is used on the road versus on the dynamometer rolls. This discrepancy between the energy consumption results from the variation of the road and drivers in the Range Event. The configuration of the vehicles is still the dominant factor in the allocation of

energy and performance of the vehicle. In Chart 10, the number of vehicles in each hybrid type did not show any trends in the amount of electrical energy used compared to the total energy. The CS hybrids stayed within the lower end (less than 20%) of the amount of energy used.

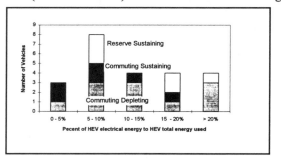

CHART 10. Breakdown of CD, CS, and RS Hybrids by Percentage of Electrical Energy to Total Energy Used in HEV Mode.

The control strategies of these vehicles require the systems to maintain a constant SOC on the battery pack, so the total electrical energy used should be small. The CD hybrids ranged from the very low to an excessive amount of electrical energy used. This scattering of results indicates the system configuration of the CD hybrid was the primary indicator of the amount of electrical energy used. The RS hybrids did not fall into any one percentile range.

A final analysis centered on the acceleration performance characteristics of the hybrids. Further breakdown of the vehicles by system configuration provided more information on the vehicles. The parallel configurations in all three hybrid types had consistent acceleration times. The parallel configurations had slightly faster acceleration times than the series vehicles. Since the power of both the ICE and the EM go to the wheels instead of one system powering the other, the parallel systems had lower acceleration times. The combined power of the EM and ICE ranged between 32kW and 107kW, as seen consistently throughout each parallel, hybrid type. The variation of the power ratings for the EM and ICE does not seem to have any impact on the acceleration times for the parallel configurations.

The differences between the hybrid types in the series configuration is more apparent. Throughout the series configurations, the size of the EM is significantly higher than the ICE (as much as 6 times larger). This is especially the case with the CS hybrids, where their overall acceleration performance is faster. The CD hybrids also have larger EMs than ICEs, but the difference is not nearly as large (factor of 2.8). The slowest series configurations are the RS hybrids.

CONCLUSIONS

The 1994 HEV Challenge had three distinct hybrid electric vehicle types participate. The raw data presented in this paper provides a general overview of the vehicles at the competition. The Commuter-Sustaining hybrid vehicles had slightly lower energy economy, higher usage of electrical energy, and slightly faster accelerations then the Commuter-Depleting or the Reserve-Sustaining hybrids. The Reserve-Sustaining hybrids were the weakest performers in all areas, but this is most likely due to the short amount of time teams had to fully develop their vehicles. The second year vehicles, both CD and CS hybrids, were more reliable and demonstrated better overall performance. The raw data presented shows a large range of vehicle design, systems integration and performance from the HEV Challenge. These vehicles were hand-built with technology currently available and affordable. The control strategies of these vehicles show promise, but they require further development.

The raw data and the vehicle descriptions provided by the teams were useful in breaking down the vehicles based on the SAE J1711 guidelines, but they were not sufficient. The HEV Challenge provided the testing ground for collecting data on a multitude of hybrid electric vehicle technology. What is apparent is that these vehicles are complex and the method of collecting data and testing these vehicles is just as complex. Each year this process is modified and further refined. The 1995 HEV Challenge will provide another opportunity to test these vehicles and collect more comprehensive data on the most successful hybrid designs in energy economy, performance and reliability.

ACKNOWLEDGEMENT
This paper was made possible through the support of the U.S. Department of Energy, Assistant Secretary for Energy Efficiency and Renewable Energy, under contract W-31-109-ENG-380.

REFERENCES
1. SAE HEV Task Force, *Recommended Practice for Measuring the Electric Energy Consumption, All Electric Range, Fuel Economy, and Exhaust Emissions of Hybrid Electric Vehicles -- SAE J1711*. Draft SAE J1711, Detroit, MI, Version September 16, 1994.

2. SAE HEV Test Procedure Task Force, "Notes form 1/24/94 meeting of the SAE HEV task force," Detroit, MI, January 1994.

3. Timothy Roethemeyer, Brandon Masterson, Marc Stiler, and the UIUC HEV Team, "University of Illinois Hybrid Electric Vehicle: An Electric Vehicle for Today," Urbana-Champaign, IL, May 1994.

4. Augenstein, Team APEX, "California State Polytechnic University, Pomona," Pomona, CA, May 1994.

5. Shawn Sarbacker, Bailey White, Joel Miller and Phillip Chen, "Leland Stanford Junior University 'The Winds of Freedom II'," Stanford, CA, May 1994.

6. Jeffrey Bratcher, Brent Crittenden, Jeff Earhart, Shawna Salyer, Roy Sanchez, Robert Tolentino, Schott Wilkes, Davie Brenner, Boyd Burnett, Ookyong Kim, Dale May, Casey Osborne, Gary Romero, Roland Shafner, "Texas Tech University Hybrid Electric Vehicle Challenge Final Report," Lubbock, TX, May 1994.

7. Patrick Barber, David Bell, Richard Bonomo, Scott Costelllo, Barton Heldke, Nathan Hendon, Clark Hochgraf, Robert Rossi, C. Thomas Wiesen, "The University of Wisconsin - Madison Paradigm Hybrid Electric Vehicle," Madison, WI, May 1994.

8. Wayne Taylor, Chris Atkinson, "The Design and Development of an Efficient Series Hybrid Electric Vehicle at West Virginia University," Morgantown, WV, November 1994.

9. Marten Byl, Paul Cassanego, Gregory Eng, Troy Herndon, Keith Kruetzfeldt, Gregory Reimers, and Dr. Andrew Frank, "Hybrid Elecetirc Vehicle Development at the University of California, Davis: The Design of AfterShock," Davis, DA, May 1994.

10. Jordan Wilkerson, Fred Householder, Mark Caggiano, Dr. David Holloway, "The University of Maryland at College Park Methanol Hybrid Electric Vehicle," College Park, MD, May 1994.

APPENDIX

Table 1. Vehicles listed by hybrid type with EM and ICE size and hybrid configuration.

School	EM Power (kW)	ICE Power (kW)	Hybrid Config.
Commuter-Depleting			
Cal Poly-San Luis Obispo	18	36.5	Parallel
CO School of Mines	32	16.4	Series
Concordia University	89.5	14.2	Series/parallel
Cornell University	29.8	18.6	Series
Jordan College	n/a	18.6	Series/parallel
Lawrence Tech. Univ.	31.3	39.5	Parallel
Michigan State Univ.	38.5	63.4	Series
Penn State	21	18.6	Series
Stanford University	55.9	22.4	Series
Texas Tech	21	29.8	Parallel
U.S. Naval Academy	20.1	16.4	Series
University of Alberta	23.8	41	Parallel
University of Tennessee	32	14.8	Series
University of Tulsa	22.4	9.1	Series
Washington Univ.	59.7	13.4	Parallel
Weber State Univ.	37.5	65	Parallel
Commuter-Sustaining			
NYIT	44.7	14.9	Parallel
Univ. of Cal. Davis	45	13.4	Parallel
Univ. of Cal. - SB	8.9	38.8	Parallel
Univ of ID/WA State	89.5	14.8	Series
University of Illinois	62	16.4	Series
University of WI	74.6	14.9	Series
West Virginia Univ.	36.1	41	Series
Reserve-Sustaining			
Cal. State Univ.-Chico	50	33.6	Series
Cedarville	32	67.2	Series
GMI	22.4	14.9	Series
Univ. of Maryland	13	48.5	Parallel
Univ. of Texas-Austin	53.7	53.7	Parallel
Univ. of W. Ontario	22.4	52.2	Parallel
West. Michigan	30	38.8	Parallel

Table 2. Ground Up Class Vehicle Data

Field	Cornell University	CSPTU, Pomona	Lawrence Tech.	Michigan State University	New York Inst. Tech.	University of Texas, Arlington	UC Santa Barbara	USPSU, San Luis Obispo	Univ. of Idaho/ Washington State	University of California, Davis	University of Tennessee	University of Tulsa
VEHICLE INFO												
CAR_NUMBER	16	37	5	19	15	32	39	25	27	40	21	20
HYBRID_CONFIGURATION	Series	Series	Parallel	Series	Parallel	Parallel	Parallel	Parallel	Series	Parallel	Series	Series
VEHICLE_WEIGHT (kg)	1221.1	1116.3	1623.4	1490.9	1229.7	1091	1237.4	1261.4	1832.1	1198.4	1216.5	1625.22
CHARGING_EFFICIENCY	0.87	0.79	0.44	0.75	0.75	0.75	0.79	0.68	0.85	0.82	0.76	0.73
ENGINE_MANUFACTURER	Kohler	Briggs & Straton	Geo	Suzuki	Kawasaki	Honda	Geo	GEO	Kohler	Briggs & Straton	Kohler	Honda
ENGINE_SIZE (cc)	725	480	1000	1000	617	600	1000	993	622	570	624	359
ENGINE_POWER (kW)	18.6	12	39.5	63.4	15	74.5	38.8	36.5	15	13.4	15	9.1
FUEL_TYPE	M85	R GAS	R GAS	M85	R GAS	M85	E100	R GAS	R GAS	R GAS	R GAS	R GAS
TANK_CAPACITY (l)	42.4	38	37.8	28	x	37.8	30.3	11	56.8	34	30.3	30
MOTOR_MANUFACTURER	Unique Mob/Adv. DC	Advanced DC	Unique Mobility	GE / LEM	Advanced DC	Solectria	Solectria	Solectria	AC Propulsions	Unique Mobility	Unique Mobility	Baldor Electric
MOTOR_TYPE	Brushless DC	DC Brush	18 pole PM DC	AC induction	DC	3phase Brushless DC	AC induction	AC induction	AC induction	DC	DC	AC induction
MOTOR_POWER (kW)	30	33.5	31.3	38.5	44.7	22.4	9	18	89.5	45	32	
BATTERY_TYPE	Pb-acid	Pb-acid	Pb-acid	NiMH	Pb-acid	Ni-Cad	Pb-acid	Pb-acid	Pb-Acid	Ni-Cad	Pb-Acid	Pb-Acid
VOLTAGE	168	120	192	340	96	170	144	120	336	156	180	348
BATTERY_CAPACITY (kWh)	16.8	13.12	19.2	11.56	8.31	6.8	12.47	12.79	13.61	14.04	10.08	6.96
GENERATOR	Fisher	Fisher Elec.	x	Fisher Elec.	Unique Mobility	x	x	x	Fisher Elec.	x	Leece-Neville	Honda
EMISSIONS — ZEV												
DISTANCE (km)	11.23	12	0	10.66	0	0	0	0	10.49	12.08	7.76	6.32
AMP-HOURS	-8.12	-15.02	0	0	-17.34	0	0	0	-6	0	0	-3
kWh	-1.34	-1.69	0	0	-1.73	0	0	0	-1.53	0	0	-0.76
km/kWh	-8.38	-7.1	0	0	0	0	0	0	-6.86	0	0	-8.32
EMISSIONS — HEV												
DISTANCE (km)	16.56	17.8	0	17.17	13.95	0	17.49	0	17.64	16.77	0	6.8
AMP-HOURS	0	-7.85	0	0	0	0	0	0	0	0.35	0	-1
kWh	0	-0.88	0	0	0	0	0	0	0	0.04	0	-0.35
km/kWh		-20.23	0	0	0	0	0	0	0	419.25	0	-19.43
FTP g/m												
HC	0.305	0.877	0	0.177	1.016	0	0.578	0	0.334	0.208	0	1.647
NMHC	0.775	0.775	0	0.142	0.855	0	0.182	0	0.24	0.182	0	1.549
CO	18.06	13.82	0	0.2	48.58	0	26.07	0	28.37	2.47	0	28.1
NOX	0.02	0.06	0	13.33	0.03	0	0.58	0	0.05	0.34	0	0.03
CORRECTED g/m												
HC	0	0.427	0	0.177	0	0	0	0	0.334	0.204	0	1.313
NMHC	0	0.378	0	0.142	0	0	0	0	0.24	0.178	0	1.235
CO	0	6.734	0	0.2	0	0	0	0	28.37	2.417	0	22.4
NOX	0	0.029	0	13.33	0	0	0	0	0.05	0.333	0	0.024
ENERGY ECONOMY — ACCELERATION												
EQ_GAL (kWh)	7.08	24.01	13.16	0	25.98	25.32	4.87	0	0	5.92	1.32	30.92
NET_ELEC (kWh)	0	0	1.6	0	0.84		1.15	0	0	0.64	0	0
DISTANCE (km)	9.33	9.33	9.33	10.62	10.62	8.05	9.33	6.76	0	9.33	6.76	9.33
km/kWh	0.73	0.73	0.63	0.73	0.39	0.73	1.54	0.73	0	1.42	0.73	0.73
LOW ZEV TIME	13.71	14.38	17.13	14.92	16.82	22.78	20.03	19.81	0	13.7	14.62	22.98
LOW HEV TIME	13.6	14.5	13.7	14.86	15.22	15.8	13.39	0	0	12.71	0	22.63
RANGE												
EQ_GAL (kWh)	22.53	67.75	86.5	65.73	115.77		98.88	0	101.96	53.61	4.05	22.04
NET_ELEC (kWh)	14.42	1.26	16.61	0	8.55		1.56	0	14.55	0.72		2.69
DISTANCE (km)	109.9	184.7	195	191.6	167.64		195	3.43	136.85	109.5	17.1	27.37
km/kWh	2.98	2.68	1.89	1.67	1.35		1.94	1.67	1.17	2	1.67	1.1
ELAPSED TIME	3:21:16	3:26:44	3:24:19	3:23:11	3:26:24	DNS	3:25:05	0:07:58	2:52:41	3:25:56	0:25:05	0:47:22
RALLY												
EQ_GAL (kWh)	0	64.46	64.46	0	0	0	70.78	0	35.19	14.8	0	25
NET_ELEC (kWh)	0	6.74	0	0	0	0	6.29	0	0	8.51	0	1.32
DISTANCE (km)	0	134.86	134.86	0	0	0	134.86	0	8.05	134.86	0	20.63
km/kWh	0	1.89	1.56	0	0	0	1.75	0	1.56	5.75	0	0.78
ZEV Information (km/kWh)	7.42	11.71	7.07	x	x	x	7.73	x	4.87	12.51	9.60	x

9

Table 4. Saturn Conversion Class Vehicle Data

SCHOOL	Alfred University	Cedarville College	Ecole de Technologie Superieure	GMI Engineering & Mgmt. Inst.	University of Texas, Austin	California State University, Chico	University of Maryland	University of Western Ontario	Wentworth Institute of Technology	Western Michigan University
VEHICLE INFO										
NUMBER	36	9	3	17	2	18	24	22	26	35
HYBRID_CONFIGURATION	Parallel	Series	Parallel	Series	Parallel	Series	Parallel	Parallel	Series	Parallel
VEHICLE_WEIGHT (kg)	1550	1545.8	1528	1773.5	1406.6	1510.5	1461.5	1538.6	1674.7	1492
CHARGING EFFICIENCY	0	0.22	0.22	0.22	0.22	0.22	0.22	0.22	0.22	0.22
ENGINE_MANUFACTURER	Suzuki	Honda	Subaru	Kawasaki	BMW	BMW	Geo/Suzuki	Honda	Suzuki	Suzuki
ENGINE_SIZE (cc)	750	1500	1189	617	750	750	1000	1300	993	1000
ENGINE_POWER (kW)	93	67	82	15	52.2	34	48.5	52	41	39
FUEL_TYPE	M85	M85	M85	E100	M85	E100	M85	E100	M85	M85
TANK_CAPACITY (l)	37.9	48.5	48.5	56.8	48.5	45	42	50	48.5	60.6
MOTOR_MANUFACTURER	M. Aerospace	Unique Mobility	Baldor	Magnetek	BMW	Unique Mobility	Unique Mobility	Solectria	Solectria	Advanced DC
MOTOR_TYPE	DC Brushless	DC Brushless	DC Brushless	AC	AC	DC Brushless	DC Brushless	DC Brushless	AC	DC Brushless
MOTOR_POWER (kW)	0	32	50	22	54	50	13	22.4	24	30
BATTERY_TYPE	Pb-acid	Pb-Acid	Ni-Cd	Pb-Acid	Pb-Acid	Pb-Acid	Ni-Cd	Pb-Acid	Pb-Acid	Gel Acid
VOLTAGE	120	180	288	288	120	120	153.696	96	144	108
BATTERY_CAPACITY (kWh)	0	5.18	3.74	5.76	4	4.32	2.9	7.46	11.19	5.7
GENERATOR	none	Westinghouse	Baldor	Fisher	Unique Mobility	Bendix	E.M.	Solectria	General Electric	Power Tech Inc.
EMISSIONS FTP g/m										
HC	0	0	0	0.75	0	0	0.31	0	0	0
NMHC	0	0	0	0.56	0	0	0.29	0	0	0
CO	0	0	0	54.2	0	0	2.6	0	0	0
NOx	0	0	0	0.3	0	0	0.68	0	0	0
CORRECTED g/m										
HC	0	0	0	0	0	0	0.31	0	0	0
NMHC	0	0	0	0	0	0	0.29	0	0	0
CO	0	0	0	0	0	0	2.6	0	0	0
NOx	0	0	0	0	0	0	0.68	0	0	0
ENERGY ECONOMY ACCELERATION										
EQ_GAL (kWh)	0	16.76	0	6.64	17.88	25	6.64	122.77	0	13.59
NET_ELEC (kWh)	0	21.18	0	7.425	0.9	2.9	7.42	0.27	0	0
DISTANCE (km)	0	8.05	8.05	8.05	8.05	8.05	8.05	8.05	0	8.05
km/kWh	0	0.21	0.23	0.57	0.43	0.29	0.57	0.07	0	0.59
LOWHEV	0	18.29	12.27	16.37	14.52	17.91	14.24	13.92	0	16.58
RANGE										
EQ_GAL (kWh)	0	124.01	0	6.19	49.16	139.8	41.52	96	0	81.56
NET_ELEC (kWh)	0	6.65	0	5.61	3.53	11.4	5.75	23.35	0	0
DISTANCE (km)	0.00	126.64	198.46	10.27	102.63	143.74	119.75	174.51	0.00	143.74
km/kWh	0	0.97	1.29	0.87	1.95	0.95	2.53	1.46	0	1.76
TIME	x	3:19:54	3:00:31	0:08:20	3:25:49	3:20:00	3:25:24	3:24:48	x	3:25:22
RALLY										
EQ_GAL (kWh)	0	185.27	0	0	77.27	0	75.78	205.05	0	0
NET_ELEC (kWh)	0	10.9	0	0	0.36	0	2.44	0.86	0	0
DISTANCE (km)	0	134.9	0	8.05	24.4	115.5	134.9	134.9	0	0
km/kWh	0	0.69	0	0.59	0.31	0.59	1.72	0.66	0	0
ZEV Information (km/kWh)	x	x	x	34.91	7.84	5.82	14.77	20.76	x	x

Table 3. Escort Conversion Class Vehicle Data.

SCHOOL	Colorado School of Mines	Concordia University	Jordan College	Penn State	Stanford University	Texas Tech.	U.S. Naval Academy	U.C. Irvine	University of Alberta	University of Illinois, Urbana-Ch.	University of Wisconsin	Washington University	Weber State University	West Virginia University
VEHICLE INFO														
CAR NUMBER	4	11	12	1	14	29	31	7	33	8	34	33	3	28
HYBRID_CONFIGURATION	Series	Series	Series/Parallel	Series	Series	Parallel	Series	Parallel	Parallel	Series	Series	Parallel	Parallel	Series
VEHICLE_WEIGHT (kg)	1617.9	1725.5	1728.2	1742.2	1616.1	1649.3	1778.1	1797.6	1641.1	1733.6	1731.8	1705.9	1796.2	1646.1
CHARGING EFFICIENCY	0.82	0.91	0.88	0.68	0.8	0.89	0.81	0.62	0.81	0.68	0.89	0.87	0.83	0.81
ENGINE_MANUFACTURER	Kawasaki	Brig/Strat.	Kohler	Kohler	Honda	Kawasaki	Kawasaki	Geo	Suzuki	Kawasaki	Kohler	Brig/Stat.	Ford	Kawasaki
ENGINE SIZE CC	620	540	725	725	250	650	617	1000	1000	628	624	570	1900	620
ENGINE POWER kW	16.4	14.2	18.6	18.6	22.4	30	16.4	37.3	41	16.4	15	13.4	65	15
FUEL TYPE	E100	R GAS	R GAS	R GAS	R GAS	E100	R GAS	R GAS	R GAS	E100	R GAS	R GAS	R GAS	R GAS
TANK_CAPACITY (l)	63.6	28	45.5	30.3	40	45	45	45.4	38	41.6	38	45.4	45	45
MOTOR_MANUFACTURER	Unique Mobility	Solectria/ Adv. DC	Advanced DC	Solectria	Student designed w/ FMC	Solectria	General Elec.	Electragear	Unique Mobility	Magnetek/Cent	Lincoln Elec.	Advanced DC	Advanced DC	Advanced DC
MOTOR_TYPE	Brushless DC	P. M. Brush	DC Series	AC Induction	AC Induction	AC Induction	Shunt Wound	AC Induction	PM Brushless	AC Induction	3 phase AC	DC Series	DC Series	DC Series
MOTOR POWER (kW)	32	89.5	21	21	55.9	21	20.1	11.2	32	74.5	74.5	59.7	37.5	41
BATTERY_TYPE	Ni-Cad	Pb-Acid	Pb-Acid	Pb-Acid	Ni-Cad	Gel-Cell	Pb-Acid	Pb-Acid	Ni-Cad	Pb-Acid	Pb-Acid	Pb-Acid	Ni-Cad	Pb-Acid
VOLTAGE	180	156	96	144	108	120	120	312	170	312	360	132	96	120
BATTERY_CAPACITY (kWh)	6.71	10.14	11.72	14.4	13.61	7.63	14.65	12.93	9.35	7.39	9.5	10.94	17.37	13.5
GENERATOR	Unique Mobility	Fisher Elec.	x	Unique Mobility	Solectria	x	Fisher Elec.	x	Unique Mobility	Unique Mobility	Fisher Elec.	x	x	Fisher Elec.
EMISSIONS														
ZEV														
DISTANCE (km)	12.02	11.71	11.73	0	0	2.2	11.99	0	11.97	11.7	11.99	11.97	11.3	11.91
AMP-HOURS	-15.23	-21.74	-28.16	0	0	0	0	0	-12.18	-6.24	0	0	0	-20.33
kWh	-2.78	-3.04	-2.4	0	0	0	0	0	-2.05	-1.61	0	0	0	1.24
km/kWh	-4.32	-3.85	-4.88	0	0	0	0	0	-5.85	-7.27	0	0	0	35.87
HEV g/m														
DISTANCE (km)	0	16.67	17.01	0	0	14.15	17.54	0	17.64	17.53	17.88	17.77	17.73	17.75
AMP-HOURS	0	0	0	0	0	0	-11.39	0	-1.29	2.33	0	-27.08	2.64	2.64
kWh	0	0	0	0	0	0	-1.2	0	-0.22	1.03	0	-3.45	0.66	0.66
km/kWh	0	0	0	0	0	0	-14.62	0	-80.18	17.02	0	-5.15	26.89	26.89
FTP g/m														
HC	0	1.022	1.13	0	0	11.65	1.24	0	0.339	3.591	0.977	0.56	0.109	0.05
NMHC	0	0.8871	0.83	0	0	10.533	1.02	0	0.307	2.872	0.785	0.515	0.086	0.046
CO	0	61	66.95	0	0	266.47	67.36	0	1.979	118.85	61.52	9.922	0.998	0.332
NOX	0	1.95	0.15	0	0	0.09	0.02	0	0.645	0.076	1.338	0.014	0.395	2.692
CORRECTED g/m														
HC	0	0	0	0	0	0	0	0	0.366	2.875	0	0	0	0.046
NMHC	0	0	0	0	0	0	0	0	0.331	2.299	0	0	0	0.043
CO	0	0	0	0	0	0	0	0	2.133	95.135	0	0	0	0.305
NOX	0	0	0	0	0	0	0	0	0.695	0.061	0	0	0	2.476
ENERGY ECONOMY														
ACCELERATION														
EQ_GAL (kWh)	9.51	0.99	3.29	2.96	14.14	34.95	13.81	0	15.79	3.32	3.29	3.29	11.84	4.93
NET_ELEC (kWh)	0	0.3	1.02	2.35	4.3	0.3	1.37	0	0.15	1.14	0	0	0.51	0
DISTANCE (km)	8.05	9.33	10.62	8.05	9.33	8.05	10.62	0	8.05	9.33	9.33	8.05	8.05	10.62
km/kWh	0.69	7.3	2.5	1.52	0.51	0.22	0.7	0	0.5	1.96	0.69	0.69	0.65	0.69
LOW HEV TIME	17.99	15.82	17.81	15.31	19.88	15.02	15.8	0	17.54	13.6	13.43	15.84	12.44	16.59
LOW ZEV TIME	17.84	19.17	17.72	15.31	20.25	16.11	16.3	0	14.04	13.63	13.8	15.79	17.63	16.56
RANGE														
EQ_GAL (kWh)	0	84.2	106.89	0.66	8.55	216.55	17.1	0	75.65	62.38	121.36	3.95	59.86	17.1
NET_ELEC (kWh)	0	8.41	9.06	8.31	5.76	0.44	4.32	0	8.19	1.75	0	0	11.78	4.1
DISTANCE (km)	13.68	174.5	191.6	58.16	27.38	174.5	44.5	0	198.4	123.2	205.3	150.5	198.4	58.16
km/kWh	1.92	1.89	1.66	6.44	1.92	0.8	2.06	0	2.36	1.92	1.92	1.92	2.7	2.7
ELAPSED TIME	0:18:33	3:27:31	3:25:12	1:46:34	0:42:02	3:26:16	1:06:00	DNS	3:25:23	3:25:19	3:24:57	3:03:03	3:26:03	2:17:02
RALLY														
EQ_GAL (kWh)	0	126.63	96.7	0	35.85	115.02	0	0	65.45	67.69	93.08	44.07	44.07	89.46
NET_ELEC (kWh)	0	0	7.68	0	4.65	0.01	0	0	6.35	0	0	0	10.94	2.29
DISTANCE (km)	0	134.86	134.86	0	41.89	41.89	0	0	134.86	134.86	134.86	88.22	134.86	134.86
km/kWh	x	0.98	1.29	5.94	1.03	0.36	5.50	0	1.87	0.98	0.98	0.98	2.44	1.48
ZEV Information (km/kWh)		8.15	5.09		x	x		x	9.00	11.96	8.03	6.37	7.14	7.87

11

950177

Testing Hybrid Electric Vehicle Emission and Fuel Economy at the 1994 DOE/SAE Hybrid Electric Vehicle Challenge

Michael Duoba, Spencer Quong, Nicole LeBlanc, and Robert Larsen
Argonne National Lab.

ABSTRACT

From June 12-20, 1994, an engineering design competition called the 1994 Hybrid Electric Vehicle (HEV) Challenge was held in Southfield, Michigan. This collegiate-level competition, which involved 36 colleges and universities from across North America, challenged the teams to build a superior HEV. One component of this comprehensive competition was the emissions event. Special HEV testing procedures were developed for the competition to find vehicle emissions and correct for battery state-of-charge while fitting into event time constraints. Although there were some problems with a newly-developed data acquisition system, we were able to get a full profile of the best performing vehicles as well as other vehicles that represent typical levels of performance from the rest of the field. This paper will explain the novel test procedures, present the emissions and fuel economy results, and provide analysis of second-by-second data for several vehicles.

INTRODUCTION

The Hybrid Electric Vehicle (HEV) Challenge, sponsored by the U.S. Department of Energy (DOE), is a collegiate-level engineering design competition that involved 36 universities and colleges from across North America. The winner is found through a comprehensive test of the student-built HEVs in the areas of efficiency, performance, range, design, and emissions.

The HEV Challenge in 1993 was hosted by Ford Motor Company. In 1994, the automotive sponsor was the Saturn Corporation. Three separately competing classes made up the field in 1994. 1993 competitors from the Ford conversion class and the Ground-Up class were back again to compete. Added for 1994 was the Saturn conversion class.

Teams take a new production vehicle, or fabricate a ground-up vehicle, and add batteries, electric motors and controllers and, in most cases, a different internal combustion engine. The challenge is to make them all work together harmoniously to provide gains in fuel efficiency and reduce emissions while maintaining vehicle performance and utility.

The HEV also adds the capability of driving with zero emissions (ZEV mode). The Ford class converted production Ford Escort wagons and the Saturn class converted SL2 sedans to HEV operation. Members of the Ground-up class hand-built their own unique hybrid vehicles.

The Ford and Ground-up classes had similar requirements; they needed to demonstrate at least a 25-mile range at 45 mph (72 km/h) driving in ZEV mode. The Saturn class could not charge from the wall and was only required to demonstrate 5 miles of range in ZEV mode at 30 mph (48 km/h).

The emissions event was held June 11-13, 1994, at three separate vehicle emissions testing facilities; one for each class. This was the first event at the 1994 HEV Challenge and proved to be the best event to collect comparable test data from the HEVs.

EMISSIONS EVENT GOALS

Vehicle exhaust emissions are very important to a vehicle designer because, before any passenger vehicle can be sold, it must pass the appropriate emissions standards. Because one of the anticipated benefits of HEV technology is reduction of emissions compared with conventional vehicles, this charecteristic was given a high level of importance for the competition. Two hundred of the competition's 1,000 total points were based on emissions test results. The challenge for the schools to achieve low emissions with their HEVs was matched by the organizers' challenge to provide a concise, accurate, and equitable test procedure for their HEVs. An added dimension in measurement and testing was introduced with the contribution of the electric drivetrain. Although there are definite challenges in testing HEVs for emissions (and fuel economy), a new HEV Challenge emissions test procedure was desired for a good competition event and excellent data collection.

In the 1993 HEV Challenge, held at Ford Motor Company facilities in Dearborn, Michigan, the emissions event was based on tailpipe emissions collected during a hot 505 cycle after battery depletion miles were accumulated in ZEV mode. While this can give some relative comparison among vehicles, the data do not enable comparisons with conventional tests and do not fully address battery state-of-charge issues. It was decided by the organizers that a cold-start emissions test procedure should be employed for the 1994 competition that included an Federal Test Procedure (FTP) emissions test that would account for battery SOC differences.

To date, formalized HEV test methods exist only in various draft forms. The California Air Resources Board (CARB), the Society of Automotive Engineers (SAE) HEV Test Procedure Task Force, and each automobile company has its own idea about HEV testing procedures. The exact methodology is a controversial and political issue because differences in the test procedures could greatly affect how HEVs compare with conventional vehicles.

Although there was a definite need for a comprehensive test, the overriding factors that influenced the emissions event at the 1994 HEV Challenge were time and facilities. The draft SAE HEV procedure described a test that could last as long as five (5) days. Limited, donated dynamometer time dictated a short, concise testing procedure. The organizers had to balance the comprehensiveness of the testing with the available facilities and time.

Issues such as ZEV range affecting vehicle life cycle emissions and charging habits were ignored for the Challenge test procedures. The procedures used for the HEV Challenge emissions event were based on the SOC correction concepts proposed by members of the SAE HEV Test Procedure Task Force. SOC corrections are made to emissions test results, thus eliminating the net contribution of the battery energy. Extrapolation of the emissions results can predict emissions with zero SOC differences by careful monitoring of the battery during the test cycles.

FORD AND GROUND-UP CLASSES - The Ford and Ground-Up classes were tested a few days ahead of the competition at Ford's Certification Test Laboratory in Dearborn, Michigan and Chrysler's Highland Park facility in Highland Park, Michigan respectively.

The Ford and Ground-up classes were required to have three separate modes of operation. In HEV mode the vehicle can draw energy from either the batteries or engine depending on the design of their control system, In ZEV-mode the vehicle can drive normally as a ZEV. A third mode, APU-on-mode bypasses the control system to keep the engine on.

Day one of this test procedure included a ZEV mode test using the Urban Driving Dynamometer Schedule (UDDS), a battery depletion cycle, in HEV mode until the engine starts (if applicable), then a prep cycle (505 or full UDDS, depending on the amount of available time) in HEV mode to warm up the engine. Day two included a cold-start FTP test in APU-on mode or HEV mode, depending upon control strategies. See Table 1 for a summary of this procedure.

The FTP emissions and fuel economy results were corrected for SOC using delta Ampere-hour (ΔAh) information from the ZEV test and the HEV FTP test. The SOC difference at the end of the FTP test indicated the magnitude that the emissions and fuel economy results need to be corrected (higher or lower). The amount of energy put into

or taken out of, the battery pack during the FTP test was applied to the emissions and fuel economy results as either a "tax" or a "bonus." If, for example, extra energy was put back into the batteries, we can extrapolate extra ZEV distance that could be driven without emissions until the ΔAh reaches zero. The net grams per mile (g/mi) emissions and consumed miles per gallon (mi/gal) are adjusted based on this correction distance.

Table 1: HEV Dynamometer Emissions Testing Procedure for Ford and Ground-Up Classes

DAY 1

ZEV Test	UDDS in ZEV-mode
Battery Depletion	Run in HEV mode until engine turns on
Engine Prep	UDDS in HEV mode while engine is on
Soak	Overnight

DAY 2

HEV Test	FTP test in HEV-mode

Figure 1 is a plot of the net integrated ampere-hours in and out of the batteries during the entire procedure. These data were plotted to graphically demonstrate the SOC corrections employed for this test procedure. The West Virginia HEV is a series hybrid with an on/off engine control strategy. The test started with the engine off, then the engine turned on at 2 minutes, then shut down two thirds into the test.

The accumulated Ah into the battery during engine-on precipitated down toward the zero ΔAh point after the engine was shut down. However, at the end of the test, a positive ΔSOC remained. The accumulated Ah indicated a differential amount of extra SOC that could potentially be used to drive without fuel consumed or pollutants emitted. The ZEV efficiency data tell us how much extra distance to credit the FTP emissions, in g/mi, and fuel economy, mi/gal.

FORD AND GROUND-UP DAS AND DYNAMOMETER SETTINGS - A new data acquisition system (DAS) was developed for the 1994 HEV Challenge. This system was developed by Instrumental Solutions (IS), of Ottawa, Canada. As a backup, last year's system from Cruising Equipment (CE), of Seattle, Washington, was used when incomplete or unreliable data was obtained from the IS system. The new DAS was designed to acquire vehicle speed, sense engine-on, voltage and amperes of the battery system and generator (if series HEV) and integrate Ah and kilowatt-hours (kWh). However, the new system was very susceptible to noise generated by the high-power electronics, had calibration problems, and had limited resolution (8 bit). Last year's system was more robust with better resolution (10 bit), but was only designed to acquire battery pack data (Voltage, Amperes, kWh, Ah).

During the emissions event at Chrysler and Ford, data were logged in memory from the IS system, which was then downloaded after the test. The CE meter has a digital display,

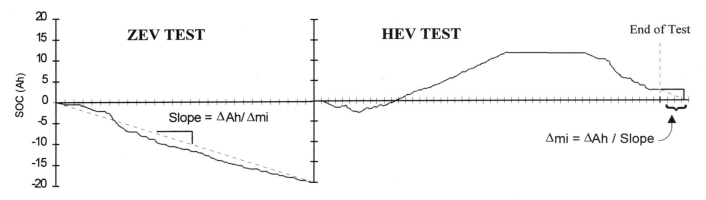

Figure 1: Graphic Representation of State-Of-Charge Correction for West Virginia Using Real Test Data

and real-time information was logged with a laptop computer or a special data memory module. Because the CE did not log speed data, the standard speed trace was later superimposed on Figures 2, 3, and 5.

The dynamometer inertia weight was set to the vehicle weight plus the standard payload. The dynamometer road load setting at 50 mph (80.5 km/h) was based on the stock body style. The Ground-Up class performed calculations of their estimated road load based on vehicle geometry and frontal area using a Dynamometer Power Consumption model. Unfortunately, there was no possible way to perform coast-down testing for each competition vehicle.

SATURN CLASS - The Saturn class was given the task of building a power-assist HEV. The Saturn HEVs were only required to have a minimum 5-mile ZEV range and were not allowed to charge off-board during the competition; the vehicle could use only on-board fuel energy. The power-assist description implies a parallel, power-peaking configuration, but several teams chose to build series systems. Because a parallel HEV with a small electric motor may not be able to drive in ZEV over the UDDS, the Saturn HEVs needed a different test than the Ford and Ground-Up procedures.

The Environmental Protection Agency's (EPA) National Fuel and Vehicle Emission Laboratory volunteered its facilities to be used during the 3 weeks prior to the competition for testing the Saturn HEV Challenge vehicles. The draft SAE HEV test procedure for power-assist hybrids prescribes a 3-day test. However, because EPA could not schedule multiple-day testing, the agency formulated a special test procedure that would account for differences in SOC.

The test included a typical vehicle prep performed the day before a cold start, multiple-cycle emissions and fuel economy test. The redundant cycle data of emissions and fuel economy may be correlated with differences in SOC, thus enabling SOC-corrected results.

In theory, this procedure can work but, the results from the two HEVs tested did not provide enough information to make the necessary correlation for SOC corrections. The University of Maryland HEV had a near-zero ΔSOC after the first three bags of the test (one FTP test). The other tested HEV, GMI Institute of Engineering and Management, could

not be SOC corrected because it had a SOC-accumulating engine generator set that never powered down.

SATURN DAS AND DYNAMOMETER SETTING - At EPA a multi-channel DAS product from National Instruments (called Labview) collected information from the battery and generator and accepted inputs from the dynamometer to collect the real trace and the actual trace.

As with the Ford class, the inertia setting for the Saturn HEVs was based on measured vehicle weight plus the standard payload and road load of the stock vehicle.

OUTCOME OF TESTING

For various reasons, not all vehicles were tested. Table 2 is a breakdown of the entire field of vehicles showing the number of many vehicles tested, the number that achieved 1994 EPA levels, and the number for which we have full test data. Problems with the data acquisition system and the vehicles themselves prevented analysis of all the tested vehicles.

Table 2: Breakdown of Vehicles for Emissions Testing

Total Number of Participants	36
Showed up to Emissions Event	23
Performed Whole Test	18
Passed 1994 EPA Standards	4
Tested EV-Only	3
Tested Engine-Only	1
Malfunctioned During Testing	3
Full Test Data of Battery, Emissions, and Fuel Economy	9

THE VEHICLES - Of the 18 vehicles tested, only the nine vehicles listed in Table 2 have full test data for battery, emissions, and fuel economy. This number is low, but the vehicles included are a good representation of the entire field of vehicle types. Poor results or incomplete data prohibits complete comparisons.

Looking at the vehicles listed in Table 3, we can see the trends in designing different kinds of HEVs. Parallel hybrids

Table 3: Attributes of Nine HEV Competition Vehicles

Class	School	Fuel	Vehicle Wt. (kg)	Series/ Parallel	Engine	Motor	Battery	Total kWh	Battery Wt.(kg)
Ford	U of Alberta	RFG	1644	P	Suzuki 1.0L	Brushless DC, 32kW	NiCd	9.4	284
	U of Illinois	E100	1737	S	Kohler 0.6L	AC Ind., 63kW	Pb-Acid	7.4	320
	Weber St. U	RFG	1800	P	Ford 1.9L	Series DC, 37kW	NiCd	17.4	370
	West Virg. U	RFG	1649	S	Kawasaki 0.6L	Series DC, 41kW	Pb-Acid	13.5	272
Ground-Up	Cal. Pol. Pomona	RFG	1118	S	Brig/Strat, 0.48L	Series DC, 34kW	Pb-Acid	13.1	262
	UC Santa Barb.	E95	1237	P (split)	Suzuki, 1.0L	Ind. AC, 9kW	Pb-Acid	12.5	246
	U.C. Davis	RFG	1200	P	Brig/Strat, 0.57L	Brushless DC, 45kW	NiCd	14.0	340
Saturn	U of Maryland	M85	1464	P	Suzuki 1.0L	Brushless DC, 13 kW	NiCd	2.9	141
	GMI Eng. & Man.	E95	1773	S	Kawasaki, 0.6L	AC Ind., 22kW	Pb-Acid	5.8	182

typically had smaller electric motors and more powerful engines than the series HEVs. The parallel HEVs typically used automotive engines; the series HEVs utilized small utility engines. The Saturn HEVs, which were not required to drive long distances in ZEV-mode, had smaller battery packs.

CONTROL STRATEGY EFFECTS - Only a portion of the vehicles had the potential for the engine to automatically turn on and off during the emissions event. We were not able to fully investigate how this kind of operation affects the test results and the vehicle performance. In addition, the data acquisition equipment that monitored the engine was not fully reliable.

The West Virginia HEV (a series configuration) was equipped with an engine that provided enough power to accumulate a charge with the engine off during roughly one third of the HEV test. The efficiency of their engine/generator set enabled them to achieve 44 MPG (18.7 km/L), corrected to 48 mi/gal (20.4 km/L) the highest tested fuel economy in any class.

The University of Alberta entry did have a working electrically heated catalyst activated by the ignition. They were allowed to key-on for a few seconds before the test was started.

SOC CORRECTIONS - As mentioned earlier, SOC corrections were not made for the Saturn HEVs. Of the two Saturns tested, one had a very small deviation from zero net change in Ah, and the other had high enough emissions that a SOC correction would have been academic.

Table 4 shows the applied SOC corrections. A positive SOC correction means that energy was put into the batteries; this causes the final results of the emissions levels to *decrease* and the fuel economy to *increase*.

With the exception of two vehicles, the degree of corrections applied to the raw emissions results for the Ford and Ground-Up classes was fairly low (see Table 4). The engine in the Illinois HEV never turned off during the test; they subsequently accumulated a large amount of battery SOC during the test, which earned them a +19.9% correction. The -54.4% SOC correction indicates a problem with the California Poly Pomona HEV (a series HEV). Their

engine/genertor set did not supply enough energy during the test to keep up with the average load of the electric motor. The second-by-second test data from the generator output and the battery utilization presented later will show details of their problem.

Table 4: SOC Corrections

Team	ΔAh in ZEV test	ΔAh in HEV test	%SOC* Correction
Univ. of Illinois	-6.24	+2.33	+19.9%
Univ. of Alberta	-12.18	-1.29	-7.7%
West Virginia	-20.33	+2.64	+8.0%
Weber State	not tested	0.00	0 %
Cal Poly Pom.	-15.02	-7.85	-54.4
UC Santa Barb.	0.0	0.0	0%
Cal. Davis	-11.50	0.35	-1.9%
GMI	n/a	+6.44	n/a
Maryland	n/a	+0.05	n/a

* A positive SOC correction indicates an adjustment of g/mi lower and FE higher.

Because the electric motor was not utilized during the HEV mode test in two of the parallel hybrids, these vehicles did not need SOC correction.

Three of the eight tests showed a negative net change in SOC (energy taken from the batteries). The data show that all but one vehicle remained within 1.0 kWh of the starting conditions of the HEV test.

EMISSIONS RESULTS

As a whole, the emissions results from the 1994 HEV Challenge vehicles were less than impressive. Many of the vehicles were using alternative fuels that required reworking of their engines. Most used small utility engines that do not have intrinsic design characteristics for good emissions control.

Table 5: Emissions Event Scoring Schedule

THC	0.41	0.41	0.41	0.41	0.41	0.41	0.41	0.41	0.41	0.41	0.41	0.41	0.41	0.41	0.41	0.41
NMHC		0.36	0.33	0.3	0.25	0.2	0.16	0.13	0.11	0.09	0.07	0.06	0.06	0.05	0.04	0.04
CO	3.4	3.4	3.4	3.4	3.4	3.4	3.4	3.4	3.4	3.4	3.4	3	2.55	2.17	1.88	1.7
NOx	1	0.8	0.63	0.5	0.4	0.35	0.31	0.27	0.23	0.21	0.2	0.2	0.2	0.2	0.2	0.2
Points:	50	60	70	80	90	100	110	120	130	140	150	160	170	180	190	200

Event scoring was based on simultaneous control of total hydrocarbons (THC), non-methane hydrocarbons (NMHC), carbon monoxide (CO), and oxides of nitrogen (NO_x). A team scored the assigned points in a particular bracket if the emissions results were below all four listed pollutant levels in the bracket. The scoring schedule is shown in Table 5.

The emissions results of our nine vehicles are listed in Table 6. All four teams that did score in the emissions event are listed. The other results are typical of the rest of the HEVs that did not score. Many schools had CO values ranging from 15 to 100 g/mi. Only one HEV ran lean; this vehicle had high NO_x (13.33 g/mi) and low CO (0.2 g/mi) readings. Vehicles either had adequate emissions control, or were far from meeting any current emissions standards.

Table 6: Emissions Results from HEV Challenge Test Procedure

School	SOC Corrected Values				Emissions Points (/200)
	THC (g/mi)	NMHC (g/mi)	CO (g/mi)	NO_x (g/mi)	
Un. of Illinois	2.87	2.29	95.13	0.061	0
Un. of Alberta	0.366	0.331	2.133	0.695	70
West Virginia	0.046	0.043	0.305	2.476	0
Weber State	0.109	0.085	0.332	0.395	90
Cal Poly Pom.	1.354	1.197	21.34	0.093	0
Santa Barb.	0.578	0.182	26.07	0.58	0
Cal. Davis	0.204	0.178	2.417	0.333	100
Maryland	0.31	0.29	2.6	0.68	60
GMI	0.75	0.56	54.2	0.3	0

Based on the emissions results, we should not conclude that hybrid electric vehicles are less capable of achieving lower tailpipe emissions. The technology for emissions controls for smaller engines is many years behind that for production car engines. The student teams that scored well in emissions did very well considering the challenges of using alternative fuels and small engines.

All four vehicles that scored in the emissions event were parallel hybrid types. Three of the schools used automotive engines. However, the teams with series configurations that showed promise in the emissions event admitted that their emissions control systems were not operating at their full potential.

FUEL ECONOMY RESULTS

Four hybrids were able to demonstrate superior fuel economy: University of Alberta with 32.09 mi/gal (13.6 km/L); West Virginia University with 48.1 mi/gal (20.4 km/L); University of California, Davis with 35.1 mi/gal (14.9 km/L); and University of Maryland with 39.8 mi/gal (16.9 km/L). The fuel economy results of our nine HEVs are listed with the production equivalents in Table 7. The listed fuel economy results are corrected for SOC (see Table 6) and for gasoline equivalent gallons.

Table 7: Vehicle Efficiencies for Competition HEVs and Various Comparison Vehicles

Class /Type	Team	ZEV % off trace[f]	ZEV Efficiency (mi/kWh)	HEV % off trace	HEV Efficiency (MPGs)[a]
Ford	Alberta	1.28	3.63	-1.39	27.65
	Illinois	-1.03	4.52	-1.99	b
	Wst. Virg.	+0.69	5.97	-0.76	48.1
Ground -Up	Cal Poly Pomona	+1.55	4.42	-0.46	14.65
	UC Davis	+2.15	3.95	-6.29	35.07
	Santa Barb.	--	--	-2.24	b
	Tulsa	-46.47	5.18	-61.98	25.75
Saturn	Maryland	--	--	-1.29	39.8
	GMI	--	--	-1.12	33.6[c]
Gasoline	Escort Wgn.	n/a	n/a	-	33
	Saturn SL2	n/a	n/a	-	27
EV	EV Geo[d]	unknown	6.75	n/a	n/a
	Ecostar[e]	+1.8	4.18	n/a	n/a

[a] Gasoline Equivalent Gallons
[b] Data exists, but was not available at time of printing.
[c] SOC Correction not possible. A Correction would boost FE.
[d] Tested at CARB, April 1994.
[e] Taken from 1994 American Tour de Sol Efficiency Testing.
[f] The measured vehicle distance driven compared to the test speed trace distance.

It is hard to draw any conclusions from the Ground-Up FTP (city) fuel economy results because there are no gasoline-equivalent vehicles with which to make a comparison. The vehicle weights vary a great deal. Some vehicles used a sturdy, welded-steel, tube frame, while others fabricated a light-weight, aluminum sub-frame. The average fuel economy of the Ground-Ups tested was 24 mi/gal (10.2 km/L), but two ground-ups were able to achieve greater than 30 mi/gal (12.8 km/L).

An indication of a vehicle's ability to follow the trace is shown by the "% off trace" column, which is the measured vehicle distance driven compared to the theoretical trace distance. Some vehicles had trouble maintaining the power demands required for the vehicle to keep up with the prescribed speed trace. Obviously, if a vehicle falls short of the prescribed driving speeds, its fuel economy may be artificially high. At the event, HEVs were run at best effort.

The Tulsa HEV was added in Table 7 to illustrate the potential problems with testing underpowered vehicles. The very large "% off trace" values (-49% and -61%) indicate that the inability of the vehicle to follow the trace must be taken into account in the 25.75 mi/gal (10.94 km/L) result. Similarly, the UC Davis vehicle, (a parallel HEV with a small engine), which demonstrates the ability to follow the trace in ZEV mode (ZEV: +2.15%), shows that the vehicle could have been aided by the motor to drive the trace in HEV mode (HEV: -6.29%).

In almost all cases, the vehicles were able to follow the trace better in ZEV mode. The reasons for this may have to do with throttle response for parallel systems, and more accurate torque response from driver input from the EV drivetrain. It may also mean that series systems have more power from their batteries in ZEV mode with a full charge than with the engine on and a partially depleted battery pack.

ZEV EFFICIENCY RESULTS

Because the Ford and Ground-up emissions test procedure had a ZEV portion, we were able to look at ZEV efficiency under the same city cycle used in the FTP emissions test. The electrical efficiency results varied from 2.4 mi/kWh to 5.97 mi/kWh (9.61 km/kWh). Results from seven HEVs, two EVs, and two conventional vehicles are listed in Table 7.

REAL-TIME DATA ANALYSIS

During the ZEV and HEV tests, we collected second-by-second data of the energy going into and out of the battery pack. In some vehicle tests, the DAS collected data from the battery and engine generator. This information shows us the power demands from the electric drivetrain during the ZEV test and during the HEV test. The net effect of the motor demands subtracted from generator output can also be seen in some vehicles. With these data, regenerative braking can be observed for each braking event and power management can be characterized.

University of Illinois - Figure 2 is a second-by-second plot of the ZEV test, which was one part of the HEV Challenge emissions testing procedure. Values of battery current and voltage were collected on a laptop computer from outputs given by a CE meter. The battery power trace in the plot is calculated from the battery current and voltage values.

The University of Illinois vehicle uses a Magnetek electric motor[2] with a home-built controller that provides nominal rating of 22.4 kW. This series-configuration HEV uses sealed Pb-Acid batteries.

The dynamics of the electric propulsion system can be seen throughout the UDDS. The batteries are experiencing 15-25 kW of load during acceleration and 10-15 kW of regenerative braking power during the braking events.

Power trace plots in ZEV mode such as in Figure 2 will show immediately whether or not the vehicle has regenerative braking capabilities. The characteristic power bumps during the decelerations indicate regenerative braking energy put back into the batteries.

An analysis of the Ah in and out of the batteries during the ZEV test indicates a projected range increase of 16.7% by utilizing regenerative braking. This Ah analysis assumes that ΔAh correlates with ΔSOC and that ΔSOC is proportional to the added amount of potential ZEV range. Using kWh would not be a good indication of SOC because energy measured in and out of the batteries is subject to energy losses each way (equal to the current squared times the resistance of the battery pack).

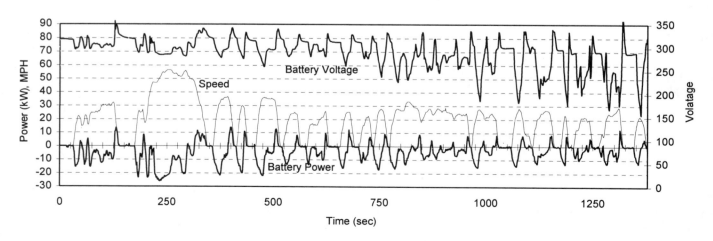

Figure 2: Battery Power and Voltage Trace During UDDS of University of Illinois ZEV Test

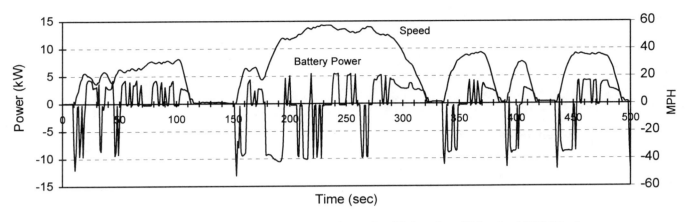

Figure 3: Power Trace During First 505 Seconds ofUniversity of Maryland HEV Test

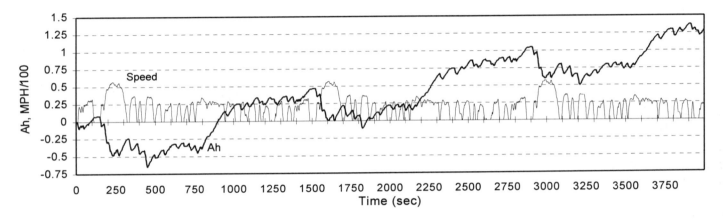

Figure 4: Ah Trace During Three UDDS cycles of University of Maryland HEV Test

One interesting note about the voltage trace of the University of Illinois vehicle: it appears that the resistance of the battery pack increased throughout the test. It is possible that the team did not have a fully charged battery pack at the emissions event, causing the batteries to operate in the lower SOC range where Pb-Acid batteries are less efficient.

We know from inspecting their vehicle and drive system[2] that their vehicle should have been very efficient in ZEV mode; less than exceptional efficiency results were obtained from the ZEV test (4.52 mi/kWh, 7.27 km/kWh), perhaps because of increasing losses from the battery during the test.

University of Maryland - Figure 3 is a plot of the first 505 seconds of the emissions test from the Maryland HEV. This vehicle was a parallel hybrid that used a small UNIQ Mobility electric motor/generator to complement a 1.0-liter engine. The control strategy kept the SOC of the batteries very close to the same level by adding and taking power from the engine throughout operation[3]. As seen from the plot, the magnitudes of the power spikes were similar for the entire cycle; throughout the test, the batteries give out roughly 10 kW during acceleration modes and accept about 5 kW of power generation.

When the speed incrementally increased or decreased, a power spike (indicating the addition or substraction of torque

to the engine) was seen from the battery power trace. This highly active control system produced the very jittery battery power trace in the graph.

Unlike the ZEV test, when a test in HEV mode is examined, what is seen is the power demand trace of the motor/generator as it is coupled to the engine and vehicle. The positive battery power bumps under decelerations look similar to the regenerative braking bumps seen in ZEV tests, but if we look closely, we can see they are sustained for longer periods and sometimes during areas of stable speed, not just deceleration.

On the basis of the University of Maryland design paper[3] and discussions with the team, we know that the motor supplies energy back to the batteries during light loads at speed and during deceleration events. However, at a stop the engine power level is brought to near idle so that engine noise and vibration are not disconcerting to the driver. The engine was effectively buffered from harsh transients; this approach made possible their significant gains in fuel economy.

Figure 4 is the Ah trace throughout three UDDS tests. The net usage of the batteries during the first UDDS was matched well, but as the cycles progress, the motor/generator was accumulating SOC. This continued until the computer-monitored SOC reached a set point, as determined by the control strategy, to use less of the generator's output during the light load conditions. Note the scale of this graph;

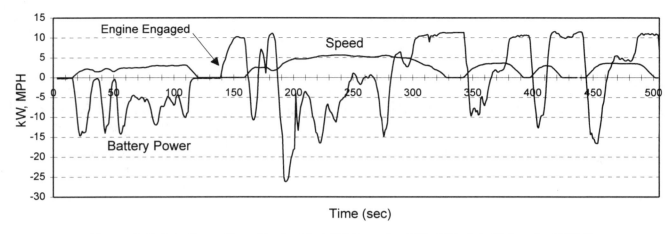

Figure 5: Battery Power Trace During First 505 Seconds of West Virginia University HEV Test

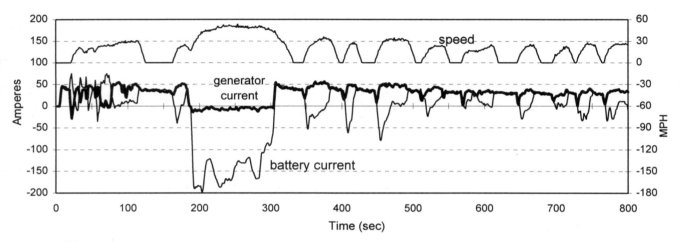

Figure 6: Battery and Generator Current Trace During First 800 Seconds of Cal. Poly. Pomona HEV Test

the battery capacity is roughly 19 Ah, and during this extended test, the vehicle stays within 1.5 Ah. This illustrates the effectiveness of the control strategy to keep the net usage of the batteries to a minimum.

West Virginia University - Figure 5 is a plot of the first 505 seconds of the West Virginia FTP emissions test. This series HEV utilizes a series-wound DC motor with a Kawasaki 0.6L water-cooled engine and a Fisher alternator. The West Virginia team used Pb-Acid batteries[1].

As mentioned before, the vehicle control system engaged the engine roughly 120 second into the test (this point is labeled on the graph). The power to drive the vehicle came solely from the battery during the first acceleration "hill." After that, the generator was observed giving power to the batteries.

The rest of the battery power trace shows the generator power subtracted by the electric drivetrain demands. At a stop, the engine generator set is putting out a constant 11kW. The other DAS system was also monitoring the generator and confirmed that output was constant during the test. Utilizing the engine at an efficient and powerful point proved successful, with a corrected 48.1 mi/gal (20.4 km/L) fuel economy result.

California State Polytechnic, Pomona - The trace in Figure 6 is a plot of the data taken from the IS DAS for the California Poly Pomona HEV test. This time, the outputs of the generator and battery are expressed in current. This robust HEV used components that emitted minimal noise and subsequently allowed relatively smooth data traces of the speed, generator current, and battery current. However, the plots shown in Figure 6 did require (three point) data smoothing.

The Pomona HEV used a Briggs and Stratton engine coupled to a Fisher alternator and a basic series-wound DC motor[4]. This vehicle has proven to be fairly successful because of its robust and simple design.

This figure demonstrates operational characteristics similar to those shown in Figure 5, but there was an apparent problem in the generator current trace. At high loads, particularly during the second acceleration "hill," the generator current quickly dropped to zero. During subsequent accelerations, there was a dip in the generator current.

While we do not know for sure what caused this to happen, it seems that under high loads (perhaps induced by low bus voltage) the generator momentarily did not produce any power. This adversely affected the vehicle efficiency in two ways. The engine momentarily did not produce power while it was running, thus making the vehicle deplete the batteries while consuming fuel producing a negative SOC correction. Also, the generator was not providing power under the highest load conditions where the batteries need it most. Battery efficiency is lowest under high load conditions, thus losses were increased without the needed contribution from the generator.

CONCLUSIONS

The DOE-sponsored HEV Challenge competition is a significant project because it puts a significant number of HEVs on the road. Engineers have modeled and studied the capabilities of hybrid electric drivetrains in vehicles, but there are very few real HEVs accessible for testing and data collection. The creative energies of student engineers and the resources of 36 colleges and universities have produced HEVs that have set performance benchmarks and demonstrated the potential of this important future vehicle technology.

The emissions event provided an opportunity to obtain data from many vehicles with a standard test procedure. The HEV test procedure used for ZEV-capable HEVs proved to work well by quickly testing HEVs and applying an SOC correction to the results.

The potential for increased emissions and fuel economy can only be realized if full utilization of the HEV's load-leveling properties can be accomplished. The best vehicles from the 1994 HEV Challenge show benchmark efficiency and emissions results that establish levels of efficiency and emissions performance that represent starting points for future HEVs.

Two student vehicles were able to achieve roughly 40 mi/gal (17 km/L) or greater in the city driving cycle; this represents an increase of roughly 30-40% in fuel economy over the stock vehicles. Three competition vehicles were able to achieve electrical efficiency results better than a production EV for the city driving cycle in ZEV mode. The data from the road events loosely match the efficiency test results, but mechanical failure and control strategy effects from these student-built prototype vehicles generate variance in the comparisons.

Results from the emissions event illustrate the need for highly developed internal combustion engines for HEVs with state-of-the-art emissions-control technology. Such engines are well within the current state of knowledge, but they have not been fully developed for these applications.

Development of effective control systems remains a formidable task in unlocking the potential of HEVs and satisfying the particular goals that HEV technology will be designed to accomplish. Although the computer technology exists, such control systems are only now being developed.

Many worthwhile lessons were learned from this ambitious, but detailed emissions test procedure for the student-built HEVs. With use of a different DAS, a new Saturn test procedure, and improved SOC correction calculations, 1995 promises to build on what was accomplished in 1994.

ACKNOWLEDGMENT

The work for this paper was supported by the U.S. Department of Energy, Assistant Secretary for Energy Efficiency and Renewable Energy, under contract W-31-109-ENG-380.

REFERENCES

1. W. Taylor and C. Atkinson, "The Design and Development of an Efficient Series Hybrid Electric Vehicle at West Virginia University," design paper submitted for the 1994 HEV Challenge competition (June 1994).

2. T. Roethemeyer, B. Masterson, M. Stiller, "University of Illinois Hybrid Electric Vehicle: An Electric Vehicle for Today," design paper submitted for the 1994 HEV Challenge competition (June 1994).

3. J. Wilkerson, Fred Householder, Mark Caggiano, D. Holloway, "The University of Maryland at College Park Methanol Hybrid Electric Vehicle," design paper submitted for the 1994 HEV Challenge competition (June 1994).

4. Augenstein, "California State Polytechnic University, Pomona," design paper submitted for the 1994 HEV Challenge competition (June 1994).

950178

Electric Vehicle Performance in 1994 DOE Competitions

**Spencer Quong, Michael Duoba, Robert Larsen,
Nicole LeBlanc, Richard Gonzales, and Carlos Buitrago**
Argonne National Lab.

ABSTRACT

The U.S. Department of Energy (DOE) through Argonne National Laboratory sponsored and recorded energy data of electric vehicles (EVs) at five competitions in 1994. Each competition provided different test conditions (closed-track, on-road, and dynamometer). The data gathered at these competitions includes energy efficiency, range, acceleration, and vehicle characteristics. The results of the analysis show that the vehicles performed as expected. Some of the EVs were also tested on dynamometers and compared to gasoline vehicles, including production vehicles with advanced battery systems. Although the EVs performed well at these competitions, the results show that only the vehicles with advanced technologies perform as well or better than conventional gasoline vehicles.

INTRODUCTION

DOE alternative transportation competitions offer an excellent opportunity to analyze different types of EVs in a low-risk, low-cost setting. With up to 50 vehicles at each competition and a wide range of technologies, the events show the effect of different components and designs on performance.

These events also offer an opportunity to showcase alternative-fuel vehicles and their technologies to the public. Competitions are held throughout the year at several different locations across the nation; this increased visibility will improve the awareness and public image of EVs. Participants include schools, private, and corporate manufacturers. The student competitors also gain experience in automotive technology, energy efficiency, and alternative transportation.

This paper analyzes the results from three types of test conditions at the competitions: closed-track, on-road, and dynamometer testing. The document also analyzes the effect of the vehicle parameters on the performance of the vehicle and compares the results of the different tests.

ELECTRIC VEHICLE COMPETITIONS

All the EV competitions are designed to test the vehicles' performance, efficiency, and range. Three of the competitions occurred on closed tracks: Solar/Electric 500 (S/E 500) in Phoenix, Clean Air Grand Prix (CAGP) in Atlanta, and EV Grand Prix (EVGP) in Richmond. Participants in these events consisted of private, corporate, and scholastic groups. Only colleges and universities were part of the CAGP, and the participants in the EVGP were from high schools. All the EVs in the closed-track events were converted from conventional vehicles. Teams scored points in several events including acceleration, handling, range, and efficiency. The acceleration event was defined as the time the vehicles took to travel 0.2 km. The handling event consisted of a timed slalom or autocross course. The range event measured how far a vehicle could travel in a fixed time. Finally, the efficiency event measured the amount of energy used by each vehicle at constant speeds. Oral and written design review events were also part of the student competitions.

The two on-road competitions provided a different setting in which to evaluate EVs. The World Clean Air Road Rally (WCARR) took place on the surface streets and highways of the Los Angeles area, and the American Tour de Sol (ATdS) traveled for seven days from New York City to Philadelphia. The scores of the competitors were based upon the time their vehicle took to complete each leg compared to the perfect time. That is, a team lost points if the vehicle was late or early compared to an ideal time. The teams could also score additional points by completing "range laps" at the end of the day.

In addition to the rally, some of the vehicles in the ATdS were tested on a dynamometer to measure their performance. Although the testing had no effect on the scores of the participants, the acceleration, energy efficiency, and power consumption of the vehicles was measured.

BACKGROUND

DATA ACQUISITION SYSTEMS - In each of these competitions, some or all the vehicles used a kilowatt-hour meter to measure the energy consumption. The meter, from Cruising Equipment Co., measured the current from the battery pack using a shunt and the voltage through a 100:1 voltage divider on the battery pack terminals. The energy was calculated by integrating the voltage and current readings. The meter sampled the vehicle data at a rate of 128 units per second, and recorded the current and voltage at a frequency of 1.2 kHz. The meter had a resolution of 0.5 V and 1 A. Real-time information could also be recorded by attaching a computer or memory module to the meter [1].

The data measured on the dynamometer before the ATdS used a National Instruments Labview system. This device was also used to collect real-time information from some vehicles at the Richmond competition. The Labview system used A/D converters to monitor the battery voltage. The current from the battery pack was measured using a shunt (50 mV/500 A) and had a two-stage low-pass filter. The system measured 256 samples per second and recorded the data at a rate of 1 Hz. Software averaging was also used to reduce noise. The accuracy was 0.25 % of full scale (500V/500A).

ELECTRIC VEHICLE THEORY - The power necessary to power an electric vehicle depends on the sum of four forces (rolling resistance, aerodynamic, gravitational, and acceleration) multiplied by the velocity and the efficiency. The equation that describes these forces is:

$$P = VE(F_{rr} + F_D + F_g + F_a) \qquad (1)$$

where

F_{rr} = Rolling resistance force
F_D = Aerodynamic drag
F_g = Gravitational force
F_a = Acceleration force
E = Vehicle efficiency

Because the aerodynamic drag is cubicly dependent on the velocity of the vehicle (i.e., $F_D = f(V) = 1/2\rho C_d A V^2$), the drag strongly affects the performance of the vehicle at higher speeds as shown in Figure 1. The vehicle will consume more power to overcome aerodynamic drag than the other forces at higher speeds [2].

CLOSED-TRACK COMPETITIONS

The competitions at Richmond (EVGP) and Atlanta (CAGP) were on a closed-track, which allowed the organizers an opportunity to test the vehicles under partially-controlled conditions during the efficiency and range events. At both competitions, the vehicles used DC-drive systems and lead-acid batteries. The nominal battery pack voltage was limited to 96 V at Richmond, and 120 V at Atlanta. All the EVs were conversions and were required to have roll-cages, which increased the weight of the vehicles.

During the efficiency event, the participants followed a pace car around the track at three constant speeds. At Richmond the vehicles drove at 88, 64, and 40 km/h, and at Atlanta the vehicles traveled at 88, 56, and 40 km/h. Once the vehicles completed a fixed distance (8 km at Atlanta and 12 km at Richmond) at each speed, they stopped and the in energy use was recorded from the kilowatt-hour meter. Figure 2 shows the results of efficiency event by comparing the weight to the energy efficiency (km/kWh) of the vehicles. To compare the vehicles at the two competitions, the results from the 56 km/h efficiency event at Atlanta were projected to reflect the energy efficiency at 64 km/h using regression techniques. As expected, the energy efficiency decreased as the vehicle weight increased. The trend line at 88 km/h shows that for every 125 kg increase in vehicle weight, the energy efficiency decreased by one km/kWh. At 64 and 40 km/h, the slope of the trend line was 1/200 km/kWh per kg.

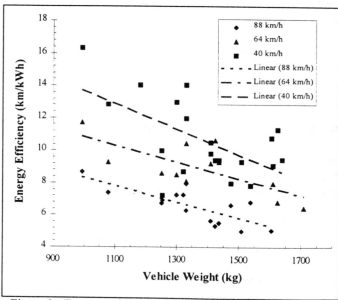

Figure 2: Energy efficiency versus vehicle weight during the efficiency event at the EVGP and CAGP.

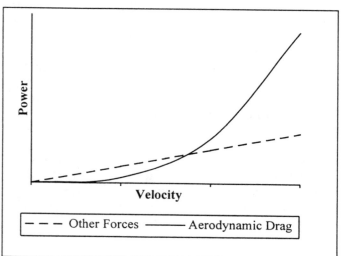

Figure 1: Effect of aerodynamic drag compared with other forces on the power consumption of a vehicle.

Driving style and variations in speed resulted in the wide variations of data, some of which were not included in the analysis. For example, the team with the best energy efficiency coasted through the turns to conserve energy, which resulted in an artificially high efficiency of 30.9 km/kWh at 40 km/h. Only the vehicles that completed the required distance at each speed were recorded.

At Atlanta, the ranges of the vehicles were measured by demonstrating which vehicle could travel the farthest in two hours. Vehicles were removed from the track if they had an average lap speed of less than 40 km/h. Figure 3 compares the range of the vehicles to the vehicle and battery weights. EVs that did not complete the event due to technical problems are not included in the graph. Also, Car #00 was still able to complete laps at the end of the two hours.

Figure 3 shows that vehicle weight and battery capacity are important in determining the range of the vehicle. For example, Car #14 had a battery capacity of 22.1 kWh, but only traveled 78.8 km due to its vehicle weight (1,605 kg). In contrast, Car #4 traveled 101.0 km, yet had half the capacity (11.0 kWh) and weighed 1,255 kg. Although Car #4 came in fourth place, its lighter weight allowed it to compete with vehicles with larger battery packs (Car #72, 93, 00).

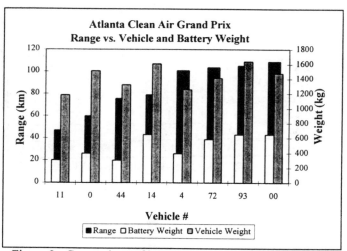

Figure 3: Comparison of battery weight, vehicle weight, and range on CAGP vehicles.

As stated above, the aerodynamic drag accounts for a larger portion of a vehicle's energy at higher speeds. Figure 4 shows the energy economy during the efficiency events for three different shapes of vehicles: small cars, trucks, and sports cars (sports cars were defined as having sloped rear ends). All three types of vehicles show a decrease in energy economy as speed increases. Due to the more aerodynamic shapes and sizes of the sports cars, their efficiency decreases 20% from 40 to 88 km/h, compared with 45% and 40% for trucks and small cars, respectively. This corresponds to the expected EV performance as shown in EQ (1).

Figure 5 shows a histogram of the 0.2 km acceleration runs of the vehicles at the Richmond and Atlanta events. Since many

of the vehicles used similar drive systems (General Electric or Advanced DC Brushed Motors), a large number of acceleration times are close to 17 s.

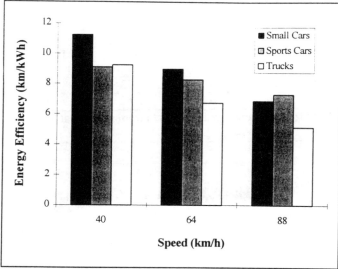

Figure 4: Comparison of vehicle efficiency at different speeds to vehicle shape at Richmond and Atlanta.

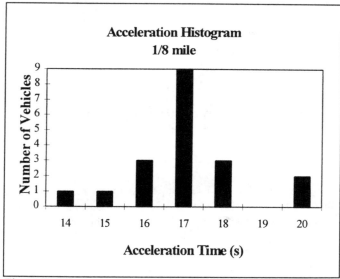

Figure 5: Histogram of acceleration times at EVGP and CAGP competitions.

Real-time data were also collected from one vehicle during the efficiency event (shown in Figure 6). Information was gathered during the 40- and 56-km/h runs. Table 1 shows a summary of the data for Car #35. The information collected includes the voltage, energy, and current. As expected, the current and energy draws were greater at the higher speed. The voltage drop from the battery also increased as the speed increased due to the internal resistance of the battery pack. Figure 6 also shows that no regenerative braking was present during the runs (current and slope of energy curve were both always positive). The plateau in the middle of graph is the time between the runs for which the vehicles stopped to record their energy consumption from the meter.

Overall, the closed-track competitions offer an opportunity to test EVs on-the-road under semi-controlled conditions. The results from the EVGP and CAGP showed a close correlation to expected values. Driving style and variations in speed account for the deviations from expected results.

Run	Avg. Speed (km/h)	Total Energy (kWh)	Avg. Power (kW)	Average Efficiency (km/kWh)
40	37.0	0.37	1.13	32.6
56	56.3	0.54	2.52	22.3

Table 1: Summary of real-time data from Car #35 at the EVGP.

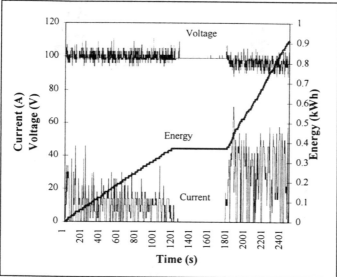

Figure 6: Instantaneous data from Car #35 Raleigh County School, during the efficiency event.

ON-ROAD COMPETITIONS

The WCARR and ATdS competitions were rally events and both occurred on surface streets. These on-road events offer the opportunity to measure the performance of the vehicles under typical driving and road conditions. Unfortunately, due to the nature of an on-road rally, the driving style, road conditions, and traffic conditions may vary for each vehicle.

Thirty-five vehicles were monitored during the two competitions. As previously discussed, the ATdS road rally was seven days long and the WCARR lasted three days (data were collected for two days). Only five vehicles were monitored during the Los Angeles competition. These consisted of privately owned EVs with lead-acid batteries and DC drive systems. The competitors in the ATdS were divided into four classes: American Commuter (AC), Tour de Sol Commuter (TdS), Production (Prod), and Open. The AC class had the most participants and consisted of registered and practical vehicles with no battery limitations. The TdS class included three teams and had a limitation on solar array size and battery capacity depending on the number of passengers. The Production class was the most interesting with participants from Ford, Chrysler, Electricar, and Solectria. The EVs in this class

had to be driven "as sold." The Open class consisted of all other vehicles, including two and three wheel EVs (3, 4).

The ATdS and WCARR routes and driving conditions were significantly different. The ATdS took place on back-roads with few traffic controls or other cars. The average speed during the rally portion of the ATdS was generally higher than during WCARR, which took place in city driving conditions. The WCARR rally had more accelerations and stops, which resulted in a slower average speed. Thus, the efficiencies and range of the WCARR EVs were considerably less than the ATdS vehicles. In both competitions, the EVs were driven with a more-efficient style than used by a typical driver to save energy and increase range.

Some of the vehicles with advanced technologies or excellent performance are shown in Table 2. These included and Solectria Force with nickel metal-hydride batteries and the University of California, Davis EV with a zinc-bromine battery. The efficiency (eff.) was averaged over the rally portion of the seven-day competition. The range was the longest distance the vehicle traveled between charges and included the rally and the extra laps at the end of the day.

Vehicle	Class	Eff. (km/kWh)	Range (km)	Battery
Ford Ecostar	Prod	8.74	304	Sodium-Sulfur
Chrysler TEVan-NJ	Prod.		101	Nickel-Iron
Chrysler TEVan-PECO	Prod.		109	Ni-Cd
Solectria ForceRS	AC	11.65	344	Ni-MH
Bolton HS	AC	7.40	228	Pb-Ac
UC Davis	AC	8.07	281	Zn-Br

Table 2: Performance of some vehicles at ATdS. (3)

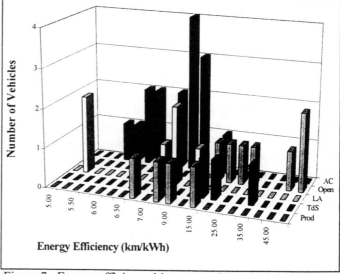

Figure 7: Energy efficiency histogram of EVs in the ATdS and WCARR (LA) during the rally.

Figures 7 and 8 show a histogram of the energy efficiency and maximum range of the EVs in the competitions. The Open and TdS classes tended to have a better efficiency because these vehicles were extremely lightweight and aerodynamic compared to the practical vehicles in the other classes. In contrast, the Production and AC classes tended to have a longer range because these vehicles could carry more batteries (LA refers to the WCARR vehicles).

Average daily efficiency varied from 5.23 to 65.74 km/kWh and the maximum range was between 29 and 344 km. The most efficient vehicle was from Team New England and was a small, three-wheeled, one-person vehicle. The vehicle with the longest range was the Solectria ForceRS with nickel metal-hydride batteries.

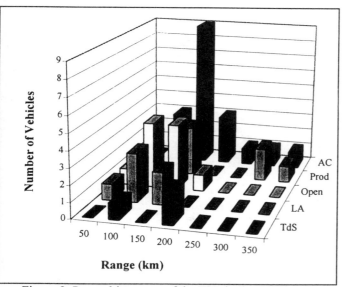

Figure 8: Range histogram of the EVs in the ATdS and WCARR (LA) competitions.

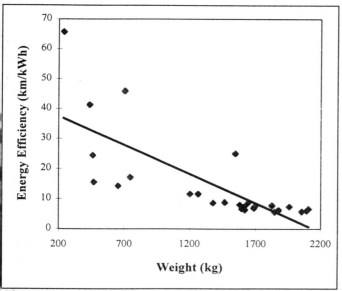

Figure 9: Average energy during the rally portion of the ATdS compared to vehicle weight.

Figure 9 shows the comparison of vehicle weight and vehicle efficiency during the ATdS competition. In this event, the trend line on the graph shows that for every 50-kg increase in vehicle weight, the efficiency decreases by 1 kWh. The energy efficiency per weight decreased compared with the closed-track events because of accelerations, traffic, and other road conditions.

Figure 10 shows the instantaneous data gathered from Sungo, Car #32 during Day 2 of the ATdS rally. The Sungo used lead-acid batteries and a DC brushless motor. This allowed the vehicle to capture 21% of the energy used through regenerative braking during the time shown in Figure 10. The regenerative braking is in effect when the current and the slope of the energy line is negative (4).

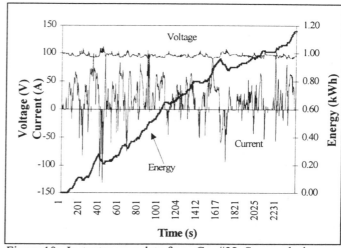

Figure 10: Instantaneous data from Car #32, Sungo, during one portion of the ATdS rally.

Overall, rally-style competitions show the effects of real-life driving and road conditions on the performance of EVs. Unfortunately, the information gathered depends on driving style, traffic, and traffic controls. Yet, some of the vehicles at the rallies showed impressive performance.

DYNAMOMETER TESTING

Before the start of the ATdS nine vehicles were evaluated on a dynamometer at the New York City Environmental Protection facility (5). Due to the limited test time, each vehicle was tested for approximately one hour. Valuable information was gathered on all the vehicles during the testing including energy efficiency, acceleration, and power consumption at constant speeds. In addition, three gasoline vehicles were tested as a reference.

Real-time data collected during the testing included battery voltage, current from the battery pack, and other dynamometer measurements. The Labview system previously discussed collected all the data. A hall-effect sensor rather than the shunt used in the other vehicles, measured the current from the TEVans and Ecostar.

The dynamometer settings for the EVs were difficult to evaluate. The few teams that performed extensive coast-down testing on their vehicles produced accurate results. For those EVs that did not perform these tests, the horse power load was set to the original certified value of the converted vehicle. The weight settings used the actual vehicle weight plus a standard payload. In all cases, the road load was verified by matching the coast down on the dynamometer.

Three tests were performed on each vehicle: urban driving schedule (UDS), acceleration, and steady-state speed. Table 3 shows the results of the UDS testing. The energy efficiency refers to the amount of energy the EVs used during the UDS cycle. Percent regenerative (regen.) energy is the amount of energy captured during the UDS through regenerative braking compared with the total energy used. "Equivalent MPG" compares the fuel efficiency of the gasoline vehicles to the EVs. To convert the electrical energy into equivalent gallons of fuel the following equation was used:

$$MPG = EE \times G \times \eta \qquad (2)$$

where

    EE = Electrical Energy Efficiency

    G = 33.8 kWh of electrical energy/Gallon gasoline

    η = Electrical System Efficiency compared to Gasoline System Efficiency

    = 0.226

The electrical system efficiency refers to the difference in the energy loss of converting oil into electricity at the plug, to converting oil into gasoline at the pump. This includes gasoline production, oil power plant losses, and distribution losses. The reference by Wang and DeLuchi (6) uses 0.324 as the system efficiency, but does not include battery and charger efficiency. The value of 0.226 was derived by using a battery efficiency of 75% and charger efficiency of 93% (5). The battery efficiency value may be low when considering EVs with advanced battery systems.

Vehicle	Type	Energy Efficiency (km/kWh)	% Regen. Energy (%)	Equivalent MPG (mpg)
Ford Escort	Gas			28.40
Dodge Caravan	Gas			20.60
Geo Metro	Gas			36.20
Chrysler TEVan1	EV	3.18	5.24	15.12
VW Rabbit	EV	5.95	0.00	28.26
SAAB 99	EV	4.74	0.00	22.53
Chrysler TEVan2	EV	3.20	5.00	15.20
Ford Festiva	EV	5.37	1.20	25.51
Geo Storm	EV	6.00	4.24	28.49
MG B	EV	4.94	0.00	23.45
Ford Ecostar	EV	6.72	17.30	31.93

Table 3: Results of the UDS testing during the ATdS.

The data in Table 3 show that the production vehicles captured a significant amount of energy from regenerative braking. Also, some of the conversion vehicles and the Ford Ecostar have equivalent fuel efficiencies comparable to the gasoline vehicles.

The performance of the vehicles was also measured at constant speeds from 16 to 96 km/h at 16-km/h increments, as shown in Figure 11. Again, Equation 2 was used to convert the EV electrical efficiency to equivalent mpg. The gasoline vehicles were not tested at 16 km/h because it was difficult to maintain the steady-state speed. Also, the Ford Festiva could not reach 96 km/h during the testing. In most cases, the internal combustion (IC) vehicles tested at the ATdS were more efficient than their EV counterparts when the energy system efficiency was considered (except for the Ford Ecostar). The electric vehicles are more efficient when comparing the vehicle, not the system.

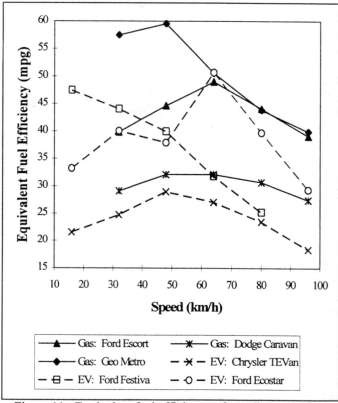

Figure 11: Equivalent fuel efficiency of gasoline and EV at steady-state speeds.

During the steady-state speed tests, instrumentation also recorded the power required to maintain the speeds (Figure 12). The plateau in the Ford Ecostar plot may be due to changes in the motor performance at different speeds or anomalies in the measurements (the Ecostar used a direct-drive system).

Figure 13 shows the fuel consumption of the control gasoline vehicles at the same constant speeds. One important fact is that the gasoline vehicles consume fuel at idle, but the EVs use no energy when their speed is zero. The fuel consumption rate was measured by capturing the emissions at each speed and using the carbon count of the exhaust to calculate the amount of fuel used.

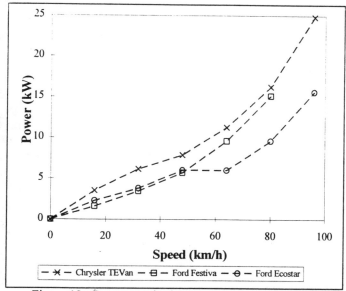

Figure 12: Power required at constant speeds for EVs.

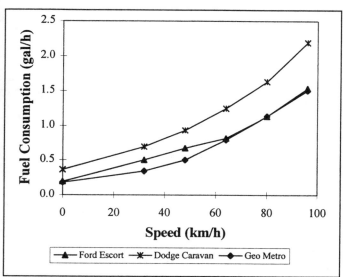

Figure 13: Fuel consumption of gasoline vehicles at constant speeds.

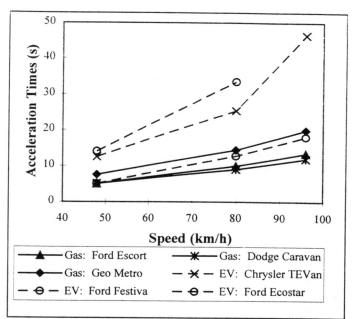

Figure 14: Average acceleration times of EV and gasoline vehicles at ATdS.

Vehicle	UDS Eff. (mi/kWh)	Rally Eff. (mi/kWh)	% Change
VW Rabbit	3.70	4.33	17.1%
Ford Festiva	3.34	5.38	60.8%
Geo Storm	3.73	5.53	48.3%
MG B	3.07	4.53	47.4%
Ford Ecostar	4.18	5.43	30.1%
SAAB	2.95	3.95	33.7%

Table 4: Comparison of UDS and on-road energy efficiency during the ATdS.

The vehicles also performed two acceleration runs on the dynamometer. Figure 14 shows the average of these two runs. The EVs performed better than their IC counterparts during this test. The Ford Ecostar had an impressive 0-96-km/h time of 18.1 s.

Although the dynamometer testing provides an excellent baseline measurement of EVs, it does not account for variations in performance due to driving and traffic. Table 4 compares the UDS and on-road efficiencies. The average percentage increase in the on-road efficiency was 39.6%. This large variation in performance is caused by the efficient driving styles of the competitors to extend their ranges (for example, coasting long distances to stop and slow accelerations). Also the UDS has more accelerations and stops than the rally route.

Most of the EVs tested on the dynamometer before the ATdS performed well, but not as good as the IC cars, except for the advanced Ford Ecostar with sodium-sulfur batteries.

CONCLUSION

Overall, student competitions not only offer an opportunity to educate future engineers, but also allow the testing of a wide range of vehicles with varying technologies. The closed-track competitions provided a semi-controlled atmosphere in which to test the EVs. The efficiencies of the vehicles in these events were affected by the vehicle weights, battery weights, and the vehicle aerodynamics. The ranges of the vehicles were strongly dependent on battery and vehicle weights. Both efficiency and range measurements provided results which correlated to expected values.

The on-road rallies also show on-road performance, but in a more realistic setting with traffic and different driving conditions. The on-road competitions, especially at the ATdS, have shown the benefits of advanced battery technology such as sodium-sulfur and nickel metal-hydride batteries. In general, the smaller vehicles had better efficiencies, but shorter ranges than the heavier vehicles with larger battery capacities.

In contrast to on-road measurements, dynamometer testing offers the opportunity to test the vehicles in a controlled atmosphere and provides a reference for comparing different vehicles to each other, including EV and gasoline cars. The EVs performed the same as conventional vehicles in efficiency and worse in power consumption, but were equal to or better than their gasoline counterparts in acceleration. Still, the testing showed that advanced EVs in the future have the potential of equaling or surpassing current IC technology. By comparing the results of the dynamometer testing to the on-road data, the effect of driving style and road conditions is easily seen. All the EVs had better performance on-the-road than during dynamometer testing.

ACKNOWLEDGMENTS

The work for this paper was supported by the U.S. Department of Energy, Assistant Secretary for Energy Efficiency and Renewable Energy, under contract W-31-109-ENG-380.

REFERENCES

(1) Cruising Equipment Co., *Installation Manual: Kilowatt-hour + Meter*, Seattle, WA, January 1994.

(2) Cairns, Elton J. and Earl Hietbrink, "Electrochemical Power for Transportation," *Comprehensive Treatise of Electrochemistry, Volume 3*, J. Brockris et al. (eds.), Plenum, New York, 1981, p. 421.

(3) Northeast Sustainable Energy Association, *American Tour de Sol*, Greenfield, MA, 1994.

(4) Quong, S., et al., "Energy Efficiency of Electric Vehicles at the 1994 American Tour de Sol," in *S/EV 1994 Conference Proceedings*, NESEA, Greenfield, MA, 1994, presented at Solar and Electric Vehicles '94 October 3-5, 1994, Providence, RI..

(5) Duoba, M. and, S. Quong, Unpublished Information, *Argonne National Laboratory*, Argonne, IL, September 1994.

(6) Wang, Q. and M. DeLuchi, "Impacts of Electric Vehicles on Primary Energy Consumption and Petroleum Displacement," *Energy, 17:* 351-366, 1992.

950179

Design and Analysis of a Hybrid Electric Vehicle Chassis

John G. Aerni
Prince Corp.

Clark J. Radcliffe and John L. Martin
Michigan State Univ.

ABSTRACT

Design of a hybrid electric vehicle chassis for the 1993 and 1994 HEV Challenge is presented. Computer finite element modeling and solid modeling techniques were used in developing the chassis. The main design parameters are presented and described. Final chassis design was tested, using finite element analysis, to ensure overall structural integrity and occupant safety. The chassis proved to be safe and reliable, under the rigors of competition driving, in the 1993 and 1994 HEV Challenges.

INTRODUCTION

Michigan State University took part in the HEV (hybrid electric vehicle) Challenge competition, sponsored by Saturn, The Society of Automotive Engineers (SAE) and the U.S. Department of Energy (DOE). The 1994 HEV Challenge brings with it the Ground-Up and Escort Conversion classes featured in the 1993 Ford/DOE/SAE HEV Challenge, and it offers a new class, the Saturn Conversion class. The 1994 Challenge allows the Ground-Up and Escort classes, which were range-extender vehicles with significant zero-emission-vehicle (ZEV) range in the 1993 challenge, to optimize their vehicles. The new Saturn Conversion vehicles are power-assist hybrids competing within their own class. Power-assist hybrids have shorter ZEV range with the electric energy storage used to boost the auxiliary power unit (APU) power for short intervals. Vehicles in all three classes compete in a variety of dynamic and static events to evaluate performance and overall engineering design.

Michigan State is one of 12 universities competing in the "ground-up" portion of the Challenge. Student teams must complete 100% of the vehicle, though componentry may be purchased from companies that manufacture the required materials. Michigan State University's entry for the HEV Challenge, "Spartan Charge" (Figure 1), has a series power train configuration, and can operate as a zero-emission vehicle (ZEV) for short commuting distances of less than 50 miles. Low-emissions were obtained with a methanol powered engine carried on board to recharge the batteries to extend the overall range of the vehicle. Charging was accomplished with a three-cylinder four-stroke Geo Metro engine which turns an alternator to produce electricity to power an electric motor and recharge the batteries.

Design and construction of the vehicle's chassis allowed students to gain the most knowledge when a high-technology computer-aided approach was taken in the development of the chassis' structural systems. Computer modeling packages and the role they played in design, development and strength analysis are described. Governing parameters, decisions made concerning the final design, and construction of the chassis are also discussed. Computer finite element modeling analyses, that were used to verify the structural integrity of the vehicle, showed that passenger safety was ensured.

COMPUTER MODELING

Utilizing a computer-aided design software package, I-DEAS (Integrated Design Engineering Analysis Software) by Structural Dynamics Research Corporation, was the most efficient way to develop the HEV chassis. I-DEAS is an integrated package of mechanical engineering software tools that provides a variety of applications for product design. Lawry [5,6] provided useful guides that were helpful in developing and analyzing the finite element and solid models of the chassis. Utilizing the available computational capabilities of I-DEAS aided in the design of the structural systems.

I-DEAS is made up of a number of "Families" of applications, each subdivided further into "Tasks" all executed from a common menu and sharing a common database. Applications include Solid Modeling, Finite Element Modeling & Analysis, System Dynamics, Drafting, and Manufacturing. Our needs included Finite Element Modeling and Solid Modeling.

FINITE ELEMENT MODEL - Chassis overall design was first constructed in the Finite Element Modeling package. A monocoque mid-section, straddled by space-frames in the front and rear were roughed out on paper and then translated into a finite element model. Aluminum was used for the monocoque and was modeled using isotropic thin-shell elements, while the steel space frames were conveniently modeled by beam elements. Thicknesses and material properties of the thin shells could easily be governed, in addition to the beam element's cross-sections.

Figure 1. Michigan State University's Hybrid Electric Vehicle, Spartan Charge.

In developing the Finite Element model of the chassis the construction geometry task of the Finite Element Modeling Family was used. Corners of the monocoque and major tube intersections were defined in a global coordinate system and represented by points on the graphic display. All points were then connected by lines which determined the planar intersections of the monocoque and the geometric orientation of the beam sections. Two dimensional surfaces, created from the construction geometry, represented the aluminum monocoque surfaces, while individual lines defined the tubular space frame geometry. An auto-mesh feature was utilized to develop an array of finite elements from the construction geometry. This methodical approach is powerful for the inevitable event of mesh refinement. Old mesh configurations can be deleted and a refined mesh can be obtained from the previously created construction geometry. Construction geometry was a useful task in developing a base geometry from which finite element models could be built.

A series of finite element strength analyses ensued after the creation of the preliminary model. Excessive high local stresses and deflections were reduced and material thicknesses were optimized in an iterative manner which was especially helpful in optimizing the front and rear space frames. A collection of beam cross-sections were created. Larger cross sections were used in high stress areas and tube geometry could be easily relocated and analyzed. Finite element modeling is flexible, in that separate sections, such as space frames, could be loaded and analyzed as separate entities.

Space frames were modified and analyzed easily because they were modeled with one-dimensional beam elements. Torsion and braking loads were chosen to simulate extreme operation conditions. Locations where the space frames bolt on to the monocoque were held fixed. Appropriate forces were applied to the wheel locations which were then transferred to the frame through the suspension geometry that was modeled using rigid members. Figures 2 and 3 show an exaggerated view of the effects of braking and torsion on the front space frame. Dashed lines represent the unloaded frame and solid lines represent the frame under load.

Several different loading cases were used in verifying the structural integrity of the vehicle since the objective of the finite element analysis was to create a structurally sound and safe chassis. These loading schemes will be discussed in moredetail in the Finite Element Modeling section.

SOLID MODEL - Final chassis geometry that resulted from the finite element analyses was used to produce a computer solid model that was constructed in the Solid Modeling Family. This solid model exactly replicates what the chassis will look like when it is constructed which was useful for surfacing the body shell, checking component clearances and spacing, verifying vision requirements, and deciding mounting locations. Impressive drawings for presentations and displays were generated from this model. Figure 4 shows the computer solid model of the chassis.

The first entity created in I-DEAS Solid Modeling was the monocoque which was created using blocks representing the sheets of aluminum with the same thickness and geometry. Once the monocoque was created, an aluminum color was created from a color palate and a shiny gloss applied to give the object a natural appearance. This monocoque served as a basic foundation for the remaining components to be built around and attached to.

Front, rear, and roll-cage space frames were created around the monocoque which were composed of square and

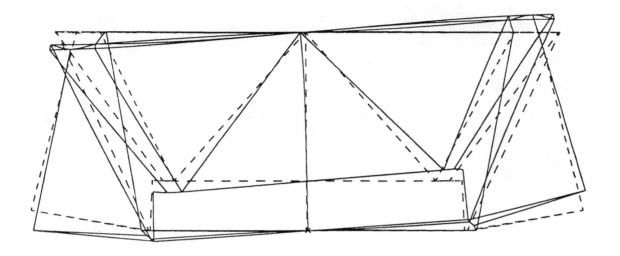

Figure 2. Front Space Frame Under Torsion Load. (Front View)

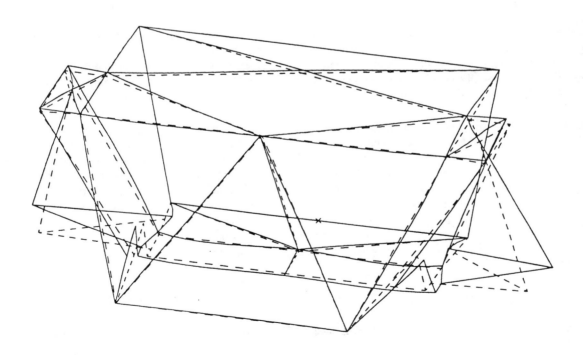

Figure 3. Front Space Frame Under Braking Load. (Front Isometric View)

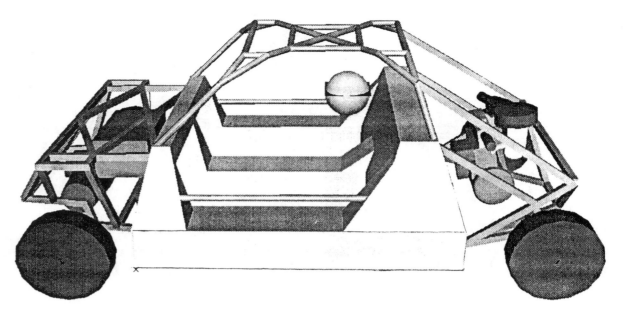

Figure 4. Computer Solid Model of Chassis.

round tubing with accurate tube sizes and wall thicknesses. Points in space were located in Construction Geometry and used to define vectors around which the tubes were created. A steel tubing color scheme was developed and applied to give a life-like appearance.

All major components to be mounted in the chassis were meticulously created to give an accurate picture of spacing and clearance concerns. These components included the Geo Metro Engine, alternator, electric motor, transmission, inverter, wheels and dash board. They were positioned in the chassis and colored to give an accurate visualization of the final product.

Space for the drivers head was created as a sphere and placed in the passenger compartment. Head placement was oriented at a vertical height the same as a fiftieth percentile male occupant to ensure that the visibility requirements, as stated in the HEV Challenge Rules and Regulations [3], were met.

Computer aided engineering is becoming an everyday practice in the engineering world. Using finite element and solid modeling techniques reduces the need for other costly testing methods. Products can be produced more efficiently and in less time using a computer aided approach. Using the computer to help engineer the structural systems enabled us to become familiar with a powerful tool that is available to today's engineers.

CHASSIS DESIGN

The vehicle chassis links the mounting points for the vehicle's front suspension, steering, engine, transmission, rear suspension, final drive, fuel tank, seats for occupants, and in our case, motor controller, electric motor, and batteries. It requires rigidity to maintain accurate handling, lightness to reduce inertia and rolling resistance, and toughness to sustain punishing fatigue loads from the road, power unit, and driver. This section describes the design decisions made to develop the final hybrid electrical vehicle chassis.

A number of key design parameters were observed during the chassis design phase. These parameters include:
- Passenger Accommodations
- Materials for Fabrication
- Battery Housings
- Packaging

Each of the design parameters played a major role in the design of the chassis and will be described separately.

PASSENGER ACCOMMODATIONS - Ergonomics play a vital role in the design of interiors for today's auto makers. Automobile operators are becoming more and more demanding for new interiors to be functional as well as comfortable. To accommodate the needs of the passengers the chassis' mid-monocoque was designed to provide ample space for comfort and clear visibility.

Rough passenger compartment dimensions and measurements were taken from a compact car. Seats were positioned in their furthest back position. These were used as a general layout for the passenger compartment. This helped in deciding the distance from front to rear firewall, height of ceiling, seat accommodations, dash position and passenger placement. Vision requirements, defined in the HEV Challenge rulebook [3], were observed in the design and verified through the computer solid model of the chassis. Spartan Charge's passenger comfort, visibility and accessibility to controls were rewarded with a first place in Ergonomics award.

MATERIALS FOR FABRICATION - Choice of materials was decided upon considering manufacturability, recyclability, material properties, safety, and ability to model accurately using finite element analysis. Composite materials and conventional metals were considered for use in the chassis. Composite materials are very attractive because of their material properties, but a composite chassis would have been difficult to manufacture. Plus, the anisotropic material properties of composite plies are more difficult to model on the computer.

Basic chassis design was planned while considering the tools available for it's construction. Some of the advantages of composite materials become less appealing when considering the more difficult manufacture methods associated with these materials. The Farrell Hall machine shop, which is part of the Agricultural Engineering Department where the vehicle was constructed, had a large variety of machines and experienced mentors to aid in conventional metal construction. Therefore, basic metal construction techniques, such as welding, bonding, and riveting, were used in manufacturing the chassis.

Though composite structures have a low density, which is crucial to reduce excess weight, an equally important property to consider is toughness. Toughness is a measure of the combination of strength and ductility. Toughness is the area under the material's stress-strain curve which represents the amount of energy a material can absorb before failure. This property has to be considered to ensure the long term reliability of the vehicle. Although composite structures are generally lighter and stiffer they also are unforgiving and more susceptible to design flaws. Also, local high stress areas or manufacturing defects in a composite structure can easily develop a crack that can go undetected which can then propagate and eventually result in a sudden catastrophic failure. According to Smith [7], the energy-absorbing qualities of a well-designed and well-fabricated aluminum monocoque outweigh the weight saving and stiffness of a composite monocoque. Composite structures must absorb impact by controlled fracture rather than by plastic deformation. Designing controlled fracture is very difficult and requires many crash tests. Conventional metals provide the added security of local plastic deformation in a high stress area which will reduce the strain energy in that small location thus allowing the surrounding material to absorb the added loading.

Tubular steel and sheet aluminum were chosen to be used to construct the chassis because of their toughness and simpler computer modeling advantages. These metals are both recyclable and easy to manufacture with the available shop tools and machinery. Smith [7,8] and Fournier [4] provided helpful manuals for design and manufacturing techniques of aluminum and steel. 5052 sheet aluminum was chosen because of it's excellent resistance to corrosion and workability properties, Bray [1]. Lightweight sheet aluminum was easy to bend and the joints were bonded and riveted to construct the passenger monocoque. Square tubular steel was chosen for building the space frames. The flat sides made it easier to cut and weld joints and attach component mounts.

BATTERY HOUSING - Battery selection had not been made prior to the chassis design phase. So in designing the chassis, two types of batteries, lead-acid and nickel-metal-hydride, had to be applicable which were of different sizes and weighed 750 and 875 pounds respectively. This meant that battery housings had to be designed to accommodate both battery types. Also these battery housings had to be completely sealed from the passengers, able to support the heavy battery weight, provide proper battery ventilation, be serviceable, and positioned low and close to the middle of the vehicle so as not to hamper the dynamic performance of the vehicle. Figure 5 shows the battery configuration in the mid-monocoque section.

Five identical battery packs were chosen to aid in serviceability. Because the packs are identical they are interchangeable, and any pack could be put into any housing. Each battery pack's electrical characteristics could be monitored. If one of the five battery packs was malfunctioning it could easily be replaced. Housings were designed so that the batteries are loaded into the vehicle from underneath the chassis. This ensured that the batteries would be completely sealed off and inaccessible to the passengers.

Box sections were utilized in the aluminum monocoque to house the batteries and to lend structural rigidity to the chassis.

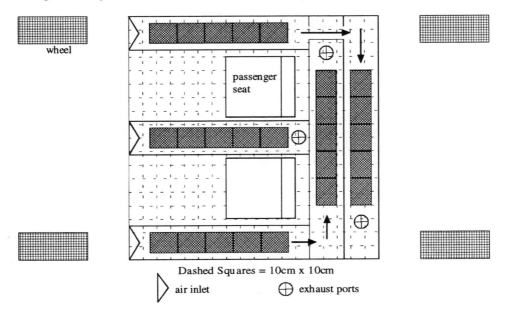

Dashed Squares = 10cm x 10cm

▷ air inlet   ⊕ exhaust ports

Figure 5. Battery Pack Placement and Ventilation in the Mid-Monocoque.

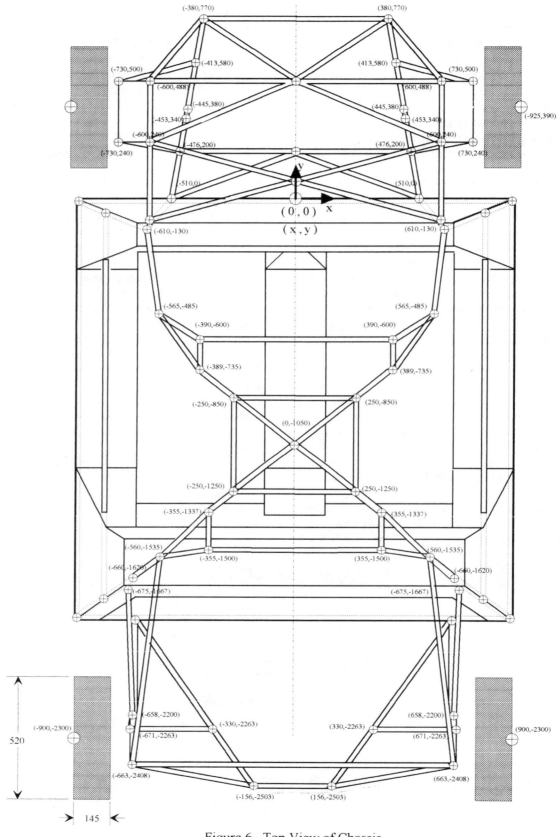

Figure 6. Top View of Chassis.

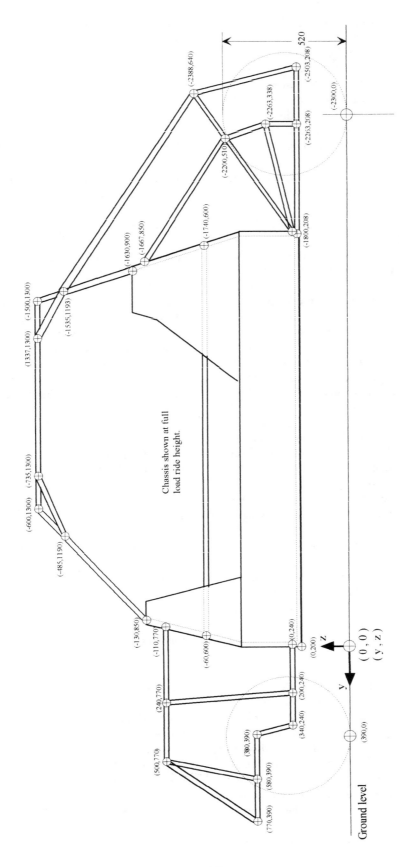

Figure 7. Side View of Chassis.

Chassis shown at full load ride height.

Ground level

(0, 0)
(y, z)

Therefore, chassis stiffness was increased by strategically placing the box sections around the perimeter of the monocoque. All box sections were constructed with four internal stiffening ribs for the extra strength needed to hold the heavy batteries.

PACKAGING - Major components were packaged into the chassis using the I-DEAS computer model. Chassis space frames were designed to accommodate the Geo Metro suspension while the overall size of the space frames were adjusted in the model to provide the needed space for the major components. A front wheel drive vehicle was decided upon with the electric motor and its controller (inverter) in the front space frame. This electric motor was fitted to a Geo Metro transmission, also conveniently located in the front, which was directly coupled to the front wheels. The Geo engine and alternator were placed in the rear space frame behind the storage compartment. Figure 4 shows the solid model and its use in component packaging.

FINAL CHASSIS DESIGN - Final MSU Spartan Charge chassis configuration was specified from the previously described design parameters. After considerable research and thought, a mid-chassis aluminum monocoque passenger compartment and front and rear steel bolt-on space frames were decided upon. This modular space frame/monocoque design can prove to be very convenient for small collision repairs. In the event of a small crash, the space frame will deform to absorb the crash energy leaving the monocoque unharmed which would enable the damaged space frame to be removed and a new space frame installed with relative ease.

The monocoque was made of recyclable sheet aluminum and was reinforced around the perimeter with an internal space-frame. Large box sections along the sides dramatically improve the torsional stiffness of the chassis and double as battery housings. This monocoque will contain five uniform battery packs that are inserted into the monocoque from the bottom. The sides and top of the box sections are then bent from one sheet of aluminum to ensure that the batteries are completely sealed and inaccessible from the passenger compartment.

Both space-frames were constructed of square mild steel tubing that were easy to weld mounts to. The steel bolt on and off space frames contain all of the major propulsion components except the batteries. Figures 6 and 7 show the final chassis design and display the coordinates of major structural member intersections in millimeters.

STRUCTURAL INTEGRITY

Through the use of finite element analysis (FEA) on I-DEAS the structure was proven to be sound and able to stand up to extreme operating conditions. All of the FEA analyses were performed using a linear static analysis. Structural integrity was confirmed with three analyses: *Torsional Stiffness*, *Mid-Span Bending*, and *Hitting a Bump While Braking*. In each analysis the entire chassis was modeled. Analyses verified that the chassis would be adequately stiff and strong to operate safely under extreme operating conditions.

TORSIONAL STIFFNESS - Torsional stiffness of the entire chassis was determined using rigid beams to conservatively model all suspension geometry while the rear wheels were held fixed. A 100Nm torque was then applied to the front wheels. The displacement results were used to calculate the angle difference between the front and rear axles. To determine the torsional stiffness in Nm/degree, the 100Nm torque load was divided by the angle difference between axles.

Fenton [2] states that the torsional stiffness of a vehicle chassis should be a minimum of 6500Nm/degree to prevent unsafe handling due to excessive dynamic deflection. Calculations indicated an angle difference between the front and rear axles of 6.03×10^{-3} degrees. Dividing this number into the 100Nm torque gave a torsional stiffness of 16,580 Nm/degree which is well above the published requirement for safe operation. It should be noted that a number well above the minimum is desirable to account for common 'over stiff' computer results from a finite element model of just over 5000 elements. Considering the amount of material used in the chassis it is hard to accept the large number obtained for torsional stiffness. Thus, we went with our design on the premises that an over designed chassis is acceptable but an under design could be devastating.

MID SPAN BENDING - Deflections at the middle of the chassis were made using component weights as indicated in Table 1. Component weights were placed in their appropriate position on the chassis, and wheel locations were held fixed. Fenton [2] states that mid span bending should not exceed 1.27mm. Analysis on the MSU Spartan Charge chassis indicated the mid span bending was 0.45mm. Considering compensation for common 'over stiff' computer results for our model, this result indicated that the vehicle was within acceptable deflection levels.

Table 1. Approximate Vehicle Component Weights used to Calculate Mid-Span Bending.

Component	Weight (lb)	Weight (Newtons)
I. C. Engine	130	580
Inverter	80	355
Electric Motor	160	710
Transmission	50	220
Dash	75	335
Batteries	800	3560
Passengers	400	1780
Seats	50	220
Fire System	10	45
Electrical, Fuses, Wiring	50	220
Fans	10	45
Fuel System	60	265
Body	150	670
Alum. Monocoque	250	1110
Top Roll Cage	35	155
Alternator	40	180
Steering	50	220
Doors	60	265

HITTING A BUMP WHILE BRAKING - This simulation shows the effect of both front wheels of the vehicle hitting a bump or curb while braking. Loads were calculated based on equations in Ref. [2]. Dynamic measurements on small passenger automobiles have shown peak accelerations of 3g recorded in the vertical direction. Longitudinal braking forces are limited by the adhesion of the tire to the road, thus a limiting figure of 1g is acceptable. It is suggested to multiply these accelerations by a 1.5 factor of safety to arrive at the corresponding maximum accelerations of 4.5g vertical and 1.5g horizontal. Then, as the driver applies the brakes while hitting a bump, the resulting forces will be

Vertical load due to bump $= R \times 4.5$

Rearward load due to bump $= R \times 4.5 \times \tan \Theta$

Load transfer due to bump $= R \times 4.5 \tan \Theta \times y/2B$

Load transfer due to braking $= 1.5 \, Wy/2B$

Rearward load due to braking $= 1.5R + 1.5 \, Wy/2B$

These add up to give the reaction at each of the front wheels

$$\text{Vertical} = 1.5\left\{ 3R\left(1 + \frac{y}{2B}\tan\Theta\right) + \frac{Wy}{2B} \right\} = 22.5\text{kN}$$

$$\text{Rearward} = 1.5\left\{ R\left(3\tan\Theta + 1\right) + \frac{Wy}{2B} \right\} = 28.0\text{kN}$$

where

W = weight of vehicle (3000 lb, 13360 N)

B = wheel base of vehicle (275 cm)

y = height of center of gravity above ground (35 cm)

R = single wheel reaction force, assuming under breaking 2/3 of the vehicle weight shifts to the front wheels (1000 lb, 4450 N)

Θ = angle between vertical and the line between impacting bump and axle, typical for hitting roadside curb (45°)

The breaking while hitting a bump force components were 22.5 kN vertical and 28.0 kN in the rearward direction. These forces were applied to the front wheels, while the rear was held fixed.

The front space frame, constructed of a steel with a 340MPa yield stress, was below yielding stress levels. But the extreme loading condition revealed that the maximum stress (136MPa) in the aluminum monocoque near the bottom front corner of the doors was near, yet below, the yield stress for the aluminum (145MPa) that we are using. This analysis confirms that under the most extreme driving conditions, hitting a curb while braking, the chassis will not plastically deform.

OCCUPANT PROTECTION

The ground-up MSU Spartan Charge vehicle is designed for occupant protection under the HEV Challenge Rules and Regulations document. Essential safety features of concern include protection in the event of frontal impact, side impact, and rollover. Containment of the batteries is addressed which is a very important issue in electric vehicles. In addition to previously mentioned vehicle structure design, I-DEAS contributed significantly to safety verification. Occupant protection FEA analyses were performed using the maximum reasonable loads, plus safety factors, to simulate the vehicle behavior in the event of a rollover or crash situation.

As specified in the Sports Car Club of America (SCCA) vehicle regulations, all the bars or safety structures that an occupant can come in contact with are padded with a minimum of 2.5cm of foam. There are no sharp exposed corners or edges where an occupant could be injured, plus five point seat belt harnesses are installed for the driver's and passenger's protection.

ROLLOVER PROTECTION - Occupants must be protected from contact with the ground in any rollover attitude. A roll bar near the occupants and a forward roll hoop are in place to protect against roof crushing. The roll bar is braced with braces of identical tubing attached at the top of the roll bar at 57 degrees from vertical and room is allocated so that the helmet of the tallest occupant of the vehicle is at least five (5) centimeters below the surface defined by the roll bar and the front roll hoop. Continuous closed sections of steel tubing welded to the internal steel space frame, around which the monocoque is constructed, make up the roll bar and roll hoop. Seamless SAE 4130 medium-carbon chromium-molybdenum steel tubing had an outside diameter of 1.5 inches and a nominal thickness of 0.095 inches.

The rollover finite element design was analyzed on I-DEAS with a relevant rollover load set. Required loading according to the United Nations Standard for rollover stated in Fenton [2] was 0.6 times the vehicle weight placed at each of the windscreen pillars. To give a higher factor of safety, a load of two times the vehicle weight was directed at 30° from vertical on the front drivers side A-pillar to determine the local stress in this critical area. Nodes representing the bottom of the vehicle were fixed. The highest stress in the rollover cage (650 MPa) is below the yield stress (820 MPa) for the alloy steel that was used and was located at the bottom of the drivers side front roll hoop.

SIDE COLLISION PROTECTION - Frame members extending from the roll bar to the roll hoop at a height above lap level protect vehicle occupants from a side collision. Steel side bars constructed from SAE 4130 medium-carbon Chromium-molybdenum steel tubing with an outer diameter of 1.5 inches and a wall thickness of 0.095 inches were incorporated in the door so as not to hamper vehicle egress. These bars were integrated into the doors of the vehicle, and were secured with a mechanical coupling at each end that served as the door latch. The sliding lock collar which is operated by a door handle was also constructed from SAE 4130 round stock. As an integrated whole, the bar and the coupling transmit impact forces from a side collision to the rest of the frame. Occupant safety is significantly enhanced with this feature.

The aluminum battery box structure is an energy absorbing crush zone also offering side collision protection. Each battery box is reinforced with one inch square steel tubing around the bottom outside face. Battery box openings along the bottom are reinforced with one half inch square solid 5454 aluminum bar stock. Four vertical stiffeners reinforce each battery box compartment against lateral forces.

For conducting a linear static stress analysis, a load of two times the vehicle weight was directed horizontally into the side of the car in an area corresponding to the middle of the passenger door. A node set representing the side of the vehicle opposite the intended impact area was restrained against movement in any direction. Maximum stresses on the side of the car were 140 MPa, below the 145 MPa yield stress for aluminum. Figure 8 shows the finite element model stress

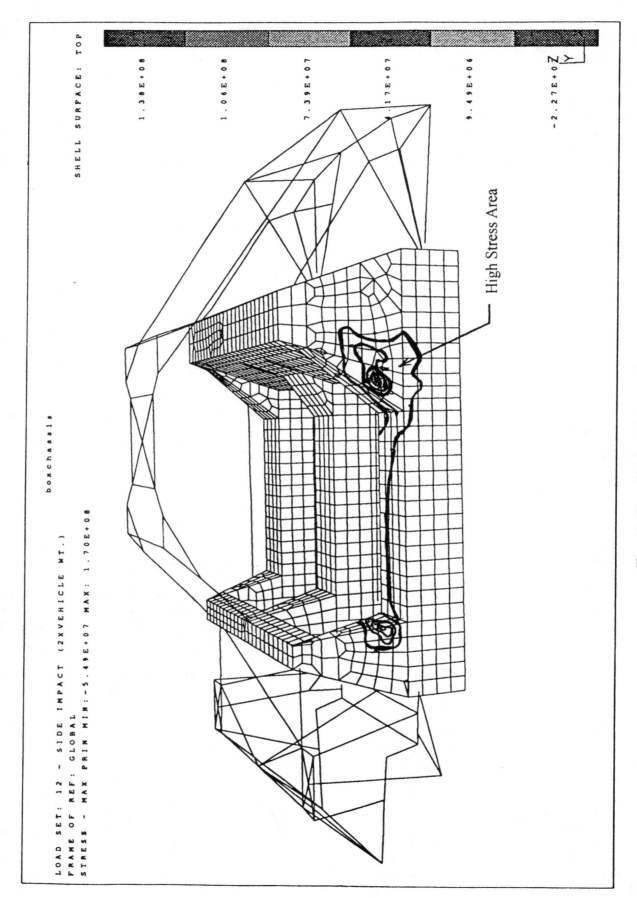

Figure 8. Stress Plot for Side Impact Test.

contours, the smallest closed contours having the maximum stress. Maximums occur at the interface where the loaded steel side impact bar comes in contact with the thinner wall aluminum sheet.

FRONTAL IMPACT PROTECTION - Occupants are protected from frontal impact from a minimum 300 mm crush zone, as specified in the rules, which is located between the plane defined by the nose of the vehicle and the vertical plane defined by the brake pedal hinge. However, the space needed for the electric motor, transmission, and motor controller was not to be included in the minimum crush zone dimension. The side bar door coupling, the roll bar/cage arrangement, and the monocoque all contribute to the overall stiffness and strength of the passenger compartment. These features are very important to the prevention of significant passenger compartment deformation in the event of a head on impact.

Fenton [2] states that in a frontal impact, the passenger compartment should retain its shape after a 30 mph solid barrier impact. An FEA analysis on I-DEAS involved forces based on the required 30mph (13.4 meters per second) impact velocity. The force was calculated by using

$F = m \times dV/dt = m \times \Delta V/\Delta t$

m = Vehicle mass (1360 kg)

ΔV = Change in velocity from 13.4 meters per second to 0 (13.4 m/s)

Δt = The average time it takes for a vehicle to completely stop upon hitting a barrier at 13.4 m/s (0.15 s)

A force of 121 kN was directed horizontally into the front of the car and a node set representing the rear of the monocoque was restrained against movement. As expected, stresses in the front space frame of the chassis, where the crush zone is located, were well above yield stress, so significant plastic deformation would take place as kinetic energy dissipates. However, the passenger compartment was stressed at yield stress, which complies with Fenton's statement that no significant plastic deformation should occur in the passenger compartment. The maximum stresses in the passenger compartment were around 145 MPa at the space frame/monocoque interface, just reaching the 145 MPa yield stress for aluminum.

BATTERY CONTAINMENT - Physical isolation of the batteries from the passengers involves several levels of protection, the primary of which involves the separation of the batteries from the driver and passenger by the 0.062 inch thick walls of the fully enclosed battery box structure. Battery tray openings are reinforced with one half inch square solid 5454 aluminum bar stock to prevent local deformation. Four vertical stiffening ribs reinforce each battery box compartment against lateral forces. These physical isolation and strengthening features stiffen up the structure in addition to offering passenger and driver protection from the batteries and side impacts.

CONCLUSION

The HEV Challenge provided a unique opportunity to design and construct a hybrid electric vehicle chassis. Chassis design parameters were identified as: passenger accommodations, materials for fabrication, battery housings, and packaging. These were discussed and appropriate decisions were made which resulted in a structurally sound HEV chassis. The design was constructed for the 1993 and 1994 Hybrid Electric Vehicle Challenge. The HEV Challenge gives students the chance to apply their design and analytical skills to real world problems.

A high-technology computer-aided approach was utilized in the chassis' structural system development. Computer solid modeling and finite element modeling were used extensively in the chassis design. Solid modeling was especially helpful in packaging the components, deciding mount locations, verifying vision requirements, surfacing the body, and provided an accurate visual aid. Finite element analyses were instrumental in determining structural member locations and cross-sections. Structural integrity finite element analyses were performed to ensure that the chassis would be safe and able to withstand the excessive rigors of competition. I-DEAS proved to be a valuable tool in the development of the chassis.

REFERENCES

1. Bray, Jack. Aluminum Mill and Engineered Wrought Products, Reynolds Metals Company.

2. Fenton, J. Vehicle Body Layout and Analysis, Mechanical Engineering Publications, London.

3. Ford Motor Company. HEV Challenge Rules and Regulations, 1992.

4. Fournier, Ron & Sue. Metal Fabricator's Handbook, Price Stern Sloan, Inc. 1990.

5. Lawry, Mark. I-DEAS Student Guide, Structural Dynamics Research Corporation, 1990.

6. Lawry, Mark. I-DEAS Finite Element Modeling, Structural Dynamics Research Corporation, 1990.

7. Smith, Carroll. Engineer to Win, Motorbooks International. 1984.

8. Smith, Carroll. Prepare to Win, Aero Publishers, Inc. 1975.

950491

A Hybrid Vehicle Evaluation Code and Its Application to Vehicle Design

Salvador M. Aceves and J. Ray Smith
Lawrence Livermore National Lab.

ABSTRACT

This paper describes a hybrid vehicle simulation model which can be applied to many of the vehicles currently being considered for low emissions and high fuel economy. The code operates in batch mode with all the vehicle information stored in data files. The code calculates power train dimensions, fuel economy for three driving schedules, time for 0 - 96 km/h at maximum acceleration, hill climbing performance, and emissions.

This paper also documents the application of the code to a hybrid vehicle that utilizes a hydrogen internal combustion engine. The simulation model is used for parametric studies of the vehicle. The results show the fuel economy of the vehicle as a function of vehicle mass, aerodynamic drag, engine efficiency, accessory load, and flywheel efficiency. The code also calculates the minimum flywheel energy and power to obtain a desired performance. The hydrogen hybrid vehicle analyzed in the paper has a range of 480 km (300 miles), with a predicted gasoline equivalent fuel efficiency of 33.7 km/liter (79.3 mpg).

INTRODUCTION

Modeling is an important tool in the design and evaluation of vehicles. Direct testing of vehicles is expensive, time consuming and difficult. While it is recognized that vehicle testing is always necessary, models can provide accurate estimates of vehicle performance at a reduced cost and effort. Modeling also provides a method for testing new concepts and ideas at early stages in the vehicle development process.

This paper describes a vehicle evaluation code. This code has been developed to analyze electric and hybrid vehicles. Electric and hybrid vehicles are currently receiving great attention, due to concerns about emissions and energy efficiency. Electric vehicles are the best developed technology that can be used to meet the 1998 zero emission vehicle mandates imposed by the State of California, and hybrid vehicles offer the potential for very high energy efficiencies, long driving ranges, and low emissions or zero emissions for fuel cell hybrids.

Several electric and hybrid vehicle models exist in the literature. Interest in electric vehicles in the late 1970s and early 1980s resulted in many models;[1-5] and the current interest has resulted in the development of a new generation of vehicle codes. These include, among others, a code that applies to pure electric vehicles, focusing especially on battery simulation;[6] a code to simulate stirling engine hybrids;[7] and a code applicable to electric vehicles, range-extender hybrids, and conventional cars.[8] A survey of existing vehicle simulation codes has also been published recently.[9] The new models differ from the older models in the characteristics of the individual components being simulated, as well as in the vehicle configurations being analyzed, because progress in power electronics now makes possible not only more efficient components, but also more efficient configurations than those available in the past. All these models incorporate a wide range of degrees of detail and complexity. As with all models, increasing the accuracy results in an increased complexity of the model, as well as in an increased need for vehicle component data.

The Hybrid Vehicle Evaluation Code (HVEC) described in this paper has been developed to evaluate many of the vehicle configurations currently being considered for low emission and high energy efficiency vehicles. HVEC is capable of analyzing vehicles with different combinations of primary power supplies (engines, fuel cells), and energy storage devices (batteries, flywheels, ultracapacitors).

HVEC applies only to electric vehicles and series hybrids in which the primary power supply and the storage system provide only electric power to the traction motor. No mechanical connection between primary power supply, storage, and traction motor is allowed. Due to this limitation, HVEC cannot be applied to simulate conventional vehicles. Figure 1 shows a schematic of the vehicle configuration that can be simulated with HVEC.

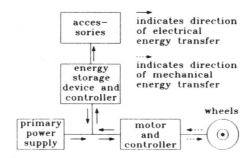

Figure 1. Schematic of the vehicle configuration that can be simulated with HVEC. Primary power supplies are engines or fuel cells. Storage systems are flywheels, ultra-capacitors or batteries.

DESCRIPTION OF THE CODE

As stated previously, HVEC applies only to electric and series hybrid vehicles. The vehicle configurations that can be analyzed with HVEC are listed in Table 1, along with a brief description of each. Table 1 includes some of the configurations that present the most interest for high efficiency and low emissions vehicles. These configurations also represent the most common combinations of primary power supplies and energy storage devices. Table 1 does not list separate configurations for ultracapacitors, because these are presently simulated in the same way as flywheels (although most likely with different parameters).

The code operates in batch mode, with all the information for the vehicle provided in a data file. The user starts by selecting a vehicle configuration from the list given in Table 1. After this is done, the user selects the names for the vehicle data file and two result data files (a short, summary file; and a long, more detailed file). The user can select these files by either typing in a file name, or by selecting the default file names given by the code. A list of all the information required to describe a vehicle, taken from an example data file, is shown in Table 2, for an engine-flywheel hybrid (configuration 4).

HVEC starts by calculating weights and volumes for the power train components. Weights and volumes are calculated from values and correlations given in the literature,[10,11] or from correlations derived from manufacturer's equipment catalogs. The power train weight is then used to calculate the test vehicle weight, according to the following equation[3]:

$$TVW = BCVW + (1 + MPF)*(PTW - BCPTW)$$

Table 1. List of vehicle configurations that can be analyzed with HVEC, including a brief description of each. Ultracapacitors are simulated in the same way as flywheels, and therefore the list does not include separate configurations for ultracapacitors.

1. Electric vehicle. Conventional battery-powered electric vehicle.
2. Flywheel vehicle. Electric vehicle which uses a flywheel instead of a battery for energy storage.
3. Battery-flywheel hybrid. This vehicle uses a flywheel for leveling the battery load and for regenerative braking.
4. Engine-generator-flywheel hybrid. This vehicle uses an engine operating at a fixed power, in an on-off mode, to keep the flywheel at an appropriate state of charge. The flywheel provides the power peaks, stores the engine energy not required for traction, and provides all the traction energy when the engine is off.
5. Engine-generator-battery hybrid. This vehicle operates in exactly the same way as the engine-flywheel hybrid, with the flywheel replaced by a battery for energy storage.
6. Fuel cell-flywheel hybrid. The operation of this vehicle is also the same as the operation of the engine-flywheel hybrid, with the fuel cell providing a constant power, in an on-off mode.
7. Fuel cell-battery hybrid. In this vehicle, the fuel cell also operates at a constant power in an on-off mode. Energy storage is provided by batteries.
8. Fuel cell vehicle. In this vehicle, the fuel cell directly drives the motor. HVEC assumes that this vehicle cannot do regenerative braking.

In this equation, TVW is the test vehicle weight, BCVW and BCPTW are base case weights for the vehicle and the power train, given in the vehicle data file, PTW is the vehicle power train weight, calculated by the model, and MPF is the mass propagation factor, an empirical coefficient which accounts for the fact that a heavier power train requires a heavier structure to carry it. Base case weights can be estimated from existing prototypes. This formulation allows the study of performance changes due to heavier or lighter power trains.

Table 2. Information required for the vehicle specification data file for vehicle configuration 4 (engine-flywheel hybrid), for a hydrogen hybrid vehicle with an optimized engine.

Title of run	LLNL Hydrogen Hybrid Vehicle

Enter type of electric motor
1. dc motor
2. Brushless, permanent magnet motor
3. ac induction motor I
4. ac induction motor II
5. User-Defined motor   4

    Is there regenerative braking?   1
    1=yes, 0=no

Vehicle characteristics
1.	base-case vehicle test weight, kg (empty weight + 136 kg)	1,250
2.	base-case power train weight, kg	263
3.	mass propagation factor	0.3
4.	frontal area in m^2	2.04
5.	aerodynamic drag coefficient	0.24
6.	coefficient of rolling friction	0.007
7.	2nd coefficient of rolling friction, s/m	0.0

Motor characteristics
11.	motor maximum continuous torque, N-m	100.0
12.	motor maximum RPM	11,000.0

Transmission characteristics
21.	transmission efficiency	0.95
22.	velocity for changing to 2nd gear, m/s	100.0
23.	velocity for changing to 3rd gear, m/s	100.0
24.	1st gear reduction ratio, RPM/(m/s)	300.0
25.	2nd gear reduction ratio, RPM/(m/s)	0.0
26.	3rd gear reduction ratio, RPM/(m/s)	0.0

Moment of inertia contributions
31.	tire radius, m	0.30
32.	moment of inertia for 4 tires and axles, kg m^2	5.0
33.	moment of inertia for motor and transmission, kg m^2	0.06

Energy storage
42.	flywheel storage capacity, J	7.2×10^6
43.	flywheel specific energy storage, J/kg	1.8×10^5
44.	flywheel maximum specific power, W/kg	5,000.0
45.	flywheel turnaround efficiency (output/input, including electronics)	0.90

Engine characteristics
Enter a number for engine type
1. Gasoline engine
2. Natural gas engine
3. Hydrogen engine   3

51.	Engine power at peak efficiency, W	31,000
52.	peak engine efficiency fraction	0.46
53.	peak generator efficiency fraction	0.95
54.	maximum continuous engine power, W (for hills)	40,000
55.	engine efficiency fraction at maximum power	0.40
56.	generator efficiency at maximum engine power	0.90
57.	length of test drive, m	500,000
58.	penalty for engine start up, J	36,000

Accessories
Air Conditioning load is 10% of steady-state load at 50 mph
Do you want air conditioning? (1=yes, 0=no) 1
61.	additional accessory load	500
62.	energy transfer efficiency between flywheel and accessories	1

File control
Do you want a file (POWER.DAT) with drive power results? (1=yes, 0=no)   0
Do you want a file (FLYWHEEL.DAT) with flywheel results? (1=yes, 0=no)   0
Do you want a file (ACCELRTN.DAT) with 60 mph accel data? (1=yes, 0=no)   0
How many cycles for each schedule do you want in the files?   0

Parametric studies
Do you want to do a parametric study? (1=yes, 0=no)   0
Enter variable number that is to be varied within a range   0
Enter minimum value of range   0
Enter maximum value of range   0
Enter number of interval subdivisions   0

HVEC then simulates a test drive of the vehicle over three driving cycles. The driving cycles are: a constant 88 km/h (55 mph) drive, the EPA Federal Urban Driving Schedule, and the Highway Driving Schedule. For vehicle configurations 1, 2 and 3 (limited range vehicles), each driving cycle is repeated until the vehicle energy or power is not enough to meet the requirements of the drive. For vehicle configurations 4 through 8, the driving cycles are repeated until the vehicle travels a specified distance and the energy storage system has the same state of charge as it had at the beginning of the drive. This distance is chosen to be long enough to yield good average values over many cycles. No consideration is given to the possibility of having vehicles 4 through 8 run out of fuel. It is assumed that they have a fuel tank that is large enough to drive the specified distance. However, the test drive for vehicles 4 through 8 can stop before reaching the specified length of the test drive if the primary power source (engine or fuel cell), or the energy storage system, does not have enough power to meet the requirements of the driving schedule. HVEC requires all vehicles to precisely meet the velocity-time relations imposed by the driving cycles.

HVEC uses basic vehicle dynamics equations[12] to calculate the required motor power during vehicle operation. The user can specify vehicles with or without regenerative braking (except for fuel cell vehicles with no electrical storage capability, configuration 8). In hybrid vehicles, HVEC controls the energy flows in and out of the primary power supply, the storage system, and the motor, with strategies aimed at yielding maximum energy efficiency. In hybrid vehicles with an engine or a fuel cell, the engine or fuel cell initially operates at a fixed power to charge the storage system. When the storage is fully charged, the engine or fuel cell is turned off, and the storage provides all the energy for propulsion and for accessories. This process continues until the storage is discharged to some preset level. At this point, the engine or fuel cell is turned on to start a new recharge cycle. On-off cycling of engines and fuel cells may cause efficiency losses and/or energy consumption. A cold engine may have higher friction than a warm one, because oil viscosity is higher at low temperature. Low polluting engines may require electric heating of the catalytic converter before start up. To take into account these effects, the model allows the user to specify a penalty for engine or fuel cell start up (number 58 in Table 2). This penalty indicates an amount of electric power that is deducted from the storage device

every time the engine or fuel cell is switched on. Deep storage cycles are desirable to reduce the cycling frequency of the engine or fuel cell. However, the depth of discharge for batteries is usually limited to 80% to avoid battery damage. Flywheels and ultracapacitors are discharged until they have a specified amount of energy, which may be necessary if acceleration is required (such as for passing) before the engine or fuel cell can start operating. While HVEC assumes that engines and fuel cells in hybrid vehicles usually operate at a fixed, normal power, HVEC also allows engines and fuel cells to work at a high power setting, which is used exclusively for long hill climbing, for which the storage system may not have enough energy to provide the desired performance. As the vehicle operates most of the time at normal power, the engine and generator, or fuel cell, are optimized for this condition, and the efficiency of the system may be lower at the high power setting.

At the end of each test drive, HVEC gives the results for distance traveled, energy consumption, fuel economy in km/liter (and mpg), and a summary of system efficiencies and energy losses for the driving cycle. After completing the three test drives, HVEC calculates the time for 0-96 km/h acceleration, and hill climbing performance: range on a 5% and on a 30% hill for vehicles 1, 2, and 3; and continuous hill climbing slope at a 96 km/h speed for vehicle configurations 4 through 8.

Finally, the code calculates vehicle emissions. For electric and flywheel vehicles (configurations 1, 2, and 3), emissions are calculated by assuming that the electricity required to charge the battery or flywheel is generated at a natural gas power plant. For vehicles with an engine, the user can choose between a gasoline engine, a natural gas engine, or a hydrogen engine. Emission values for the gasoline engine are assumed equal to the CARB LEV (California Air Resources Board Low Emission Vehicle) limits. For the natural gas engine, the code uses the CARB ULEV (Ultra Low Emission Vehicle) limits, which have been recently demonstrated.[13] For the hydrogen engine, HVEC uses the emission rates measured by Homan,[14] for a hydrogen engine operating very lean. Fuel cells are assumed to have no emissions, except for CO_2 production. For CO_2 calculations, hydrogen is assumed as being generated by steam reforming of natural gas at a 67% efficiency. If the hydrogen is obtained from a renewable source, net CO_2 production is zero.

HVEC allows the user to specify if any of three additional result data files should be generated. These files include information on the driving cycles, on the storage system, and on the maximum acceleration test, respectively. HVEC also has an option which allows running for multiple values of a single variable. This option is very useful in parametric analyses, optimization, or for vehicle synthesis, where the performance specifications are given, and the goal is to find vehicle characteristics that are compatible with these specifications. This option allows rapid assessment of fuel economy sensitivity to design variables.

VEHICLE COMPONENT SIMULATION

This section describes the procedure used to simulate the major vehicle components.

ELECTRIC MOTOR AND CONTROLLER - The efficiency of the electric motor and controller is calculated by using performance maps provided by manufacturers. The performance maps are specified in data files as tables of efficiency values as a function of torque and RPM. HVEC then uses Lagrangian interpolation to obtain the efficiency for any combination of torque and RPM. HVEC includes data files for two ac induction motors, each made by a different manufacturer; a brushless, permanent magnet motor, and a dc motor. The user has the choice of selecting one of these motors, or generate and use a data file for a different motor.

The electric motor simulation assumes that the performance maps are scalable in terms of the maximum torque and speed, so that a single motor map can be used for a family of motors with the same characteristics and different sizes. According to Unnewehr and Knoop,[2] this is a good assumption, if the difference in sizes is not very large.

TRANSMISSION - The transmission is simulated by specifying the vehicle speeds at which an upshift or a downshift occurs, as well as the reduction ratios for each of the gears. HVEC simulates a 3 speed transmission, but the same transmission model can be used to simulate two speed, or fixed ratio transmissions if the speed for shifting into the higher gears is set well above driving cycle speeds, so that the vehicle never shifts into these gears. The model assumes a constant transmission efficiency, which is also specified by the user.

ENGINE AND GENERATOR - As previously discussed, engines used in the present model operate at two fixed conditions, in an on-off mode. The two conditions are: normal power, used for regular city and highway driving schedules; and high power, used for long hill climbs. Therefore, the engine can be completely characterized by specifying the engine efficiency and power at normal and high power conditions.

The generator is also specified by two efficiency values, one at the normal power conditions, and the other at the high power conditions since generator efficiency is also a function of torque and RPM. Operating the engine and generator at fixed conditions makes it possible to optimize the system at the normal power conditions, which is the most usual operating point. The system efficiency is then higher than the efficiency of an engine and generator that have to operate over a wide range of conditions.

FUEL CELL - In hybrid vehicles (configurations 6 and 7), fuel cells are assumed to operate at two fixed power settings, in the same mode of operation used for constant speed engine hybrids. Therefore, fuel cells in hybrid vehicles are also completely characterized by the efficiency and power at the high power mode and at the normal power mode. In pure fuel cell vehicles (configuration 8), fuel cells directly provide all the power to drive the traction motor. This configuration is evaluated by using fuel cell efficiency data as a function of generated power. Fuel cell information is stored in a data file. HVEC includes data for a proton exchange membrane fuel cell.[11] The user can choose this data file, or generate and use a data file that is appropriate for a particular fuel cell type or characteristics. HVEC does not allow regenerative braking for pure fuel cell vehicles, due to the high cost and technical difficulties associated with fuel cell electrolyzers.

FLYWHEEL OR ULTRACAPACITOR - Flywheels or ultracapacitors are defined by specifying the energy storage capacity, the energy storage density (per unit mass of the system), the maximum specific power (maximum power divided by total system mass), and the turnaround efficiency (output energy/input energy), which is assumed constant. Turnaround efficiency includes the flywheel or ultracapacitor and all required electronics for power conditioning. HVEC keeps an inventory of the energy stored in the system, and controls the operation of the engine or fuel cell based on this value.

BATTERIES - Batteries are, among all the vehicle components used by HVEC, the component that presents the greatest difficulty to simulate with a good degree of accuracy. Battery performance is a function of many parameters, such as materials and construction methods, battery age, battery discharge rate, battery discharge history, and temperature. All these factors significantly affect the battery performance.

HVEC uses the battery descriptions and routines previously used by Marr et al.,[6] for an electric vehicle simulation model. This model uses basic equations for the electric circuits, along with experimental correlations for cell internal resistance and zero load voltage as a function of battery depth of discharge, to evaluate the energy and power available. Battery temperature effects are not included in the model, but can be incorporated if experimental data are available.

Battery information is stored in data files. HVEC includes data files for the following types of batteries:

- Tubular lead-acid battery
- Nickel-Iron battery
- Sodium-Sulphur battery

Other types of batteries may be more desirable for electric or hybrid vehicles. However, lack of data at the present time precluded data files for these other types. The user can generate a battery file that is appropriate for a particular application. It should be recognized that this is a difficult procedure, because a battery model is usually appropriate only for the specific type of battery for which the experimental results were obtained.

When battery data are limited, and high accuracy is not required, the flywheel model can be used to simulate a battery. The flywheel model only requires information on specific energy, specific power, and turnaround efficiency, which are available for most battery types. This approach has been used by some researchers in the past,[7] and can be used to obtain initial estimates to vehicle range, energy consumption, and performance.

CODE VALIDATION

Validation of vehicle simulation models is difficult due to the great number of variables that affect vehicle performance. A rigorous code validation requires a statistical analysis, in which the code results are compared to the average vehicle performance obtained over many test drives, to reduce the effect of random variations in vehicle parameters or driving conditions.[15]

HVEC has not been validated according to this criterion. However, HVEC has been applied to simulate the performance of two current electric vehicle prototypes for which the required vehicle and performance parameters are known. The results of the analysis indicate an agreement within 10% between the experimental and calculated values, for fuel economy as well as for time for maximum effort acceleration. While not a rigorous validation, this agreement is considered satisfactory, and indicates that code results are a reasonable indication of vehicle performance.

APPLICATION OF THE CODE

HVEC is now applied to the analysis of a five passenger, engine-flywheel hybrid vehicle which utilizes a hydrogen internal combustion engine. This vehicle is being developed as a low emission, general purpose, long range vehicle. The vehicle operates with a flywheel and an optimized hydrogen engine with a 15:1 compression ratio. The engine is designed for lean-burn operation at constant speed, and has a predicted brake thermal efficiency of 46%. This vehicle may also be capable of a gasoline equivalent fuel economy of 33.8 km/l (80 mpg), which has been set as a goal by the Partnership for a New Generation of Vehicles (PNGV). The vehicle specifications are given in Table 2. While the values listed in the table are estimates, they are believed to be achievable with current technology. Engine and flywheel are key vehicle components that are currently under development.[16,17] Engine efficiency is expected to reach 46% based on previous research[18,19] on high compression, lean burn hydrogen engines. Flywheel data in Table 2 has been obtained from preliminary measurements.

Table 3 lists the results obtained for the vehicle. The calculations assume a lower heating value for gasoline equal to 3.18×10^7 J/l. The model predicts a very high combined fuel economy (33.7 km/l, or 79.3 mpg, 55% urban, 45% highway, almost reaching the PNGV goal), emissions lower than those obtained with an electric vehicle, if power plant emissions are taken into account,[20] and good performance (0 - 96 km/h acceleration in less than 10 s). Fuel economy is lower for the urban cycle than for the highway cycle, mainly due to the accessory load which has to be provided during vehicle operation (1000 W total; 500 W for air conditioning and 500 W for other accessories. These values are considered appropriate average accessory loads for driving conditions over an entire year). Since a vehicle in the urban driving cycle takes longer to complete the specified distance, more energy is necessary to satisfy the accessory load in this cycle. Fuel economy for a vehicle with zero accessory load is slightly higher for the urban cycle than for the highway cycle due to regenerative braking in the high efficiency power train considered. Fuel economy for the highway cycle is slightly higher than for the 88 km/h drive, because the vehicle components are selected to provide a high combined cycle fuel economy, resulting in a high power train efficiency for the

Table 3. Results obtained for the hydrogen hybrid vehicle defined in Table 2.

a) Approximate weights and volumes for power train

Component	Weight,kg	Volume,liters
Motor	24	8
Controller	20	20
Transmission	9	3
Flywheel	40	44
Engine	119	131
Generator	42	14
Fuel tank	26	90
Total	280	310
Overall vehicle wt 1272		

b) Energy information for each driving cycle

	88 km/h (55 mph)	Urban	Hwy
Number of cycles		43	32
Total time, s	20,844	57,671	23,932
Distance traveled, km	512.5	504.2	515.6
Consumed energy, MJ	439	512	441
Wh/km	238	282	237
Gasoline equiv. km/l	37.1	31.3	37.2
Gasoline equiv. mpg	87.3	73.7	87.5
Combined gasoline equivalent km/l (mpg) (55% urban, 45% hwy)	33.7 (79.3)		

c) Performance characteristics

Time to reach 96 km/h, s	9.7
Distance travelled in 10 s, m	165
96 km/h climbing slope in percent	5.5

d) Emissions in g/km. LEV and ULEV values added for comparison

	Vehicle	LEV	ULEV
CO_2:	76		
HC:	3.1×10^{-3}	4.7×10^{-2}	2.5×10^{-2}
CO:	3.1×10^{-3}	2.1	1.1
NO_x:	5.6×10^{-2}	1.3×10^{-1}	1.3×10^{-1}

highway cycle. This compensates for the obvious advantages of constant speed driving. The values for the fuel tank weight and volume listed in Table 3 correspond to a cryogenic liquid hydrogen storage system that can store 3.75 kg of hydrogen to give a 480 km (300 mile) range.

The code has also been used for parametric studies of this vehicle. Parametric studies are important because, some of the vehicle data are subject to change. It is also desirable to know how sensitive the fuel economy of the vehicle is to variations in the different parameters. This information allows the vehicle developer to spend a greater effort on improving the parameters that are the most important for obtaining high fuel economy.

Figures 2-4 show the results of the parametric analysis. Figures 2(a) - (d) are a set of fuel efficiency maps for the vehicle, with contour lines that indicate gasoline equivalent km/l, with mpg in parentheses, for the combined driving cycle as a function of engine brake thermal efficiency, versus vehicle mass, drag, accessory load, and flywheel efficiency, respectively. These figures also show operating points for similar vehicles with a hydrogen engine, a compressed natural gas (CNG) engine, and a gasoline engine. The efficiency for the gasoline engine shown in the figures is the peak efficiency for a current engine.[21] The efficiency of the natural gas engine is estimated as 35%, assuming 12:1 compression ratio and storchrometric air/fuel ratio.

Figure 2(a) shows fuel economy contours as a function of engine efficiency and vehicle test mass. The figure shows constant fuel economy lines with a small slope, which indicates that fuel economy is relatively insensitive to vehicle mass. This figure (as well as Figs. 2(b) - (d)) also shows that the CNG and gasoline hybrids have fuel economies that fall well below the 33.8 km/l (80 mpg) PNGV goal. Only the hydrogen hybrid vehicle or similar efficiency fuel cell vehicle can approach the desired goal.

Figure 2(b) shows fuel economy lines as a function of engine efficiency and vehicle C_dA product, where C_d is the vehicle drag coefficient and A is the frontal area of the vehicle. The product C_dA determines the aerodynamic drag on the vehicle. Constant fuel economy lines in Fig. 2(b) also have a small slope, which indicates that drag does not have a major effect on fuel economy, at the speeds being considered in this analysis.

Figure 2(c) shows fuel economy lines as a function of engine efficiency and vehicle accessory load. The figure shows that accessory load has a major effect on fuel economy, and this effect is observed to increase as the engine becomes more efficient. This figure points very clearly to accessory load reduction as an important way to obtain high fuel economy in high efficiency power train vehicles.

Figure 2(d) shows a fuel economy map for the hydrogen hybrid vehicle, with fuel economy as a function of flywheel turnaround efficiency and engine efficiency. The figure shows that flywheel efficiency has a strong effect on the fuel

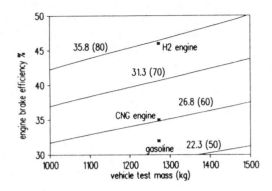

Fig. 2a

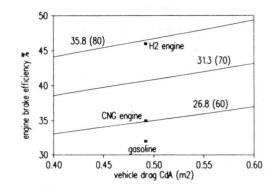

Fig. 2b

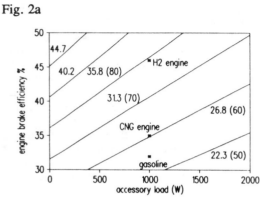

Fig. 2c

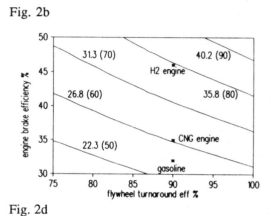

Fig. 2d

Figure 2a-d. Fuel economy maps for the hybrid vehicle in the combined cycle. The lines indicate gasoline equivalent km/l, with mpg in parentheses, as a function of engine brake thermal efficiency, and an additional parameter, chosen as mass for Fig. 2(a), drag for 2(b), accessory load for 2(c), and flywheel turnaround efficiency for 2(d). The figures also show the operating points for vehicles with a hydrogen engine, with a compressed natural gas (CNG) engine. and with a gasoline engine.

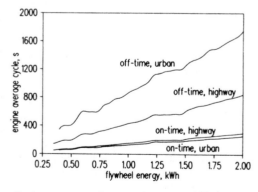

Figure 3. Average engine on-time and off-time, for the urban and highway driving cycles, as a function of flywheel energy storage capacity, for the hydrogen hybrid vehicle with a 31 kW engine power output.

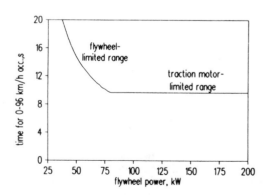

Figure 4. Time to reach 96 km/h, as a function of flywheel power capacity, for the hydrogen hybrid vehicle.

economy of the vehicle. The region in which the fuel economy exceeds 33.8 km/l (80 mpg) occupies only the upper right corner of the figure, indicating that a combination of high flywheel efficiency and high engine-generator efficiency is necessary to achieve the PNGV goal. Reaching the flywheel and engine efficiency values indicated in this figure is probably the biggest challenge in designing a vehicle that meets the PNGV goal.

Flywheel energy storage capacity and power are also important parameters for vehicle design. It is especially important to know the minimum flywheel energy storage capacity and power that results in satisfactory vehicle operation. Figures 3 and 4 show the results of a parametric analysis, for the flywheel energy storage and power capacities, respectively.

As flywheel energy storage capacity increases, it takes a longer time for it to charge and discharge. Therefore, both the average engine on-time and off-time are increasing functions of the flywheel energy storage capacity. Figure 3 shows average engine on-time and off-time, for the urban and highway cycles, for the hybrid vehicle. The linearity of the curves (except for some variations due to the irregularities in the driving cycle) indicates that the engine duty cycle (fraction of the total time the engine is on) remains constant in the whole range, approximately equal to 0.13 for the urban cycle, and 0.26 for the highway cycle. For small flywheel capacities, the average engine on-time drops to under 1 minute, where engine cycling losses may set a lower limit to the flywheel energy capacity.

Figure 4 shows required time to reach 96 km/h (60 mph), as a function of flywheel power capacity, for the hydrogen hybrid vehicle. The time for maximum effort acceleration from 0 to 96 km/h drops rapidly from 30 to 9.7 s as the flywheel power increases from 25 to 80 kW. Further increases in flywheel power do not have any effect on the time for maximum acceleration, because, for high flywheel power, maximum acceleration is limited by maximum motor power output. Maximum flywheel power equired to meet the driving cycles is about 35 kW.

CONCLUSIONS

This paper describes a vehicle simulation model which can be applied to many of the electric and hybrid vehicle configurations currently being considered for low emissions and high-fuel economy. For a given vehicle, the model calculates energy consumption and fuel economy over three driving cycles, maximum effort acceleration performance, hill climbing performance, power train component dimensions, and emissions. The results obtained with the simulation code have been compared with measurements made for two existing electric vehicle prototypes, and the agreement has been satisfactory.

The paper also describes the application of the simulation model to a hydrogen hybrid vehicle that operates with a constant speed, high compression ratio internal combustion engine. The results indicate that, for the vehicle characteristics used in the analysis, the vehicle is close to meeting the 33.8 km/l (80 mpg) PNGV goal, has high performance, low emissions, and a 480 km (300 mile) range on 3.75 kg of hydrogen.

The simulation model is also used in parametric evaluations of the vehicle. These have shown that vehicle fuel economy for the hydrogen hybrid vehicle is a strong function of engine efficiency, flywheel turnaround efficiency, and accessory load, and only a week function of mass and drag. Parametric analyses are also applied in the calculation of the minimum flywheel energy and power requirements.

ACKNOWLEDGEMENTS

This work performed under the auspices of the U.S. Department of Energy by the Lawrence Livermore National Laboratory under Contract No. W-7405-ENG-48.

REFERENCES

1)   Chang, M.C., 1979, "Computer Simulation of an Advanced Hybrid Electric Power Vehicle," SAE Transactions, Vol. 87, Section 1, pp. 890-904.

2)   Unnewehr, L.E., and Knoop, C.W., 1979, "Electrical Component Modeling and Sizing for EV Simulation," SAE Transactions, Vol. 87, Section 1, pp. 877-889.

3)   O'Connell, L.G., Anderson, C.J., Behrin, E., Cliff, W., Crisp, R., Forsberg, H.C., Hudson, C.L., Payne, J.S., Renner, R., Schrot, M.D., Strickland, G., Schwartz, M., Walsh, W.J., 1980, "Energy Storage Systems For Automobile Propulsion, Final Report," Lawrence Livermore National Laboratory Report UCRL-53053-80.

4)   Dobner, D.J., and Woods, E.J., 1982, "An Electric Vehicle Dynamic Simulation," SAE Paper 820779, Presented at the Passenger Car Meeting, Troy, MI.

5) DeWispelare, A.R., 1983, "Electric Vehicle Modeling and Simulation," Technical Report AU-AFIT-EN-TR-83-4, School of Engineering, Air Force Institute of Technology, Wright-Patterson Air Force Base.

6) Marr, W.W., Walsh, W.J., and Symons, P.C., 1991, "User's Guide to DIANE Version 2.1: A Microcomputer Software Package for Modeling Battery Performance in Electric Vehicle Applications," Argonne National Laboratory Report ANL/ESD--8, DE91 006071.

7) Schreiber, J.G., Shaltens, R.K., and Beremand, D.G., 1992, "Electric and Hybrid Electric Vehicle Study Utilizing a Time-Stepping Simulation," Proceedings of the IECEC Conference, Vol. 3, pp. 159-165.

8) Cole, G.H., 1993, "SIMPLEV: A Simple Electric Vehicle Simulation Program Version 2.0," Idaho National Engineering Laboratory Report DOE/ID-10293-2.

9) Murrell, D., 1994, "Motor Vehicle Power Train Simulations," report to U.S. Department of Energy, Office of Transportation Technologies.

10) DeLuchi, M., 1992, "Hydrogen Fuel Cell Vehicles," Institute of Transportation Studies Report UCD-ITS-RR-92-14, University of California, Davis, CA.

11) Allison Gas Turbine Division, GM Corp., 1993, "Research and Development of Proton Exchange Membrane (PEM) Fuel Cell System for Transportation Applications, Initial Conceptual Design Report," Report EDR 16194, Prepared for the Office of Transportation Technologies, Department of Energy.

12) Gillespie, T.D., 1992, "Fundamentals of Vehicle Dynamics," Society of Automotive Engineers, Warrendale, PA.

13) Cogan, R.J., Editor, 1993, "Chrysler Expands NGV Lineup," Green Car Journal, Vol. 2, p. 38.

14) Homan, H.S., 1978, "An Experimental Study of Reciprocating Internal Combustion Engines Operated on Hydrogen," Ph.D. dissertation, Cornell University.

15) Waters, W.C., 1972, "General Purpose Automotive Vehicle Performance and Economy Simulator," SAE Paper 720043.

16) Smith, J.R., 1994, "Optimized Hydrogen Piston Engines," proceedings of the SAE Convergence'94 meeting, Detroit, MI.

17) Post, Richard F., T. Kenneth Fowler, and Stephen F. Post, 1993, "A High-Efficiency Electromechanical Battery," proceedings of the IEEE, Vol 81, 3 March.

18) Oemichen, M., 1942, "Hydrogen as an Engine Fuel," Engine Laboratory of the Technische Hochschule, Dresden, Germany, VDI-Verlag GmbH, Berlin NW, V.D.I. Paper No. 68 (English translation).

19) King, R.O., S.V. Hayes, A.B. Allan, R.W.P. Anderson, and E.J. Walker, 1958, "The Hydrogen Engine: Combustion Knock and the Related Flame Velocity," Transactions of the Engineering Institute of Canada, Vol. 2, No. 4, December.

20) Smith, J.R., 1993, "The Hydrogen Hybrid Option," Proceedings of the Workshop on Advanced Components for Electric and Hybrid Electric Vehicles, Gaithersburg, MD. NIST Special Publication 860.

21) Thomson, M.W., Frelund, A.R., Pallas, M., Miller, K.D., 1987, "General Motors 2.3 L Quad 4 Engine," SAE Paper 870353.

Controlling a CVT-Equipped Hybrid Car

Andreas Schmid, Philipp Dietrich, Simon Ginsburg, and Hans P. Geering
Swiss Federal Institute of Technology (ETH)

Abstract

In order to achieve maximum fuel efficiency, the SI engine of the new CVT-equipped hybrid car developed at the Swiss Federal Institute of Technology (ETH) is operated in a high power regime (such as highway driving at speeds above 120 km/h) with its throttle in its 100-percent open position. Whenever an engine power which exceeds 11 kWs is demanded, there exists an equilibrium point between the engine torque and the torque induced by the drag. Any regulation of the vehicle speed has to be performed by altering the gear ratio of the CVT. If any acceleration is required, it is necessary to increase the engine speed. This requires that the vehicle has to be slowed down for a certain short period of time. If this characteristic behaviour of the car (which is typical for a non-minimum-phase system) is not accepted by a driver who demands and expects immediate acceleration, it might lead to critical situations. Therefore three different approaches have been investigated in order to find an appropriate control strategy. While the first is based on a rather simple interpretation of the driver's intention, approaches two and three consist of a control concept using the feedback linearization technique. All three concepts are compared in a special driving cycle with the behaviour of a conventional car equipped with a manually shifted gear.

It is demonstrated with simulations using a simple nonlinear dynamic model of the plant and a linear dynamic model of the behaviour of the driver that this vehicle can easily be handled in critical traffic situations when being conducted by a conventional driver who is obliged to adapt his behaviour to the car only slightly.

Introduction

Future Governmental regulations, the aspects of global warming, and an unbroken market demand for individual mobility combine to drive various initiatives to cut automobile fuel consumption significantly and to reduce emissions by orders of magnitude.

To achieve these improvements, different approaches have to be combined:

- reduction of total vehicle mass

- increasing energy conversion efficiency (engine, transmission, etc.)

- reduction of dissipative losses (drag, rolling resistance, etc.)

whereby the highest potential is located within the first two points.

Concept of the ETH-Hybrid III vehicle

The driveline of the hybrid vehicle developed at the Swiss Federal Institute of Technology (ETH) is designed to focus on an increased driveline efficiency. Additionally, the design aims at achieving local zero-emission driving within a limited range. The configuration of the hybrid drivetrain includes a spark-ignited (SI) 4-cylinder engine, an electric motor/generator, a flywheel (as short-time energy storage device) which is directly connected with the SI engine by clutches, and a continuously variable transmission (CVT) of the steel-belt type [1]. The set-up of the system is shown in Fig. 1

The core ideas of the concept are the combination of a CVT and a flywheel in a vehicle in order to

- shift the operating points of the SI engine toward areas of increased efficiency

- recuperate the braking energy of the vehicle

The flywheel is operated up to the maximal engine speed and at ambient air conditions. In a CVT, fixed transmission ratios as used in manual or automatic transmissions are replaced by a continuously variable band of ratios. The major advantage is the variability of the relation of vehicle and engine speed (at least within the operation range of the

CVT). This potential can be used to optimise the operating point of the SI engine (or also the electric motor including the battery system). To recuperate braking energy, an enlarged range of gear ratio is needed to charge/unload the flywheel at low vehicle speed. With a configuration of the transmission which enables a reverse flow of power along the CVT component through a gear change, the total gear ratio can be squared (i^2-transmission). In the actual application, a gear ratio range of 1 to 20.5 can be achieved.

Operation modes of the hybrid vehicle

At low power demand (typically in urban driving) the vehicle is powered by the energy of the flywheel through the CVT. The engine is operated between 1800 and 3600 rpm at full load to charge (speed up) the flywheel which turns at engine speed when locked with the SI engine by the clutches C3 and C1 (Fig. 1). At the upper speed limit (3600 rpm) the engine is declutched and shut down. The engine is clutched to the flywheel and started again after the flywheel having reached its lower speed limit (1800 rpm). This strategy is called duty cycle mode. A control strategy for this operating mode has been investigated in [2]. This duty cycle mode can increase the overall efficiency but is limited through the relation between ON and OFF cycle time, because starting and stopping the engine cause some losses. In this operation mode, the highest efficiency gain related to today's vehicles can be achieved.

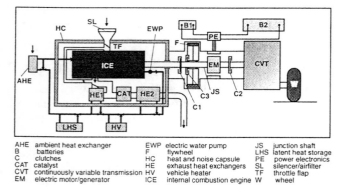

AHE	ambient heat exchanger	EWP	electric water pump	JS	junction shaft
B	batteries	F	flywheel	LHS	latent heat storage
C	clutches	HC	heat and noise capsule	PE	power electronics
CAT	catalyst	HE	exhaust heat exchangers	SL	silencer/airfilter
CVT	continuously variable transmission	HV	vehicle heater	TF	throttle flap
EM	electric motor/generator	ICE	internal combustion engine	W	wheel

Figure 1: A schematic representation of the hybrid driveline developed at the ETH

At higher power demand (typically highway-driving), the total efficiency of the driveline recommends a continuous operation of the engine. Thus the flywheel is always declutched, i.e., the vehicle is not supposed to accelerate by using stored kinetic energy. This operation mode demands the kind of strategy mainly investigated in this paper.

To minimise emissions, the SI engine, equipped with an exhaust aftertreatment (a three-way catalytic converter) and an appropriate heat management system, is always operated with a stoichiometric fuel mixture. Hence, best efficiency is gained at full load. As a consequence, the engine power output can be varied mainly as a function of engine speed.

Plant

Interpretation of the Drive Pedal

In duty cycle operation, the drive pedal must cease to be directly related to the engine torque as is the case in today's SI engines. With the flexibility of the CVT, the engine speed or the engine power, respectively, can be selected independently of the state of the vehicle in wide range of operation. The drive pedal can be interpreted as a driver's demand related to the state of the vehicle defined by the vehicle speed v_V and vehicle acceleration a.

One possibility of interpretation of the angle of the drive pedal α_{DP} is the demanded traction force F_V of the vehicle,

$$F_V \sim \alpha_{DP} \tag{1}$$

The traction force is the sum of various forces:

$$
\begin{aligned}
P_V = F_V v_V &= (F_{roll} + F_{air} + F_{acc})\, v_V \\
&= (c_r m_V g + A_V \frac{\rho}{2} v_V^2 + a(m_V + m_\Theta))v_V
\end{aligned} \tag{2}
$$

With equation (1) the characterisation of the drive pedal position is assumed to be

$$\alpha_{DP} \sim v_V^2 + a. \tag{3}$$

This approach has two advantages:

- At steady state, with no or very small acceleration only, a relation to the vehicle speed is possible. This interpretation causes the drive pedal position to be more sensitive in the low-speed range.

- In transient operation, α_{DP} is to be interpreted as demanded acceleration. The derivative of α_{DP} can then be interpreted as the fashion how to realise the transient behaviour to get to the new operating point.

In the mode of *continuous operation* of the engine, the 100% open throttle leads to the fact that the engine power P_e is a function of the engine speed ω_e only

$$P_e = f(\omega_e). \tag{4}$$

With the efficiency of the transmission η defined by

$$P_V = P_e \cdot \eta,$$

where P_V denotes the gearbox exit power, equation

$$P_V \sim f(\omega_e) \tag{5}$$

is obtained.

With this drive pedal interpretation, each change of the driver's demand for changing the vehicle speed causes an adjustment of the engine speed.

In this paper, three different controller designs are compared which are nterpreting the drive pedal position as the driver's demand for the force/torque at the wheel in order to adapt the gear ratio.

Differential Equations of the Plant

In order to achieve a good comparison of the performance of different controllers, a simple but nevertheless nonlinear model is needed. In the highway driving mode, all clutches are either locked or open. The engine torque, since it is a function of the engine speed as described above, can be approximated by a polynomial function of order 2 (cf. Eq. (6)).The driveline of the car is simplified to two rotational inertias which are connected by the CVT gearbox. The first inertia, Θ_e, is that of the engine, while the second one, Θ_v, represents the rotational inertia which, with respect to the wheel axis, is equivalent to the inertia of the total mass of the rest of the car.

The angular acceleration of the engine is given by the difference between the torque of the engine torque T_e

$$T_e(t) = \left(\alpha_e \omega_e^2(t) + \beta_e \omega_e(t) + \gamma_e\right) \tag{6}$$

and the gearbox entry torque T_α by

$$\dot\omega_e(t) = \frac{1}{\Theta_e} \cdot (T_e(t) - T_\alpha(t)). \tag{7}$$

The difference between the gearbox output torque T_z and the torque induced by the sum of all drag forces T_d which is assumed to be

$$T_d(t) = \left(a_d \omega_w^2(t) + c_d\right)$$

(ω_w denotes the rotational speed of the wheels) yields the rotational acceleration of the wheel by the equation

$$\dot\omega_w(t) = \frac{1}{\Theta_v} \cdot (T_z(t) - T_d(t)).$$

If the transmission ratio v is defined as

$$v(t) = \frac{\omega_e(t)}{\omega_w(t)}$$

the time derivative of the engine speed is

$$\dot\omega_e = v \cdot \dot\omega_w + \dot v \cdot \omega_w.$$

With the gearbox transmission efficiency η defined by

$$T_z = \eta \cdot v \cdot T_\alpha$$

the engine speed can be eliminated and the final equation of motion is given by

$$\dot\omega_w = \frac{v}{\Theta_e v^2 + \dfrac{\Theta_v}{\eta}}\left[T_e - \frac{T_d}{v\eta} - \Theta_e \omega_w \dot v\right] \tag{8}$$

This affine differential equation shows that the vehicle speed may be increased immediately by increasing the engine power as well as by applying a negative change of gear ratio. Since the engine power below its maximum value is a positive monotonous function of the engine speed, a positive change of gear ratio will increase the engine power

with a dynamical delay, whereas a negative one accelerates the vehicle by using kinetic energy of the engine.

As input of the system the relative rate of change of v

$$u(t) = \frac{\dot v(t)}{v(t)}$$

is chosen which is assumed to be proportional to the oil flow into the appropriate CVT chamber. The advantage of defining this relative quantity as input rather than the plain speed of change of gear ratio $\dot v$ is that its value in the saturation of

$$u_{max} = \left.\frac{\dot v}{v}\right|_{max}$$

is constant.

Human Driver

In the investigated case of tracking a leading vehicle the human driver reacts, as published in [4], on changes of relative speed and the derivative of speed by compareing the distance to the vehicle in front of himself with a speed dependent value(cf. Fig. 2). The dynamic behaviour of the driver is modelled as a controller of the form

$$T_{\dot\alpha}\dot\alpha_{DP}(t) + \alpha_{DP}(t) =$$
$$T_{\Delta\dot v}\Delta\dot v(t-\tau) + T_{\Delta v}\Delta v(t-\tau) + T_{\Delta d}\Delta d(t-\tau) \tag{9}$$

Here τ denotes the reaction time, Δd the distance between the modelled driver's car and the leading car, Δv the speed difference between both vehicles, and $\Delta\dot v$ its time derivative. In [4] the model is operated with averaged parameters.

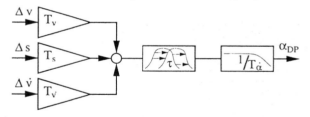

Figure 2: Signal Flow of the Driver Model

Torque at the Wheel

As mentioned above, in an ordinary vehicle, whenever no changing of gear speed is taking place, the torque at the wheel axis is the very quantity which is influenced by the driver with a negligible delay in time. If we neglect the small inertias of the wheel itself as well as those of all parts of the power train after the CVT, the torque at the exit of the gearbox T_z is approximately the torque at the wheel T_{wheel}. Thus we can state:

$$T_{wheel} \approx T_z = \Theta_v \cdot \dot\omega_w + T_d(\omega_w).$$

Taking into account the formula for the acceleration of the wheel (Eq. (8))

$$\dot{\omega}_w = \frac{v}{\Theta_e v^2 + \dfrac{\Theta_v}{\eta}} \left[T_e + \frac{T_d}{v\eta} - \Theta_e \omega_w \dot{v} \right]$$

and if

$$\varepsilon := \frac{\Theta_e}{\Theta_v}$$

denotes the quotient of the two main rotational inertias, the approximate torque at the wheel is given by

$$T_{wheel} \approx \frac{v\eta}{\varepsilon v^2 \eta + 1} [T_e + T_d \varepsilon v - \Theta_e \omega_w \dot{v}] \qquad (10)$$

The first and the second term in the bracket describe the share of the SI engine torque and that of the drag, respectively. The third term, however, reflects the influence of the variation of the gear ratio, i.e., the *dynamical part of the torque*.

In the duty cycle mode, accelerations of the vehicle are primarily based on the dynamical part, i.e., the flywheel speed decreases with increasing vehicle speed and vice versa.

In the highway mode, however, intuition does not allow a slowing down of the engine for acceleration purpose, since the engine power is certainly not expected to decrease if some additional force at the wheel is demanded. Therefore, the driver's intention while pressing down the torque pedal is interpreted in the following manner:

The vehicle must reach a state in which the torque at the wheel has reached approximately the value indicated by the pedal and where this value can be maintained over an arbitrarily long period of time. Therefore, the stationary wheel torque defined as

$$T_{ws} = \frac{1}{\varepsilon v^2 \eta + 1} \cdot \left[T_e v\eta + T_d \varepsilon v^2 \eta \right]. \qquad (11)$$

is used. It is equivalent to the wheel torque which would result if the vehicle was equipped with a conventional gearbox and was not performing any change of gears, i. e.,

$$\frac{dv}{dt} = 0.$$

Note that this torque is not identical with the acceleration $\dot{\omega}_w = 0$ of the vehicle.

The main problem of this interpretation is the non-minimum phase characteristic of the vehicle dynamics, i.e., whenever an acceleration is required, the car is first obliged to slow down in order to increase engine speed and engine power. Otherwise, if kinetic energy of the engine is used to accelerate the vehicle by applying a negative change of gear ratio, the engine power will decrease monotonously with the engine speed and therefore, the car cannot maintain its new speed but will asymptotically slow down to a much lower speed.

In order to avoid any gain scheduling, i.e., interpolation between several linear controllers designed in different nominal points of the system equations, three different, basically nonlinear approaches are compared. With the objective to guarantee a behaviour of the vehicle which is acceptable for the driver, for each approach there is a slightly different interpretation of the driver's intention. For an application in a commercial product, these interpretations could to be worked out by a fuzzy logic tool.

Objectives

A Benchmark for Drivability

In order to relate different controllers in realistic driving situations at the level of highway driving, a comparison of different driving cycles has been made (Fig. 3). Beside the common Federal Test Procedure (FTP-75) and the European Test Procedure (ECE-R15/4), two cycles are indicated that were developed during a field trial of 20 VW Golf II cars equipped with hybrid drivelines [3]. All tests assume a maximal acceleration of < 0.5 m/s^2 at vehicle velocities above 25 m/s, which allows smooth speed adjustment during highway driving.

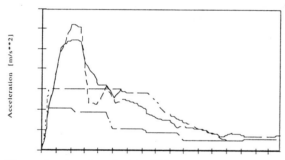

Figure 3: Acceleration in different test procedures:

ZH_City Cycle: urban driving
ZH_Agglomeration: average suburban driving
FTP-75: Federal Test Procedure (EPA)
ECE R15/4: European Test procedure.

Definition of a Driving Sequence

A typical suburban driving situation consists of following another vehicle. A second common situation is an acceleration after the end of a speed limitation on a freeway. These two situations are rather critical ones for the chosen hybrid drivetrain in the mode which is of interest, because the production of the demanded additional power differs from a common powertrain of today. This fact is the motivation to define the so-called guiding velocity trace, as shown in Fig. 4. It consists of the following sequences:

- constant driving
- moderate acceleration
- more severe acceleration
- following a leading car, the trajectory of which is assumed to be a sine-wave

The optimal distance to the preceding car varies with the speed of the vehicles:

$$\Delta Dist_{opt.} = \mathcal{c} + \gamma \cdot v_v^2 \qquad (12)$$

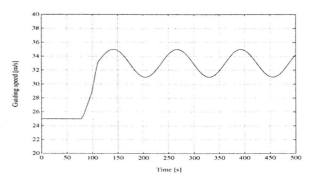

Figure 4: Guiding vehicle speed

Car with Manually Shifted Transmission (5 gears)

To compare the development of different controllers to drive the CVT car, a vehicle with a manually shifted 5-gear transmission is defined. That vehicle is driven during the whole test in the 4th gear, without any gear change. The vehicle mass of the reference car is reduced by 200 kg in comparison to the hybrid car, due to the additional equipment (flywheel, battery etc.) of the latter.

Controller Design

Approach 1: Controlling the Gear Ratio

The engine which is always running with the maximum torque is looked upon as producing an average maximum torque T_{emax} which is supposed to not be depending on the engine speed. Thus using the demanded stationary torque at the wheel T_{wsd} for an estimate for a demanded gear ratio v_d yields the simple formula

$$v_d = \frac{T_{wsd}}{T_{emax} \cdot \eta}.$$

With the time derivative of the gear ratio as input, the controller design is reduced to the problem of controlling an integrator. But since the input of the system is defined by the relative time derivative of the gear ratio

$$u(t) = \frac{\dot{v}(t)}{v(t)}$$

it is to be shown that this system can be controlled with one single linear controller. The relevant differential equation in this case is

$$\dot{v}(t) = u(t) \cdot v(t). \qquad (13)$$

Now let the optimization criterion be

$$J(u) = \int_0^\infty \left(\frac{1}{2} \left(q(v - v_d)^2 + u^2 \right) + \lambda(vu - \dot{v}) \right) dt.$$

The minimum principle of Pontryagin yields

$$u + \lambda v = 0.$$

Thus, the Hamiltonian is

$$\frac{1}{2} \cdot \left(q(v - v_d)^2 + u^2 \right) - u^2 = 0$$

which leads to the result

$$u = \pm \sqrt{q} \cdot (v - v_d).$$

Since the closed loop system must be stable, i.e.,

$$\dot{v} = -\text{sign}[(v - v_d)] \cdot \sqrt{q} \cdot |(v - v_d) \cdot v|$$

and since $v(t)$ is always a positive real number, together with equation (13) the optimal feedback law is indeed

$$u = -K_p \cdot (v - v_d).$$

Thus, the optimal feedback controller is the same as the one for controlling a simple integrator. In order to improve the performance of the control system, an additional PID controller is implemented (cf. Fig. 5). The PID controller is mapping the sum its input times a constant factor K_P, the derivative of its input times a constant factor K_D, and the Integral of its input times K_I to the input of the system u.

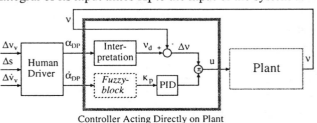

Controller Acting Directly on Plant

Figure 5: Signal Flow of the System with Control Strategy 1

The advantages of this first approach are the facts that the calculations are easy and that the controller does not need any information neither about the engine torque nor about the torque induced by the drag.

Approach 2: Input-Output Linearization

Considering the stationary wheel torque T_{ws} as defined in equation (11) as being a fictitious output y(t) of the system, its time derivative is

$$\dot{y}(t) = \frac{\partial T_{ws}}{\partial v} \cdot \dot{v} + \frac{\partial T_{ws}}{\partial \omega_w} \cdot \dot{\omega}_w.$$

With equation (8)

$$\dot{y}(t) = \left(\frac{\partial T_{ws}}{\partial v} - \frac{\partial T_{ws}}{\partial \omega_w} \cdot \frac{\Theta_e v \eta \omega_w}{\Theta_e v^2 \eta + \Theta_v} \right) \cdot \dot{v}$$
$$+ \frac{\partial T_{ws}}{\partial \omega_w} \cdot \frac{T_e v \eta + T_d}{\Theta_e v^2 \eta + \Theta_v}$$

results. (These terms are calculated with the aid of a symbolically calculating software and not listed in this paper.) However, the structure is

$$\dot{y}(t) = \alpha(\omega_w, v) + \beta(\omega_w, v) \cdot u(t)$$

with

$$\alpha(\omega_w, v) = \frac{\partial T_{ws}}{\partial \omega_w} \cdot \frac{T_e v \eta + T_d}{\Theta_e v^2 \eta + \Theta_v}$$

and

$$\beta(\omega_w, v) = \left(\frac{\partial T_{ws} \cdot v}{\partial v} - \frac{\partial T_{ws}}{\partial \omega_w} \frac{\Theta_e v^2 \eta \omega_w}{\Theta_e v^2 \eta + \Theta_v} \right).$$

By setting

$$u(t) = \beta(\omega_w, v)^{-1} \cdot (v(t) - \alpha(\omega_w, v))$$

the simple integrator dynamics

$$\dot{y}(t) = v(t)$$

are obtained. Since the output $y(t)$ represents the stationary torque at the wheel, the feedback control law

$$v(t) = -K_p \cdot (T_{ws}(t) - T_{wsd}(t))$$

is appropriate. In this case, an additional PID controller (cf. Fig. 6) is attains a significant improvement of the dynamical behaviour of the control system.

The advantage of this second approach is that the demanded stationary wheel torque is directly compared with the actual one and evaluated by the controller.

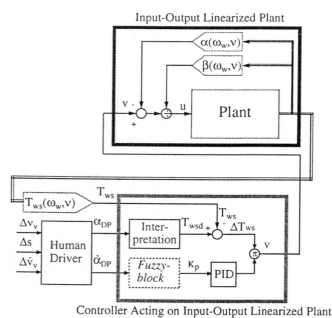

Input-Output Linearized Plant

Controller Acting on Input-Output Linearized Plant

Figure 6: Signal Flow of the System with Control Strategy 2

Approach 3: State Feedback Linearization

For the driver, the obvious states are the vehicle speed and the engine speed, whereas the gear ratio cannot be felt di-

rectly. Thus, the interpretation of the driver's wish is to be based on the two rotational speeds.

The formula for the stationary wheel torque (Eq. (11)) as a function of wheel speed and engine speed is

$$T_{ws} = \frac{\omega_e \eta}{\varepsilon \omega_e^2 \eta + \omega_w^2} \cdot [T_e \omega_w + T_d \varepsilon \omega_e].$$

It represents a surface in the $(T_{ws}, \omega_e, \omega_w)$-space. Its best linear approximation is the tangent plane in some point $(\overline{\omega}_e, \overline{\omega}_w)$ which is defined by

$$T_{ws} \approx \frac{\partial T_{ws}(\overline{\omega}_e, \overline{\omega}_w)}{\partial \omega_e}(\omega_e - \overline{\omega}_e)$$
$$+ \frac{\partial T_{ws}(\overline{\omega}_e, \overline{\omega}_w)}{\partial \omega_w}(\omega_w - \overline{\omega}_w).$$
$$+ T_{ws}(\overline{\omega}_e, \overline{\omega}_w)$$

Thus, the simple formula

$$T_{ws} = a_1 \cdot \omega_e + a_2 \cdot \omega_w + d$$

can be used. The same structure is obtained by making a linear fitting with a least square static optimization. This structure allows the expansion of the demanded rotational engine speed as a function of the demanded rotational wheel speed and the demanded wheel torque by the formula

$$\omega_{ed} = \frac{T_{wsd} - d}{a_1} - \frac{a_2}{a_1} \cdot \omega_{wd}. \qquad (14)$$

Assuming that a driver dislikes large steps, both in engine speed (acoustical impression) and in car speed (mechanical impression, jerk), the minimization of the quadratic performance index

$$\alpha_1(\omega_{ed} - \omega_e)^2 + \alpha_2(\omega_{wd} - \omega_w)^2 = \min$$

can be expected to yield an appropriate estimate of the desired point in the state space. Taking into account that in this point the value of the stationary wheel torque has to be equal to T_{wsd}, the equation

$$\frac{\alpha_1}{\alpha_2}(\omega_{ed} - \omega_e) + \frac{T_{wsd} - d - a_1 \omega_{ed}}{a_2} - \omega_w = 0 \qquad (15)$$

must hold.

By definition, the engine speed is

$$\omega_e = v \cdot \omega_w.$$

With the notation

$$\alpha = \frac{\alpha_1}{\alpha_2}$$

the estimate for the demanded wheel speed is

$$\omega_{wd} = \frac{\left[\omega_w + \frac{\alpha \cdot a_2}{a_1}\left(\frac{T_{wsd} - d}{a_1} - v \cdot \omega_w\right)\right]}{\left(1 + \left(\frac{a_2}{a_1}\right)^2 \alpha\right)}. \tag{16}$$

The value of the demanded engine speed is given by equation (14). Thus, for the demanded gear ratio, the formula

$$v_d = -\left(\frac{a_2}{a_1}\right) + \left(\frac{T_{wsd} - d}{a_1 \cdot \omega_{wd}}\right) \tag{17}$$

is obtained. Since in this case two states are demanded which describe the system completely, a total feedback linearization is required.

It is convenient to introduce the following notation for the system equations (cf. Eq. (8)):

$$\dot{\omega}_w = f_1(\omega_w, v) + g_1(\omega_w, v) \cdot u$$
$$\dot{v} = f_2(\omega_w, v) + g_2(\omega_w, v) \cdot u$$

with

$$f_1 = \frac{T_e v \eta + T_d}{\Theta_e v^2 \eta + \Theta_v}$$

$$g_1 = \frac{-\Theta_e v^2 \eta \omega_w}{\Theta_e v^2 \eta + \Theta_v}$$

and

$$f_2 = 0$$
$$g_2 = v .$$

If there exists a function

$$\lambda(\omega_w, v)$$

such that

$$\frac{\partial \lambda(\omega_w, v)}{\partial \omega_w} g_1 + \frac{\partial \lambda(\omega_w, v)}{\partial v} g_2 = 0 \tag{18}$$

and for the time derivative of $\lambda(\omega_w, v)$ the condition

$$\frac{\partial\left(\frac{d\lambda(\omega_w, v)}{dt}\right)}{\partial u} = 0$$

is satisfied.

Equation (18) represents a partial differential equation for $\lambda(\omega_w, v)$. Obviously, $\lambda(\omega_w, v)$ is separable and, with the approach

$$\lambda(\omega_w, v) = \lambda_1(\omega_w) + \lambda_2(v),$$

the two differential equations

$$\frac{\partial \lambda_1(\omega_w)}{\partial \omega_w} \omega_w \Theta_e \eta = 1$$

$$\frac{\partial \lambda_2(v)}{\partial v} \frac{\Theta_e v^2 \eta + \Theta_v}{v} = 1$$

remain to be solved. The two results are

$$\lambda_1(\omega_w) = \frac{1}{\Theta_e \eta} \ln(\omega_w)$$

$$\lambda_2(v) = \frac{1}{2\Theta_e \eta} \ln\left(\Theta_e v^2 \eta + \Theta_v\right)$$

and consequently

$$\lambda(\omega_w, v) = \frac{2}{\Theta_e \eta} \ln\left(\omega_w \sqrt{\Theta_e v^2 \eta + \Theta_v}\right).$$

Setting

$$\lambda(\omega_w, v) = y_1$$
$$\dot{y}_1 = y_2$$

yields, by definition,

$$y_2 = \frac{\partial \lambda(\omega_w, v)}{\partial \omega_w} \cdot f_1(\omega_w, v).$$

The time derivative of y_2 must be described by an equation of the structure

$$\dot{y}_2 = \alpha(\omega_w, v) + \beta(\omega_w, v) \cdot u .$$

Once $\lambda(\omega_w, v)$ is known, α and β are again calculated with the aid of symbolically calculating software tools. The results are not presented here since the expressions are too long. More detailed information, especially concerning the existence of the inverse of β, may be found in [5].

Whenever the inverse of β exists, the transformation

$$u(t) = \beta(\omega_w, v)^{-1} \cdot (v(t) - \alpha(\omega_w, v))$$

is well-defined and the new system dynamics are

$$\dot{y}_1(t) = y_2(t)$$
$$\dot{y}_2(t) = v(t) .$$

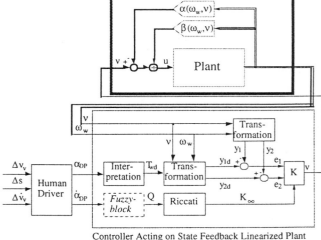

Figure 7: Signal Flow of the System with Control Strategy 3

The system is a second order integrator system which can easily be controlled if two reference values are given. These two values are determined by

$$y_{1d}(t) = y_1(\omega_{wd}, v_d)$$
$$y_{2d}(t) = y_2(\omega_{wd}, v_d).$$

The Fuzzy Block

For any industrial or commercial application, the optimization of this part of the control concept with the aid of a professional fuzzy tool is essential. To demonstrate the influence of the considering of the dynamics of the drive pedal for the controller design, the following set-up is chosen (cf. Fig. 8).

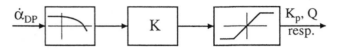

Figure 8: Scheme of *Fuzzy* Block

First, the signal is filtered in order to avoid any influence of vibrations etc. Then a proportional element (simple amplifier) generates a tuning parameter for the controller. The effect of a "harder" controller is a faster acceleration of the engine speed and, as a consequence, a significantly more marked negative jerk in the vehicle acceleration. Thus, a very "smooth" controller will provide a gentle acceleration of the vehicle whereas a "hard" controller provides a "kickdown"-like car response to any increasing angle of the drive pedal.

The saturation is needed to avoid instabilities; in a real fuzzy block the level of the saturation as well as the value of the amplifier can be tuned depending on any suitable signal which can be measured.

Results

Fig. 9 shows the simulation of the reference car in the predefined test cycle. Due to the fixed gear ratio (the engine power is limited by the engine speed) a full load acceleration can be seen. The lack of engine power leads to a rather large distance deviation. The difference between torque demand and torque at the wheel is negligible, as it was expected in the case without change of engine speed. The comparison of the actual torque at the wheel of the conventional vehicle with the Hybrid car shows a higher average value in the case of the CVT-equipped vehicle for all controller designs. This fact is caused by the increased vehicle mass of the the hybrid car.

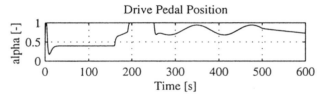

Figure 9a) Speed trace of the reference vehicle vs. a preceding vehicle

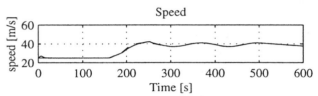

Figure 9b) Drive pedal trace to follow the reference vehicle

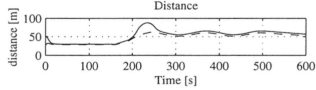

Figure 9c) Distance between the leading and test vehicle (solid), demanded distance (dashed)

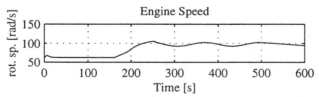

Figure 9d) Engine speed, which is related to the vehicle speed (fixed gear ratio)

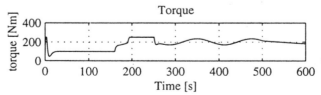

Figure 9e) Torque at the wheel

Figure 9: Performance of a reference vehicle on the defined driving sequence

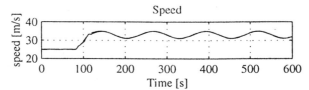

Figure 10a) Speed trace of the hybrid vehicle (solid), demanded speed (dashed)

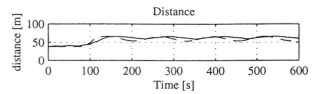

Figure 10b) Distance between the hybrid vehicle and a preceding vehicle (solid), demanded distance (dashed)

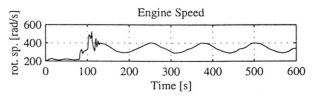

Figure 10c) Engine speed of the hybrid vehicle

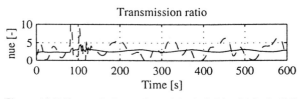

Figure 10d) Transmission ration of the hybrid vehicle (solid). and demanded transmission ratio (dashed)

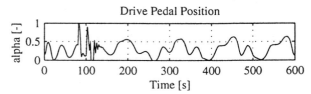

Figure 10e) Drive pedal trace to follow the reference vehicle

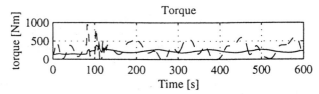

Figure 10f) Torque at the wheel (solid), demanded torque at the wheel (dashed)

Figure 10: Performance of the hybrid car with the control concept according to approach 1

The speed tracking shows very good performance, whereas the tracking of distance shows only little reaction during the initial phase of acceleration which leads to a phase angle of $\pi/2$ approximately. Neglecting the dynamic part of the torque leads to a bad correlation of the driver's intention and the actual behaviour of the vehicle.

The results of approach 2 (Fig. 11) demonstrate that the distance tracking has improved, especially in the range of high acceleration, but is still rather slow.

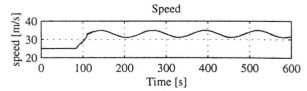

Figure 11a) Speed trace of the hybrid vehicle (solid), demanded speed (dashed)

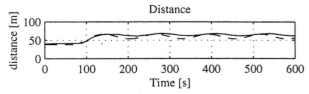

Figure 11b) Distance between the hybrid vehicle and a preceding vehicle (solid), demanded distance (dashed)

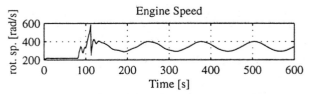

Figure 11c) Engine speed of the hybrid vehicle

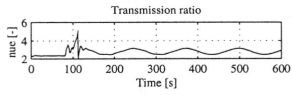

Figure 11d) Transmission ration of the hybrid vehicle (solid). and demanded transmission ratio (dashed)

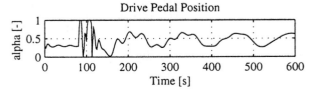

Figure 11e) Drive pedal trace to follow the reference vehicle

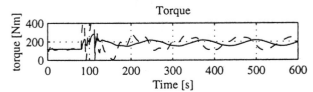

Figure 11f) Torque at the wheel (solid), demanded torque at the wheel (dashed)

Figure 11: Performance of the hybrid car with the control concept according to approach 2

The correlation between the actual torque at the wheel and driver's demand shows about the same unsatisfactory results as approach 1.

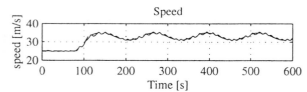

Figure 12a) Speed trace of the hybrid vehicle (solid), demanded speed (dashed)

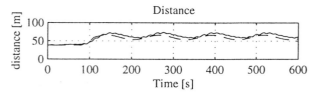

Figure 12b) Distance between the hybrid vehicle and a preceding vehicle (solid), demanded distance (dashed)

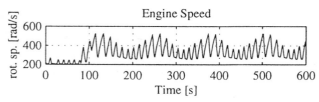

Figure 12c) Engine speed of the hybrid vehicle

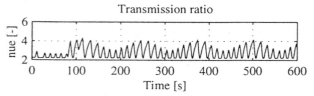

Figure 12d) Transmission ration of the hybrid vehicle (solid). and demanded transmission ratio (dashed)

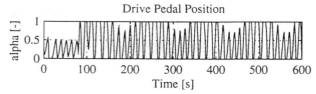

Figure 12e) Drive pedal trace to follow the reference vehicle

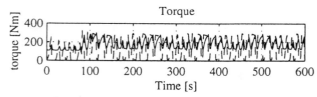

Figure 12f) Torque at the wheel (solid), demanded torque at the wheel (dashed)

Figure 12: Performance of the hybrid car with the control concept according to approach 3

In the context with the approach based on state feedback linearization (Fig. 12), a rather nervous behaviour can be recognised. The tracking of the distance shows better results on amplitude and phase. The correlation between demanded and actual torque has much improved. With that approach the driver has a relatively direct feedback of the dri-

vetrain. This is real improvement in comparison to the other two approaches.

Conclusions

- With all of the three approaches, this vehicle with its rather unusual dynamics can be driven in a realistic driving situation.

- Adaptation of the driver model parameters were neglected here for reasons of comparisons but can be expected to yield further improvements. Of course in reality the driver is capable to adapt its handling of the car quickly within a certain range of actions.

- The driving behaviour of the vehicle can be improved by adding a throttling mode during periods of slowing down and a kick-down mode for maximal acceleration.

References

[1]   *Dietrich P; Hörler H.-U.; Eberle M. K.:*

The ETH-Hybrid III car - a concept to minimise consumption and to reduce emissions, Proceedings of the ISATA Conference, Aachen, 13-17 September 93

[2]   *Shafai, E.; Schmid, A.; Geering, H. P.:*

Torque pedal for a car with a CVT, SAE Paper Nr. 941010

[3]   *Eberle M. K.:*

Ergebnisse des Zürcher Hybrid-Feldversuchs, Proceedings of int. conference on hybrid cars, Zürich, 9.11.93, pp. 57-76

[4]   *Mitschke M. und Zhenfu C.:*

Der Fahrer als adaptiver Regler, p. XVII Figure 0.7, FAT Schriftenreihe Nr 91, Frankfurt am Main, 1991

[5]   *Guzzella, L.; Schmid, A.:*

Control of SI engines with CVT's – A Feedback Linearization Approach, Proceedings ot the Third IEEE Conference on Control Application, Glasgow, 1994, pp. 633-638

Nomenclature

α	optimization coefficient
a_1	linear fitted parameter
α_1	optimization coefficient
a_2	linear fitted parameter
α_2	optimization coefficient
a_d	air drag coefficient
α_{DP}	drive pedal position
α_e	engine torque coefficient

A_v	air resistance area
β_e	engine torque coefficient
c_d	air drag coefficient
CVT	continuously variable transmission
d	linear fitted parameter
Δs	distance between vehicles
ε	quotient of inertias
f_1	first component of drift
f_2	second component of drift
F_v	traction force
g_1	first component of input vector field
g_2	second component of input vector field
γ_e	engine torque coefficient
η	efficiency of the gearbox
K_p	proportional gain
K_∞	solution of Riccati equation
$\lambda(\omega_w, v)$	fictitious output producing a maximum relative degree
m_Θ	equivalent mass of rotating parts
v	transmission ratio
P_e	engine power
P_v	traction power
q	weight parameter for Riccati equation
Θ_e	rotational inertia of the engine
Θ_v	rotational inertia of the vehicle
τ	human driver reaction time
T_α	gearbox input torque
$T_{\dot\alpha}$	human driver parameter
T_d	draft forces torque
$T_{\Delta d}$	human driver parameter
$T_{\Delta v}$	human driver parameter
$T_{\Delta\dot v}$	human driver parameter
T_e	engine torque
T_{emax}	maximum engine torque
T_{wheel}	wheel torque
T_{ws}	stationary wheel torque
T_{wsd}	demanded torque at the wheel
T_z	gearbox output torque
u	input in plant
v	input additional to transformation
v_v	speed of vehicle
ω_e	rotational speed of the engine
ω_w	rotational speed of the wheel

950493

The Effects of APU Characteristics on the Design of Hybrid Control Strategies for Hybrid Electric Vehicles

Catherine Anderson and Erin Pettit
AeroVironment

ABSTRACT

A hybrid control strategy is an algorithm that determines when and at what power level to run a hybrid electric vehicle's auxiliary power unit (APU) as a function of the power demand at the wheels, the state of charge of the battery, and the current power level of the APU. The design of this strategy influences the efficiency of the overall system. The strategy must balance the flow of power between the APU, the battery, and the motor, with the intent of maximizing the average fuel economy without overstressing the battery and curtailing its life.

The development of a system's powertrain components and the design of an optimum control strategy for that system should be concurrent to allow tradeoffs to be made while the designs are still fluid. An efficient optimization process must involve all aspects of the system, including costs, from the beginning.

In this paper, we explore the methodology behind the design of a hybrid control strategy. We also discuss the APU and battery design characteristics that are crucial to the strategy design, focusing on the interdependence of these design characteristics within the entire system. Finally, we propose a process for the development of an optimized hybrid powertrain and the corresponding control algorithm.

INTRODUCTION

A "hybrid" vehicle usually refers to one that incorporates a minimum of two independent power sources to supply the drivetrain. One of the primary advantages of this dual power supply system is it allows flexibility in power distribution between sources. This versatility enables greater optimization of the vehicle powertrain to meet the required performance of the system. In order to profit from such system flexibility, one must integrate into the system an intelligent control strategy that uses each component to the overall system's best advantage.

A hybrid control strategy is an algorithm that determines how power in a hybrid powertrain should be distributed as a function of the vehicle parameters (power demand, battery state of charge (SOC), component temperatures, etc.) and of component characteristics. One must develop this strategy carefully as part of the vehicle design process from the beginning. While the strategy determines the best operating points for the components, the range of available component characteristics provides the limits within which the strategy must operate.

This paper explores the iterative process of concurrent powertrain component and control strategy design with an emphasis on optimizing the system as a whole. We focus primarily on the auxiliary power unit and the characteristics of the powertrain components that drive the strategy design.

HYBRID VEHICLE CONCEPT

Hybrid vehicles can be divided into two main categories: *parallel,* in which both systems are used to mechanically drive the wheels; and *series*, where the power supply systems are coupled directly to a power bus which then transfers power to the wheels.

SERIES SYSTEM - The philosophy behind a series hybrid vehicle lies in its combination of a primary and a secondary energy conversion. In the primary conversion, an APU converts a highly transportable, stable chemical fuel to mechanical energy (or directly to electrical energy in certain cases) and, subsequently, to electrical energy. The most frequently considered APUs for hybrid systems include various internal and external combustion engines and fuel cells. This primary conversion device can be decoupled from the wheel power demand (unlike the engine in a conventional car) as a Load Leveling Device (LLD), which acts as an energy buffer, is included in the system. This LLD alternately stores energy (either directly from the primary conversion at low wheel power requirements or from the kinetic energy of the decelerating vehicle) and provides the propulsion motor with energy when the demand exceeds the APU power output. Some LLDs that have been proposed for use in hybrid vehicles include batteries, supercapacitors, hydraulic and/or pneumatic storage devices, and flywheels.

The secondary conversion, occurring in the inverter and motor, transforms the electrical energy from either source into the mechanical energy that drives the vehicle. Figure 1 is a schematic of the energy flow within the vehicle.

Since all the power sources and sinks are directly coupled by a DC power bus, control of the entire system can be achieved by simply commanding the APU output. The accessory and wheel loads pull required power off the bus with the LLD supplying the balance of power in the system.

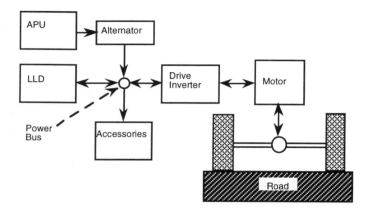

Figure 1: Series hybrid vehicle component configuration.

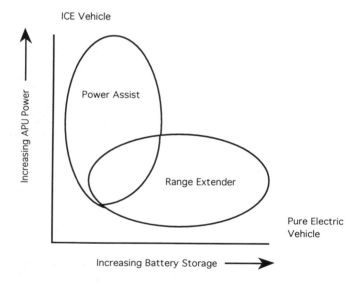

Figure 2: Comparison Chart of Power Assist and Range Extender Series Hybrid Vehicles

In addition, the series hybrid design may fall into one of two categories: "power assist" or "range extender" (see figure 2). A power assist hybrid uses the LLD to manage the power output from the APU to maximize efficiency and emissions in the APU. The usable storage capacity of the LLD is quite small (on the order of 1-5 kWh), and the APU must be capable of providing the maximum sustained power the vehicle is expected to need, with the LLD providing peak powers and transients. A range extender hybrid uses a very small APU with a substantial LLD such that the vehicle will perform similarly to a pure electric vehicle, with the additional small power source simply extending the range. Since the APU for

a range extender is small compared with the power demand, it is most often run at its maximum power level, and hybrid control strategies are fairly simple.

The primary disadvantage of the series hybrid system in most cases is the extra inefficiencies included in converting the mechanical power output from the APU into electrical power and then back into mechanical power. Often, however, the increased flexibility of the system offers more optimized components that overcome this disadvantage.

PARALLEL SYSTEM- In a parallel hybrid vehicle, there is a direct mechanical connection between the APU and the wheels through a transmission. As shown in figure 3, the electric propulsion system may either drive the same set of wheels as the APU through the transmission (Option 1), or drive the other set of wheels directly (Option 2).

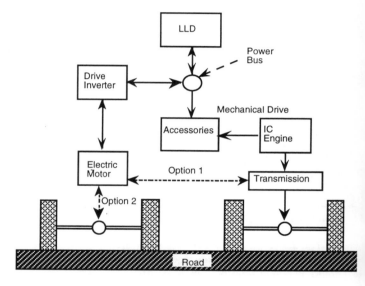

Figure 3: Parallel hybrid vehicle component configuration.

The main advantages of the parallel configuration over the series is that the power from the engine is used directly by the drivetrain with no alternator or inverter losses. However, because the APU is directly coupled to the wheels, the APU speed is determined by the vehicle speed and the transmission ratio. This direct coupling limits the flexibility of hybrid strategy design, and (without a novel clutched transmission) forces the APU to idle when the vehicle is at rest.

A parallel hybrid does have an efficiency advantage when the vehicle spends a majority of its driving time at a substantial cruise, but a vehicle that is operated on a "city driving" profile will lose this transmission efficiency advantage to inefficiencies in the APU engine. In addition, if the front and rear axles of the vehicle are driven by different power sources, the vehicle may exhibit changes in handling characteristics as the power distribution between the sources is adjusted.

The thought processes presented in this paper are sufficiently general that they can be applied to any type of vehicle. To fully explore the flexibility allowed by the hybrid system, we focus on the design of a strategy for the most versatile layout: the power assist hybrid. For simplicity, we use the example of a generalized IC engine and Pb-Acid battery for the APU and battery, respectively, as a focus for the discussion.

HYBRID CONTROL STRATEGIES

There are two distinct extremes in the spectrum of control strategies. One is a system that uses a "thermostat" algorithm to command the APU (i.e. the APU is turned on to a constant power level when the SOC of the LLD is below a certain lower threshold, and off when the SOC exceeds an upper threshold). In this mode, the LLD must accommodate all the transient power requirements. Although the APU may be operating at its most efficient point, the losses in the LLD from excessive cycling may surpass the savings from an optimized APU. For the example wheel power curve shown in figure 4, figure 5 shows the corresponding APU and LLD power requirements generated by a thermostat mode.

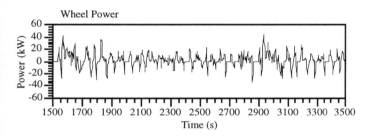

Figure 4: The power required at the wheels for a segment of the federal urban drive (LA4).

The other extreme commands the APU to follow the actual wheel power whenever possible (similar to a conventional automobile). Using this strategy, the LLD cycling will diminish, and the losses associated with charge and discharge will be minimized. The APU, however, must then operate over its entire range of power levels and perform fast power transients, both of which can adversely affect engine efficiency and emissions characteristics. Figure 6 shows the APU and LLD power requirements generated by this "following" mode for the same wheel power curve shown in figure 4. It should be noted that this is the mode a parallel hybrid vehicle always uses.

For most of the APUs and LLDs under consideration, neither of these strategies would be the optimum strategy. The ideal hybrid control strategy is one that minimizes the combined inefficiencies of both the APU and the LLD while meeting the desired performance and the emission limits (as well as any other specific system characteristics that are being used as measures of design merit). The optimum strategy is highly dependent on the characteristics of the powertrain components and the planned use of the vehicle. Unfortunately as one attempts to optimize a system, the characteristics of the components begin to conflict, driving the strategy in different directions.

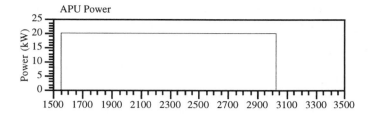

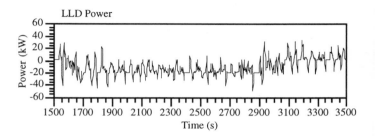

Figure 5: The APU and LLD power outputs that satisfy the wheel requirements using a constant APU thermostat strategy.

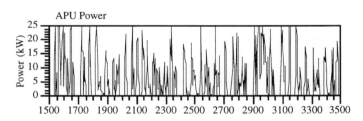

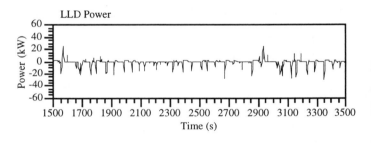

Figure 6: The distribution of power for a load following APU.

COMPONENT CHARACTERISTICS AND DESIGN TRADE-OFFS

LLDs - The LLD (in this case a battery) must be the most accommodative element in the powertrain. When there is a large power demand or production from the wheels (as during hard acceleration or braking), it must supply or accept the power required. In a hybrid application, the battery pack generally has lower capacity than it would have for a pure electric vehicles (particularly for a power assist hybrid where the APU is of considerable size). To maintain the same performance, therefore, the power density must be greater. In addition, the state of charge of the battery can be significantly affected during a short acceleration or deceleration so that the small-scale charge/discharge period (or "microcycling") that the pack sees is a more significant percentage of its capacity. Differing control strategies can place varying demands on the cycling of the battery. Using the thermostat APU strategy, the battery would be required to cycle at the frequency of the wheel power demand, while the follower APU strategy would only require the battery to cycle when the wheel power demand exceeds the APU power capability.

There are several characteristics of the battery that one must keep in mind when trying to quantify tradeoffs between the battery and the rest of the system: the charge/discharge efficiency, the total capacity of the pack, the transient capabilities, and, the hardest to determine, the life of the batteries.

Charge/Discharge Efficiencies - A battery is most efficient within a range of SOCs that minimizes its charge and discharge resistances. In figure 7, one can see the general shape of a Pb-Acid battery's internal resistance versus state of charge curves for charging and discharging the battery. A balance point must be chosen on these curves to minimize resistive losses, yet still leave room for power peaks (both motoring and regenerative braking) at the wheels. This tends to push the strategy design to keep the SOC within the 50-70% region for minimum losses in both charge and discharge. This leaves enough capacity to handle an extended period of battery discharge (such as during a long hill climb) and enough "headroom" to absorb a long period of charging such as that which occurs during a long downhill. If the SOC is not maintained within the 50-70% region, the performance may be compromised. This diminished performance may take the form of lost regenerative energy or limited power output during accelerations.

Capacity - The capacity of the pack is comparatively easy to measure, and the effects of the change of capacity on the strategy are fairly intuitive. (It should be noted that the capacity at one rate of discharge is different from the capacity at another rate, and therefore the definition of "capacity" is subject to discussion.) In general, the larger the battery pack capacity, the more the vehicle can be run like an pure electric vehicle with the APU providing supplemental power. With a large capacity, it is easier to achieve the power required for standard driving, and the pack does not have to be so rigidly constrained to a small window of states of charge. A small pack, however, must be used almost exclusively as a short-term energy buffer without significant energy storage.

Transient Capabilities - A battery can change power levels almost instantaneously, unlike the APU which is limited by its mechanical inertia. When the APU cannot respond quickly enough to fluctuations in power demand, the battery must make up the difference. The battery must be able to sustain output at a peak power during these transients until the APUs power output reaches the commanded power.

Life - Unfortunately, most available data on battery life is of limited applicability to hybrid systems. The complexities of the reactions within batteries make it almost impossible to predict battery life except as a questionable extrapolation of empirical data. Although few quantitative predictions of

battery life are available, some qualitative statements can be made:

1. A lead acid battery will degrade more (per a throughput kWh) if cycled deeply (cycled through a wide range of SOCs) than shallowly. The long term effects of microcycling (cycling over a small range of SOCs) are not fully known.
2. A battery will last longer if it has lower energy throughput.
3. Hard cycling (high power cycling), even hard microcycling, will shorten the life.

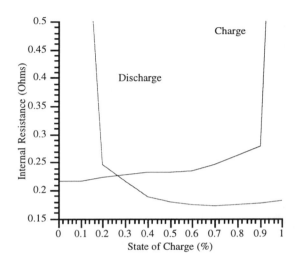

Figure 7: The charge and discharge internal resistances versus the state of charge of a battery.

Figure 8 shows the difference between the SOCs of the thermostat and follower extremes discussed above (see figures 3-5) over multiple repetitions of the federal urban driving cycle. In the thermostat mode, the APU power output is greater than the average power for the cycle causing the state of charge to continue to increase until it reaches a defined maximum state of charge (in this case 80%) requiring the APU to turn off. The follower mode, on the other hand, provides only a slight constant increase in SOC due to the battery's absorption of regenerative energy during the cycle. The deep cycled battery might only last half as long as the one kept within a tight SOC window. However, the costs of replacing the battery versus the cost of building an APU capable of fast transient response(that can protect the battery) must be weighed.

APUs - Because the APU is decoupled from the drivetrain, there is greater flexibility in its design. The design need not be performance driven as in conventional IC engines, but can be focused on other characteristics, such as emissions, that may be more important for the specific vehicle being designed. Most importantly, however, the APU characteristics must be chosen to complement the LLD requirements; thus, the need for a working strategy throughout the design process. Characteristics crucial to the design include maximum power output, transient capabilities, fuel efficiency, emissions characteristics, engine noise vibration harshness (NVH), and service life.

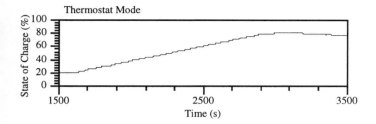

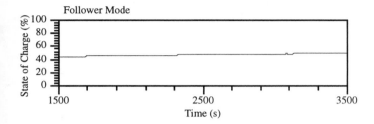

Figure 8: The state of charge during repetitions of the federal urban driving cycle with a constant APU at 20 kW in the thermostat mode (see figures 2,3) and in the follower mode(see figure 4).

Maximum Power Output - The maximum power output of the APU will affect strategy design choices in a similar manner to the capacity of the battery. With a high power capability, one may design the strategy to operate more or less like a conventional car engine in a power following mode, whereas a low power capability will force the strategy to run the engine at its highest power level so that it can keep up with current demands and store extra energy for periods of high demand.

APU Transient Capabilities - Mechanically, the transient capabilities of an engine are limited by the inertia involved in increasing or decreasing the engine speed. Although slower transients are desirable for reducing emissions, slow transients can curtail the life of the battery or potentially harm the engine. For example, slow transients can be a serious problem during a transition from a hard acceleration to a hard braking. If the APU has been commanded by the control strategy to supply a high power during an acceleration, and suddenly full regenerative braking is required, the LLD may not be able to accept the total power coming to it, unless the APU can reduce its power quickly. This limitation will cause a loss of much of the regenerative energy available. In an extreme case, the APU may be unloaded by an over-voltage condition, leading to potential overspeed. The APU control strategy must be robust, such that no combination of driver actions will result in damage to any drivetrain component.

Fuel Efficiency - The fuel efficiency of an APU generally varies as a function of the power level. The specific fuel consumption (SFC) of an engine is typically best at middle power levels and worst at the low and high power extremes. The APU operating strategy that will maximize fuel efficiency is one that runs the APU primarily in the range of powers over which the SFC is best (often termed the engine's "sweet spot"). The ratio of the highest power level to the lowest power level

used in the strategy is called the turn down ratio. The narrower this sweet spot is, and, thus, the smaller the most efficient turn down ratio is, the more the fuel efficiency requirements constrain the strategy toward a thermostat mode (see figure 9, a series of SFC graphs showing varying sweet spots.). Increasing the range of high efficiency and thus the turn down ratio and the ability of the strategy to follow drive power more closely (therefore relieving some stress on the battery) can increase the complexity and cost of the engine or lower the peak fuel efficiency. Tradeoffs must be made between engine complexity, cost, fuel efficiency, and battery lifetime. For example, if a long battery lifetime is the most important aspect of the system, then a large sweet spot is desired, possibly sacrificing engine simplicity, efficiency, or low engine emissions. In a situation where the average power is fairly constant a smaller sweet spot may be the most efficient solution.

Emissions - Frequently, one of the principle aims of a hybrid vehicle is to reduce vehicle emissions to ULEV (Ultra Low Emission Vehicle) levels. Consequently, APU emissions are very important for system success. In general, emissions are minimized when a stoichiometric air to fuel ratio is maintained by a closed loop feedback system (using an oxygen sensor for feedback). In some operating regimes, such as engine starts and transients, the stoichiometric ratio is very difficult to maintain resulting in an increase in emissions.

During a cold-start, the engine must run rich to achieve sufficient vaporization of the fuel. Rich running results in high hydrocarbons (HC) and carbon monoxide (CO) emissions, but low nitrogen oxides (NOx) emissions. A hot-start has many of the same problems as a cold start, but the time duration before the engine and catalytic converter warm up is much shorter. A hybrid strategy which minimizes engine cycling will minimize start-related emissions, but that may require that the engine have a higher turn-down ratio.

Transients present an emissions problem that is largely related to the speed of the transient. The closed loop feedback system that maintains the stoichiometric air fuel ratio is sufficient during quasi-steady state modes, however, it can only react as fast as the O_2 levels can be sensed. If the transient is too fast, the engine may run rich, increasing CO and HC emissions, or lean, increasing NOx emissions. Some of this effect can be reduced using a hybrid strategy that only allows slow transients, but this places greater strain on the LLD.

As a series hybrid vehicle decouples both the speed and the power of the APU from the speed and power requirement at the wheels, this extra degree of freedom can also be used to reduce emissions. For a given required power output, there are many combinations of speed and torque that could be used to provide that power. If the engine is run in a low speed, high load state, the fuel efficiency, noise, and hydrocarbon emissions are all improved. At high loads, however, the NOx emissions are high and traditional NOx reducing measures such as Exhaust Gas Recirculation (EGR) are more difficult. Choosing this optimum engine operating point as a function of power is an important design consideration but it is not necessarily part of the hybrid strategy design.

Noise Vibration Harshness (NVH) - Engine noise is not much of an issue as far as the performance of a drivetrain is concerned, but to avoid customer distress, it must be considered as an influencing factor on a hybrid strategy. For example, a strategy that has the engine on at full power while the vehicle is at a complete stop could be extremely disconcerting for the driver. Fortunately, the periods of low ambient (masking) noise are mostly concurrent with low power demands, so throttling back an engine at low vehicle speeds is not too much of a compromise in performance.

Life - The life of an APU can generally be extended by running it at low, constant power levels. Constant running at a sweet spot (for emissions and fuel economy) during low power demand driving, however, may cause the battery SOC to rise and the engine to be shut off. Depending on the control strategy this on/off cycling can be quite frequent. Numerous hot starts may shorten the life of an engine unless it is designed for multiple starts per trip.

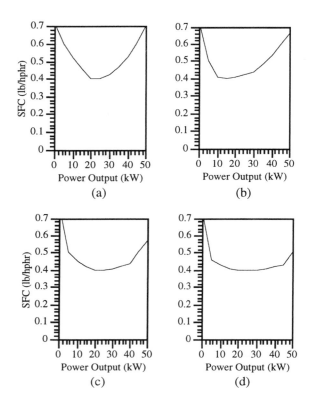

Figure 9: Four examples of engine efficiency curves. Specific Fuel Consumption versus Power Output. The "sweet spot" is smallest in (a) and largest in (d).

BRAKING CONTROL SYSTEMS - The only other system component whose specific characteristics are crucial to the optimization of the powertrain is the braking system. The added feature of regenerative braking ("regen") can improve fuel economy greatly. Unfortunately, because a typical vehicle must use all four wheels for braking to maximize control, a front wheel drive vehicle with balanced braking will not be able to capture all available regen energy. A scheme must be devised to maximize the amount of regen captured without destabilizing the car's decelerations. An optimum division of braking power between the front and the rear is a function of the degree of deceleration and the desired handling of the car. For example, a braking strategy may use regen for

all declarations up to 0.25 g, then feather in the rear brakes to prevent skidding and instability during hard decelerations.

The amount of energy available from regenerative braking influences the fuel economy greatly, especially in heavy stop and go traffic. The efficiency of the regenerative braking depends on the resistance of the battery to charging and, therefore, on the state of charge of the battery. This, once again, creates conflicting optimization factors, for the APU cannot be run at its most efficient point if it is desired that the battery stay within a certain range of SOCs. The APU must be run within its limited high efficiency range and the battery must be maintained around a state of charge that has minimum charge and discharge resistances.

COST - Inasmuch as hybrid powertrains must compete against conventional powertrains for cost and performance, the overall success of the powertrain is extremely dependent on cost. More expensive components may increase the capabilities and the life, but if that makes the system unsaleable, the improvements are useless. In the end, every tradeoff that is made in the powertrain system must be done with cost in mind.

DEVELOPMENT OF A WORKING STRATEGY

The design of hybrid systems must begin with the overall system constraints. Depending on the type of vehicle (for example, a large passenger car or a delivery truck), there are weight and volume limits. These limits include both the general physical dimensions of the car as well as the physical characteristics of the powertrain. These limits and the power requirements of the system provide an initial basis for choosing the relative sizes of the APU and the LLD. System power electronics are more efficient if constrained to within a fairly narrow bus voltage range. This additional limiting factor must also be considered in the component design. These constraints, along with the control strategy provide the system wide link between components.

All of the design factors discussed above influence the characteristics of the final vehicle; therefore, it is crucial to know the general specifications of the system as a whole. The characteristics to be optimized in the design must be prioritized to provide a path to guide the designers. A design focused on minimizing emissions will result in a very different vehicle than one focused on extending battery lifetime.

For example, a generic strategy may begin with a focus on fuel economy. A basic strategy would drive the APU at a constant peak efficiency power level (based on the first APU efficiency estimates), similar to the thermostat APU scheme discussed previously. Bringing in aspects of battery life would push the turn down ratio up (using an approximation of the engine sweet spot) until a suitable balance point between life and fuel efficiency appears, incorporating their relative importance. Emissions characteristics may then be included by slowing down the engine transient response time. The balance between the first two factors (fuel efficiency and battery life) must then be re-adjusted, resulting in a three way balance that enforces the order of priority of characteristics. This process will continue until all optimization characteristics are included, in order of their importance.

The second half of the design process focuses on interactive optimization of all the components of the system. A series of sensitivity studies will show the effects of variations in each characteristic on the whole system, including parameters contained within the strategy. Questions must be asked of the system such as: If the battery's charge resistance can be decreased by 5%, by how much will the fuel efficiency be increased? When the battery is maintained within a smaller SOC window, how much will the fuel efficiency change, and how much longer can the battery be expected to last? What happens if the relative importance of the fuel efficiency to the peak power performance is increased? As each of these questions are answered the designers can get a better understanding for which improvements in the system will provide the most benefit, economically and physically.

RECOMMENDATIONS

Compared to the design of a conventional automobile, the design of a hybrid vehicle has an extra degree of freedom. This degree of freedom requires an added component to bring the system together: the hybrid control strategy. The adaptability of a hybrid powertrain can reduce many of the component design constraints found in a traditional vehicle.

In order to take full advantage of the system flexibility, the hybrid control strategy must be incorporated into the design from the beginning of the process. Sensitivity studies should be performed throughout the design iterations so that the hybrid control strategy can guide the vehicle design towards optimization, while satisfying the initial design criteria. As was discussed previously, many characteristics of the APU and LLD are interdependent, and often create conflicting situations during optimization. The effects of these conflicting characteristics must be weighed through the sensitivity studies and engineers must judge the relative importance of each optimization characteristic.

Although hybrid vehicle development programs are aimed at developing vehicles with high fuel economy and low emissions, care must also be taken to retain vehicle acceleration performance and maintain reasonable powertrain cost. It is recommended that a systems approach to the powertrain design be taken to maximize the benefits of a hybrid system.

ECTAM™, A Continuous Comb... Engine for Hybrid Electric Ve...

W. Robert Palmer and J. Dale Allen
Spread Spectrum, Inc.

ABSTRACT

The ECTAM (External Combustion Thermal Amplification Motor) is a new engine, designed from the ground up to meet the performance needs of Hybrid Electric Vehicles and low emissions goals for future transportation. The basic design incorporates a positive displacement pinned vane rotary compressor supplying a combustion chamber with pressurized air. The air combines with fuel in the combustion phase and is ported to the positive displacement pinned vane rotary expander. In the expander the working gas pressure drops as a function of the rotative blade position. Four out of eight blades are continuously performing work as a function of the differential pressure on each respective blade. Exhaust manifold and engine housing heat energy is used to create pressurized steam which is used in cooling the continuous combustion process. This augmented steam is then mixed with the constituents of combustion and is used as a component of the working fluid which is provided to the expander. The attributes of continuous combustion, combined with continuous blade loading in this rotary system result in an intrinsically balanced and quiet engine which produces high torque at low rotational speeds. The ECTAM is compact, capable of operation using a variety of fuels and incorporates components that have the potential to be cost effectively mass produced. The prototype expander and combustor has been tested using propane. The test results have validated the potential of the components to meet the design requirements.

INTRODUCTION

Combustion engines have been operating reliably for decades. These engines take on many shapes and sizes and are the backbone of world transportation. While engine reliability has reached and exceeded most design goals, reducing pollution and increasing efficiency is still a major objective associated with automotive engines. The focus of the following research involved creating a new mechanical device which employs an improved thermodynamic cycle. Most automotive engine design activity involves changing attributes of existing engines to produce additional power, increase efficiency or reduce emissions.

The ECTAM is the result of a design process whereby new mechanical hardware was wrapped around a modified combined cycle, continuous combustion process. The desire to produce a new engine configuration incorporating these principles has been around for a long time and can be evidenced by numerous previously patented engine designs. Much effort has gone into combining a continuous combustion process into a sliding vane type approach as evidenced by the patents of Theodor Hengsbach, Minoru Takahashi, and Perry Miles [1] [2] [3]. These systems have been typically unsuccessful due to very high internal friction resulting from the sliding vane approach. Others have patented the concept of co-generation and steam injection in gas turbines [4] [5]. This process is not prevalent in a positive displacement rotary device incorporating continuous combustion as in the ECTAM. Also, the concept of using rotating hubs with independently articulating pinned blades, as with the ECTAM, has been explored in the past. This is evidenced by the patents of Robert Jensen, Raoul Mabille and William McReynolds [6] [7] [8]. However, these previous approaches use internal combustion. In the case of these internal combustion designs very high internal stresses occur. Unbalanced internal pressures cause blow-by in the blade articulation joints and the high combustion pressures result in stringent sealing requirements. Also, these previous designs are limited by manufacturing tolerances due to the method of attaching the blades to the center shaft. The alignment between the outer hub blade support elements and adjoining support hub ends dictates that if the parts are not manufactured to extremely close tolerances undesirable gapping will occur and very high point stresses will show up single contact point between the blade and blade port.

The ECTAM architecture overcomes the previously mentioned design limitations. The design includes a high volume, positive displacement rotary compressor and expander. It uses an external continuous combustion process which can be augmented by steam and water injection. The steam is generated by the heat of the expander housing. This process capitalizes on high heat transfer rates based on the latent heat of vaporization in generating the steam. The steam also serves to lower the combustion temperature and scrub the constituents of combustion. The thermodynamic energy balance indicates that high efficiencies competitive with current engines are achievable without the use of costly materials. Finally, the design simplicity of the ECTAM, combined with the ease of assembly, indicate that low cost high volume production is very realistic making the ECTAM a good candidate engine for hybrid electric vehicles and other power generation applications.

TECHNICAL DESCRIPTION

The following objectives were established for the ECTAM:

- Incorporate mechanical design simplicity by minimizing hardware elements and maintain component commonality to the maximum extent possible.
- Use existing or known materials which would lead to cost competitive high volume production.
- Use only well established and proven principles combined in a new systems architecture.
- Generate high torque at relatively low engine speeds which can be more closely matched to vehicle power requirements reducing transmission requirements.
- Maximize the effective work stroke of a positive displacement machine.
- Combine known thermodynamic cycles where appropriate to increase efficiency as has been demonstrated by existing cogeneration power systems.
- Focus on how much clean mechanical energy can be produced from a gallon of fuel.

With these generic objectives established, the initial power plant size was determined by creating a number of vehicle systems models which defined the power requirements for a broad range of potential hybrid electric vehicles. The goal was to select a power range that provided performance equivalent to that of existing full-size 1905 kg (4200 lb.) vehicles. As it turns out the same engine baseline will provide adequate performance for hybrid fleet vehicles and transit busses up to 13,608 kg (30,000 lb.), and excellent performance in smaller vehicles in the 1134 kg (2500 lbs.). weight class.

To meet these design objectives for the hybrid electric format the power range selected would provide a peak of 48 kW (65 hp) and a continuous output rating of 22 kW (30 hp).

With the design goals and power range for the initial product prototype determined the design work commenced.

A review of existing engines was conducted in order to identify fundamental design features that should be avoided in the design of the ECTAM. One drawback to the reciprocating piston engine is the sudden and extreme force placed on the pistons by the instantaneous combustion process. The hardware is required to be robust in order to minimize fatigue in the components. Noise and vibration levels are high due to the short period high concentration of energy. Furthermore, the intermittent burning of fuel in the cylinders is relatively inefficient compared to burning fuel continuously, and incomplete burning is a primary cause of pollutants.

A turbine engine (Brayton cycle) overcomes the problem of sudden and extreme force associated with reciprocating piston engines by providing to the blades a continuous stream of working fluid at a relatively constant pressure. However, turbine engines are subject to a phenomenon called "blade slip" wherein working fluid passes over or past the blade without doing any physical work. In order to minimize blade slip, more efficient turbine engines are operated at high pressures and speeds. This results in higher efficiency but limits the effective operating range of the turbine engines, i.e., they work well at set speeds, typically in excess of 60,000 rpm [9].

Sliding vane machines have blades arranged radially and contained within an inner hub. The inner hub rotates inside a larger circular outer housing. The blades are capable of moving in and out of slots cut in the inner hub. The blades thus form positive displacement expansion and compression compartments with the outer housing. This arrangement addresses the sudden and uneven combustion problems of piston engines and overcomes the "blade-slip" problem associated with turbine engines. However, this design is limited by internal friction and high part stress. These designs are usually limited to an undesirably low single rotation compression and expansion ratios of about of 3:1.

A conventional reciprocating internal combustion engine typically operates at a relatively low engine housing temperature (e.g. on the order of 82°C [180°F]). The heat of combustion is removed from the engine housing by means of a water jacket (for water cooled engines) or by cooling fins (for air cooled engines). More than fifty percent of the heat energy created by combustion of the fuel is usually lost in the form of housing and exhaust heat and is expelled to the atmosphere without performing mechanical work; thus, the thermodynamic system efficiency of such a conventional engine is inherently low.

To improve efficiency of a typical reciprocating internal combustion engine in an ideal fashion, one might simply remove the radiator from the engine. The engine would then be allowed to operate at an elevated housing temperature, i.e. 177°C (350°F). Water contained in the water jacket would be converted to steam at a pressure of about 827 kPa (120 psig). This process incorporates high heat removal rates due to the latent heat of vaporization of water at these conditions (approximately 2100 kJ/kg [900 BTU/lbm]of water). The high pressure steam could be routed into the cylinder head during the very short fraction of a second just after ignition (at the top of the power stroke). Then, the combustion process, provided it is not extinguished by the steam (which is the fundamental problem), would heat the combined mixture of fuel, air and steam to about 816°C (1500°F). This would provide a significant increase in the percentage of work which could then be performed on the piston during the expansion process. Namely, the steam would be superheated by the constituents of combustion and the total constituent of working gases would expand producing work on the piston. Unfortunately, the engine housing is not permitted to reach a temperature sufficiently high to provide adequate potential energy to the heat transfer fluid (water as an example). Also, it is extremely difficult to inject the water back into the engine cylinder following the ignition and explosion portion of the cycle, but prior to the expansion portion of the power stroke. Incorporating a water injection approach in an internal combustion type engine system would be problematic based on the difficulties associated with timing the injection and explosion processes.

A gas turbine engine, on the other hand, which employs continuous combustion, typically does not use radiators or cooling fins. Gas turbine engines are not positive displacement engines; hence, they do not have rotating blades in contact with the surface of the housing containing them. Since the rotating blades of a gas turbine engine do not come in contact with the stationary parts of the engine housing, the operating temperatures (typically 816°C [1500°F] to 1038°C [1900°F]) do not cause wear problems.

Continuous combustion and high operating temperatures would appear to make a gas turbine engine a good candidate for improved efficiency compared to a reciprocating internal combustion engine. Also, some gas turbines do inject water into the combustion gas stream in order to further increase power and efficiency. However, a fundamental limitation of a gas turbine engine is the fact that a gas turbine engine customarily has poor performance for low speed, high torque applications which require throttling. Adequate performance of a gas turbine engine is achieved only at very high and near constant engine speeds. This limits the potential for use in parallel hybrid systems and brings with it crash safety concerns.

To the greatest extent possible, the design team has attempted to combine a Brayton cycle gas turbine combustion process with a Rankine cycle heating process. This is accomplished by combining a small percentage of steam generated from the expander housing with the combustion gas. The expanding hot gas mixture is converted to rotational motion using a positive displacement rotary pinned vane expander [10]. The combustion feed air is supplied by a similar positive displacement rotary pinned vane compressor (The ECTAM engine system is shown in Figures 1 and 2).

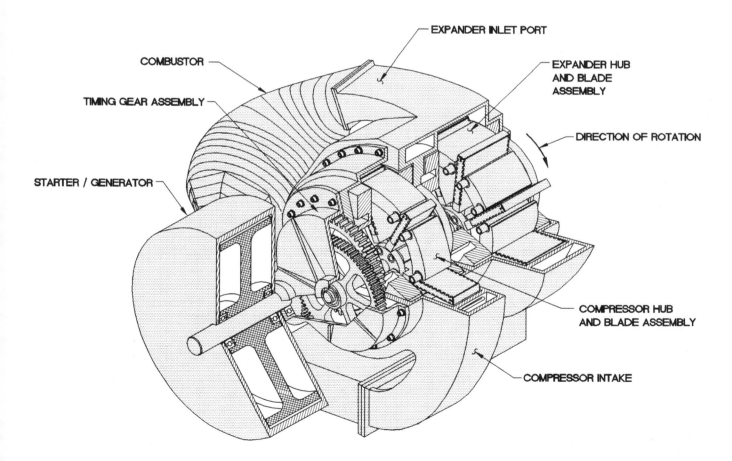

Figure 1: Isometric View of ECTAM Engine System.

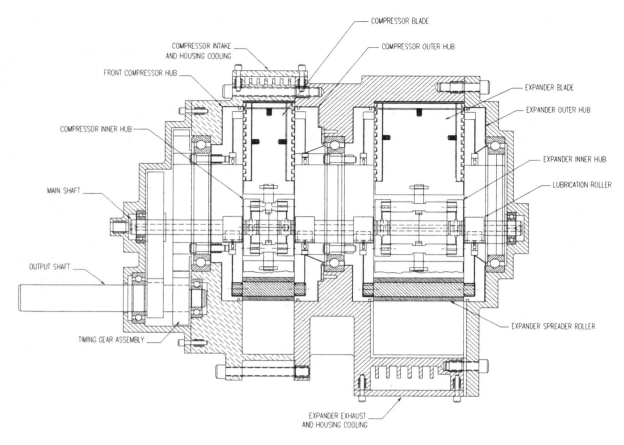

Figure 2: Cross Section of ECTAM Engine System.

THE DESIGN

THERMODYNAMIC PROCESS - The following describes the thermodynamic energy transfer process used in operating the ECTAM engine. While several embodiments of the basic design exist, this steady state summary of the energy flow process should be sufficient to convey the principle of operation. The model shown in Figure 3, reflects an efficiency of 30.5 percent. Increased internal pressures and temperatures with minimal changes to the mechanical functionality may someday yield efficiencies as high as 43%. We realize that much more engineering needs to take place along with the maturing of the technology in order to accomplish this goal (See Appendix 1 for further explanation).

Fresh ambient air at 27°C (80°F) is drawn into the low pressure side of the compressor where water vapor is injected. The water is used in cooling the compressor and increases compressor efficiency. In the compressor the feed air is pressurized to 1069 kPa (155 psia) at 252°C (486°F). The heated feed air and water vapor combination is then mixed with fuel in the combustor at an average combustion temperature of 1260°C (2300°F). In addition, the 1069 kPa (155 psia) steam generated from the cooling of the expander housing is injected into the combustion stream at the end of the flame front. Here the combined gas mixture transfers energy from the constituents of combustion to the working

gas mixture, increasing the potential energy of the steam portion and decreasing the potential energy of the combustion gas portion of the mixture. The inlet temperature at this point is maintained at 593°C (1100°F) and is controlled by the mixing ratio of air, fuel and steam. In the expander, the pressurized hot gas mixture is allowed to expand as a function of the rotative position of the blades. During expansion, the gas temperature drops to 238°C (460°F) at the point of maximum working expansion prior to reaching the exit port of the expander. At the exit port of the expander, the now 167°C (333°F) gas mixture enters the exhaust manifold containing a coil winding (heat exchanger) used to preheat the water entering the expander housing. The feed water temperature is increased from a nominal 27°C (80°F) to 149°C (300°F) prior to entering the expander housing. In the expander housing it is heated to 185 (365°F) converting to steam at 1076 kPa (156 psia).

THE COMPRESSOR - The compressor is a pinned vane positive displacement rotary system. The compressor section, see Figure 4, is mechanically similar to the expander. One difference is that 6 blades may be used instead of 8 blades, as in the expander. A two stage compressor may be used for higher pressures. A second difference is in the location of the intake and exhaust ports. Here the volume of the chambers formed by adjacent vanes decreases during rotation. The compressor inner hub is attached to and driven by the main

Figure 3: The Thermodynamic Process.

SYSTEM HEAT REJECTION AT EXHAUST 47.5%.
SYSTEM EFFICIENCY 30.5%.
SYSTEM LOSSES 22% (11 kw [14.7 hp]), (HOUSING HEAT/MECHANICAL/
COMPRESSION, EXPANSION AND PUMPING).

ENGINE SPEED: 1600 RPM   NET OUTPUT TORQUE: 90.5 N-m (67 ft-lb)
NET POWER: 15.2 kw (20.4 hp)   HEAT INPUT 49.8 kw (170,000 BTU/hr)
PUMPING: 0.4 kw (0.5 hp)   WATER FLOW: 13 Kg/hr (3.6 gl/hr)

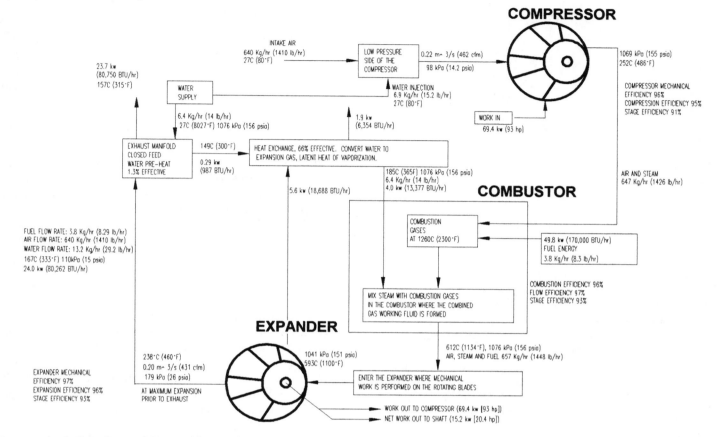

compressor is designed to exhaust to the combustor inlet at 252°C (486°F) and 1069 kPa (155 psia). The compressor and expander are together driven by a starter/generator until the speed is such that the air flow and internal pressure is adequate for ignition and sustained combustion.

THE COMBUSTOR - The external combustion chamber is designed to support a continuous combustion, multi-fuel capability. Air is fed to the combustor from the compressor at 1069 kPa (155 psia) (potentially higher for future designs). Fuel is fed to the combustor where it is pre-heated by combustion heat and mixed with air in a continuous flow process. A lean mixture is used to reduce hydrocarbon emissions and to maintain the flame temperature at approximately 1260°C (2300°F) (with the goal of minimizing the creation of NOx). Steam at 185°C (365°F) is injected into the combustor; thereby reducing the expander inlet temperature to 593°C (1100°F). The injection of steam into the combustion gas stream also helps minimize combustor emissions by scrubbing the products of combustion. The combustion gas and steam mixture then enter the expander portion of the engine. Air, fuel and steam flow rates are varied to control both the expander inlet temperature and the total flow of energy to the expander.

THE EXPANDER - The expander, shown in Figures 5 and 6, is a positive displacement pinned vane rotary system. The working gas mixture from the combustor acts directly against the blades and does not pass by them as in a turbine. The blades do not physically slide as in a sliding vane compressor. Instead, the blades are pivotally attached (pinned) at one end to the inner hub, where they extend radially through roller elements in the outer hub. The inner hub is connected to the outer hub by a gear system (shown in Figure 7). The gears cause the inner and outer hubs to rotate together at the same rotational speed, maintaining their centers of rotation.

Because the blades are attached to the inner hub there are no friction forces between the blades and outer housing. Small floating seals are used between the blades and housings to minimize gas passage from a high pressure chamber to the adjacent lower pressure chamber. The blade seals fit into grooves at the ends and sides of each blade. They are designed to be made of a low friction, high temperature material to minimize lubrication requirements and the effects of heat generated by the high speed contact between the seals and housing faces. Two possible seal materials are carbon/graphite and polyimide. The seals are held against

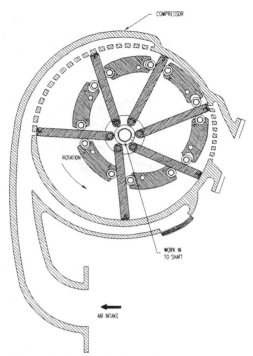

Figure 4: Sectional view of compressor

and housing faces. Two possible seal materials are carbon/graphite and polyimide. The seals are held against the housing faces by small springs located in the blades. This floating seal arrangement also compensates for thermal growth of the blades and housings. The current prototype is made with a non-circular inner face of the outer housing to accommodate the tilting of the blades. It may be possible to design the system with a circular inner face and allow the

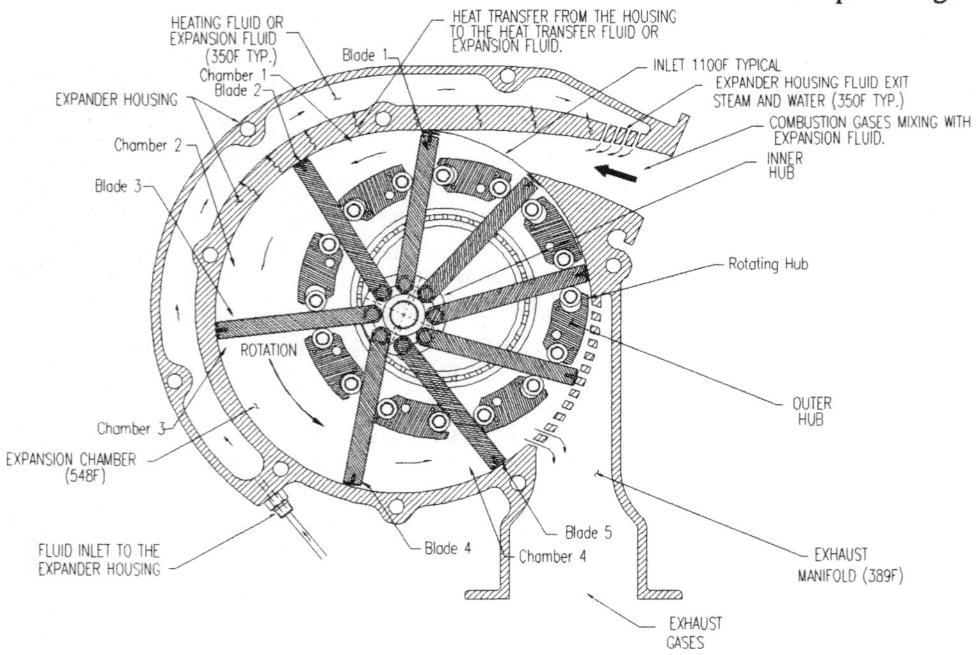

Figure 5: Expander Cross Section.

seals to compensate for the geometric changes due to the tilting motion of the blades.

It is important to note that the pressure drop from inlet to exhaust in this design is about 965 kPa (140 psi). This drop in pressure is partitioned into 4 working chambers resulting in an average chamber pressure differential of 241 kPa (35 psi). The actual pressure differential is not an average; but rather a function of temperature, pressure and volume as dictated by the rotative position of the blades. One can quickly see that the sealing requirements for the blades is less than what is required in I.C.E. designs where combustion pressure differentials typically exceed 2413 kPa (350 psi). Also, as the expanding gas leaks from a higher pressure volume to a lower pressure working volume the gas is available to perform work on the next blade in succession effectively resulting in 4 sets of light duty seals between the inlet and exhaust port. Initial testing has demonstrated that the design provides adequate sealing between blade sets and respective expansion chambers with little resulting wear.

Sealing between the blade and outer hub is accomplished by maintaining contact between each blade and its corresponding spreader rollers (front and rear). The gas pressure on the blade creates the required contact force on the forward roller. Each blade rear roller is kept in contact with the blade by springs located in the outer hubs. The expanding gas leakage past the rear roller is minimized by a contact vane type seal. The ends of this seal fit within a slot in each outer hub immediately behind the moveable rear roller (see Figures A-2 and A-3 in Appendix 2). This roller actually moves forward and backwards as a function of the blade tilt.

Seals between the outer hubs and housing are currently being redesigned. These outer hub seals are used to minimize the expansion gas leakage from the sides of the chambers formed by each blade pair. Two solutions being evaluated are contact lip seals and brush seals.

The variable blade surface area is created by the eccentric relationship between the blade hub and outer hub axes of rotation. This geometry also causes the blades to act as levers creating higher torque on the outer rotating hub than could be accomplished with sliding vane machines.

As seen from the figures, the respective expansion chamber volume varies as a function of rotative position, increasing in volume as rotation approaches the exit port. Also, as the blades rotate from the intake position the angle between two adjacent blades increases as does the distance between the inner hub and outer housing. This increasing chamber volume and decreasing fluid temperature causes the pressure in each formed chamber to

Figure 6: Photograph of Expander Section.

of pressure applied to the surface area of each blade that creates the resulting force on the outer hub. The net forces on the blades do not vary extremely as they do on the tops of pistons of an internal combustion engine. This is due to the fact that the force is caused by a gradually decreasing pressure in conjunction with an increasing working blade surface. The blade forces are converted to continuous and smooth torque on the outer hub. From this it can be observed that the transfer of energy from the expanding gas to the blade surface is along the arc length formed between the expander inlet and the expander exit ports. The gas flow direction is thus parallel to the direction of rotation of the outer hub; from which, mechanical energy is derived. This configuration serves to optimize the conversion of expanding gas energy to rotating mechanical energy.

In the expander inlet (Figure 5), the tip of the first blade sees an inlet pressure of 1069 kPa (155 psia) on one side and

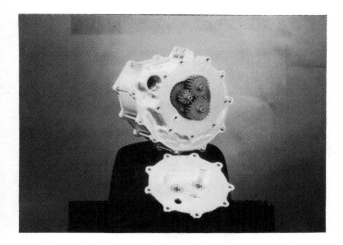

Figure 7: Photograph of Timing Gear Assembly.

a gas expansion pressure of 745 kPa (108 psia) on the back side. Blade 1 thus sees the differential pressure between the inlet and the contained expansion in chamber 1. The 324 kPa

(47 psi) differential creates a 570 N (128 lb.) force on blade 1. Chamber 1, (which is the back side of blade 1), sees 745 kPa (108 psi) and chamber 2 sees 352 kPa (51 psia). The resulting force on blade 2 is 2501 N (562 lb.). The pressure in chamber 3 drops to 172 kPa (25 psia) resulting in 2634 N (592 lb.) force on blade 3. The pressure in chamber 4 drops to 103 kPa (15 psia) resulting in 805 N (180lb.) force on blade 4. Chamber 4 is effectively vented to the exhaust port of the expander by grooves cut into the outer housing. Each resulting blade force reacts against a roller element contained within the outer hub assembly. These forces, acting simultaneously, are thus converted to rotational mechanical energy (torque) in the outer hub assembly. Power can be taken from the outer hub assembly directly to drive both the compressor and an output shaft.

Expander housing heat energy is used to create steam contained in a fluid reservoir partially formed by the exterior of the expander housing. This energy transfer maintains the housing temperature at or near 277°C (530°F) and greatly increases the internal energy of the fluid.. The steam at 185°C (365°F) and 1069 kPa (155 psia) is then fed to the combustor.

Internal cooling challenges are being addressed by the use of some high temperature materials which can be produced at competitive prices and the use of lubricants, such as water based emulsions, which can act as cooling agents as part of the lubrication cycle. The water based emulsified lubricant will aid in cooling both compressor and expander components. As the mixture makes contact with the hot internal engine parts, the water part of the mixture will vaporize leaving the lubricant part. The energy required to boil off the water and further heat the saturated mixture reduces the temperature of the internal engine parts. The steam portion then becomes part of the exhaust gas stream leaving behind the lubricant component to the greatest extent possible. The following is one example of the method of lubrication; A water based emulsified lubricant is fed through the main shaft bore to feed ports, drilled radially into the main shaft, allowing the lubricant to flow to corresponding ports in the blade hubs. These ports feed lubricant to the reciprocating blade needle bearings. Low friction materials will be used to minimize heat and load generated by friction, and part of the cooling plan involves controlling the rate of water flow through the outer housing.

HEAT EXCHANGERS - The feed water heat exchanger located at the exit port of the expander is used to preheat the water entering the expander housing. The 167°C (333°F) gas mixture enters the exhaust manifold containing a coil winding (heat exchanger). The feed water temperature is increased from a nominal 27°C (80°F) to 149°C (300°F) prior to entering the expander housing. Here the temperature of the water at the 6.4 Kg/hr (14 lb/hr) flow rate rises 122°C (252°F) and the temperature of the exhaust gases drops by 7°C (19°F). Because of the high mass flow rate of exhaust gases the heat exchanger effectiveness is assumed to be only 1.3%.

gases the heat exchanger effectiveness is assumed to be only 1.3%.

The expander housing heat exchanger is based on conduction between the housing at a nominal 277°C (530°F) and the water being heated from the inlet at 149°C (300°F) and being liberated to steam at 185°C (365°F) and 1076 kPa (156 psia). The water is contained in a fluid reservoir partially formed by the exterior of the expander housing and is then fed to the combustor. The effectiveness of this heat exchange is assumed to be 66%.

For both of these heat exchangers the percentage of available heat is fairly large compared to the portion that is transferred to the water. The design of the heat exchange elements of the ECTAM are required to be low cost and durable. This is because the efficiency increase as a function of the flow of water will not be justified by a more efficient but more costly heat exchange design. Again, the benefits of the water injection design are realized by the flexibility to rapidly control inlet temperatures and reduce the creation of NOx.

THE BENEFITS

The overriding benefit of this design approach is the potential to increase efficiency while decreasing undesirable emissions. The architecture is well suited for both parallel and series hybrid electric systems. The design features a robust, and potentially low cost engine design.

The forces on the expander blades are near constant over stroke. This is due to the fact that blade area is increasing as the internal pressure is decreasing. Engine operation is smoother and quieter relative to an internal combustion engine for a number of reasons. First, the vane loading is more uniform and in the direction of rotation. Second, the blades are continuously loaded from the intake to the exhaust ports, providing a longer expansion period from which work is accomplished. Third, the ECTAM, due to its 2 hub design, is intrinsically balanced and does not require large counter balances within the system. Fourth, of the reduction in noise can be attributed to the use of an external and continuous combustion system. The combustion process occurs well upstream of the exhaust port. Therefore, the expander muffles most of the combustion noise. The most prominent noise associated with the ECTAM is that caused by the changes in pressure as the blades pass the inlet and exhaust ports.

The ECTAM is capable of producing high torque at low speed . In operation, four blades are continuously loaded with a total force exceeding 3,559 N (800 lb.). When the reaction torque in the expander is calculated about the outer rotating hub, 506 N-m (373 ft-lb) of torque is achieved. When compressor torque is subtracted the net system torque is 91 N-m (67 ft-lb).

Engine size is a typical concern in vehicle design. This is more true in the design of HEVs (Hybrid Electric Vehicles) where, essentially, two power plants are required, the electric and engine portions. The ECTAM is designed to be a compact system to accommodate HEVs. The proof of concept prototype measures 61 cm (24")L x 61 cm (24")W x 40.6 cm

ECTAM™ ....MODEL 30

30 KW ELECTRIC GENERATOR

FUEL TYPES:	DIESEL	NATURAL GAS
	GASOLINE	PROPANE
OUTPUT VOLTAGE:	320 VDC	
	240 VDC	
	180 VDC	
SYSTEM WEIGHT:	265 LBS	
CONTROLLER:	18" x 12" x 8" (NOT SHOWN)	

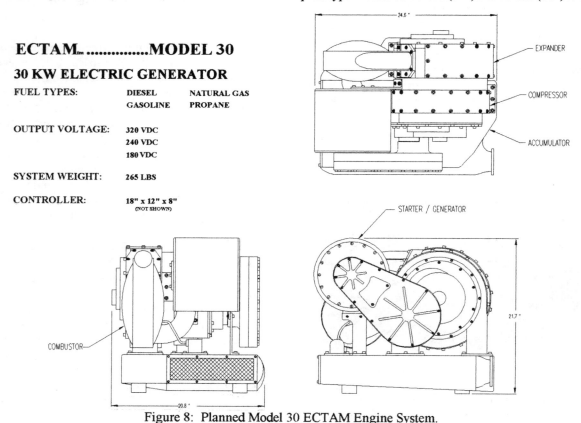

Figure 8: Planned Model 30 ECTAM Engine System.

55.1 cm (21.7")H.

The ECTAM is designed to be fairly lightweight. The current aluminum expander and stainless steel combustor combination weigh 39 kg (85 lb.). Using the prototype as a benchmark, assuming the use of both steel and aluminum parts in the production design, the weight of a 30 kW unit should be around 120 kg (265 lb.) including the starter/generator.

As part of the design criteria it was essential to configure the ECTAM for not only high volume production, but manufacturability and repair as well. The mechanical design is simple, it incorporates part type reuse extensively and is very user friendly in the maintenance department as well. Most of the prototype parts were made by local machine shops or purchased off the shelf. Volume manufacturing considerations have been incorporated and many options remain unexplored. The current expander and combustor prototype can be disassembled and reassembled by one person in about 2 hours with the use of only 2 special tooling devices (The two custom made assembly tools cost less than $400.00).

Many part manufactures, including those for the gears, bearings, seals and housings have provided design recommendations for production and some preliminary pricing. The design team has compiled an initial parts list for the 30 kW ECTAM with estimated component costs. The major components and costs for a 70,000 unit production run are summarized in Table 1.

Table 1. System Costs

SUB SYSTEM	NO. OF PARTS	TOTAL COST
EXPANDER	181	$486
COMPRESSOR	178	$441
COMBUSTOR	56	$427
HEAT EXCH.	24	$335
GEN./STARTER	12	$780
MISCELLANEOUS	143	$501
TOTAL	594	$2910

TESTING

Many initial tests have been conducted on the expander, the combustor and combinations of both. These pieces of hardware are shown in Figures 9 and 10. A commercial compressor was used to provide the inlet air where both inlet pressure and flow could be controlled. Initially the expander was spun by itself using compressed air to verify that the mechanical features such as rotation, part clearances and production of torque performed according to the design. Next, the combustor was tested to verify features such as ignition, sustained burn, water heating and exhaust port temperatures. A series of short expander and combustor tests have been performed using propane as the fuel. These tests included evaluation of the combustor exit port temperatures as a function of air, fuel and steam flow rates. It was determined that the temperature could be stabilized at 593°C (1100°F) and was controllable between 121°C (250°F) and 1038°C (1900°F) within a second by varying the flow rates.

Figure 9: Photograph of Expander/Combustor Combination

In later tests the ECTAM test assembly, shown in Figure 10, was connected to a truck rear axle at the transmission output location of the drive shaft and drove the wheels attached to the axle. This test was performed to get a better feel of the responsiveness of the system to changes in air, fuel and steam while under a small load. At this point the expander was spun up to 600 rpm with the expander housing temperatures exceeding 149°C (300°F).

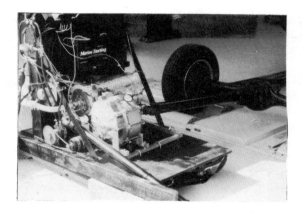

Figure 10: Photograph of ECTAM Test Assembly.

In the most recent test the rear axle was placed on a chassis dynamometer and attached to the expander, combustor and commercial compressor assembly. The data gathered to this point substantiates the physical operation of the mechanical hardware (the expander and combustor) and establishes the basis for further product development.

Plans for the future include additional tests with goals of speeds of up to 1200 rpm and long term stabilized operation under load. Controlling the expander inlet conditions is an ongoing challenge. Because slight variations in fuel, air and steam can change the inlet temperature by hundreds of degrees, it is planned to incorporate control features that don't require 3 hands to operate. The most important and most impacting goal is to fabricate and test the first complete ECTAM engine. Currently about 70 percent of the design work has been completed on the Model 30. The new design is a system baseline which aggressively incorporates improvements over the prototype. The prototype has served to be an invaluable tool which has taught the design team many things about this new technology. While there are still some challenging features which remain to be built and tested, the prototype expander and combustor has demonstrated that this new system architecture has the potential to produce the kind of clean power required for future hybrid electric vehicles.

CONCLUSIONS

The ECTAM is a new engine designed to meet the performance needs of Hybrid Electric Vehicles and low emissions goals for future transportation. The attributes of continuous combustion, combined with continuous blade loading in this rotary system result in an intrinsically balanced and quiet engine which produces high torque at low rotational speeds. The ECTAM is compact, capable of operation using a variety of fuels and incorporates components that have the potential to be cost effectively mass produced. Test results validate the potential of the components to meet the design requirements.

REFERENCES

1   Hengsbach, T., Olbrisch, G., 1975, *A Heat Engine and a Method of Operating a Heat Engine*; British Patent 1 382 603, Feb. 5.

2   Takahashi, M., 1976, *Constant Pressure Heating Vane Rotary Engine*, United States Patent 3,989,011; Nov. 2.

3   Miles, P.E., Miles, M.A., 1985, *Thermodynamic Rotary Engine,* United States Patent 4,553,513, Nov. 19.

4   Hines, W.R., 1986, *Gas Turbine Engine of Improved Thermal Efficiency,* United States Patent 4,631,914, Dec. 30.

5   Maslak, C.E., 1990, *Water and Steam Injection in Cogeneration System,* United States Patent 4,928,478, May 29.

6   Jensen, R.L., 1973, *Vaned Rotor Engine and Compressor*, United States Patent 3,713,426; Jan. 30.

7   Mabille, R., 1937, *Rotary Engine*, United States Patent 2,071,799; Feb. 23.

8   McReynolds, W.W., 1976, Rotary Internal Combustion Engine, United States Patent 3,971,346, July 27.

9   Itoh, Takane; "The Automotive Ceramic Gas Turbine-An Attractive Future Automotive Engine"; Global Gas Turbine News; November 1992.

10   Palmer, W.R., 1992, *Rotary Compressor and Engine Machine System*, U.S. Serial No. 07/940,446; filed Sept. 4.

APPENDIX 1: SUMMARY OF THE THERMODYNAMIC PROCESS

The intention of Figure 3 is to summarize the operational states and assumed losses for each critical component of the engine. This figure only represents a steady state snap shot of the projected performance at the described operating conditions. As one can imagine the closed loop calculations give widely varying results across the model as the control variables are changed. The flexibility of the design to operate under a wide range of conditions has been supported by some of the initial testing while other calculated performance features still remain to be proven by test.

The analytical models, which were used in the design of the ECTAM, clearly indicate that performance and efficiency is greatly impacted by internal temperatures and pressures. Increasing the internal pressures and temperatures increases performance and efficiency however, these increases have a compounding impact on materials and part stress. We have shown the 30% efficient version because the pressures and temperatures are within a range that can be handled by state of the art materials and finishes which are currently in production (at various levels). While 30% efficiency by itself is not record breaking, it is believed that this efficiency in a small, low noise and vibration package, incorporating continuous combustion for ultra low emissions, would be very attractive for HEV's provided the manufacturing cost can be kept competitive.

THE ANALYSIS MODELS

The first models created were used to evaluate the mechanical performance of the expander and compressor as stand alone units. Sample model calculations are found on pages 14 and 15. These calculations are based on exposed blade area, pressure differentials and physical blade position as a function of stroke (rotation). The force on the exposed blade area, which is a function of chamber pressure, is calculated and reacted against the inner and outer hub assemblies. Gears link the inner hub to the outer hub and allow the described rotational kinematics while balancing the blade load equations. The net forces and torques are calculated for all blades performing work. The resultant torque is on the large rotating outer hub. This calculation is represented pictorially in Figure A-1. The hub of the compressor is mechanically fixed to the hub of the expander

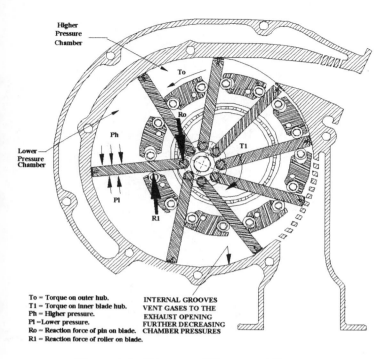

Higher
Pressure
Chamber

To

Ro

Ph

T1

Lower
Pressure
Chamber

Pl

Ro

R1

To = Torque on outer hub.
T1 = Torque on inner blade hub.
Ph = Higher pressure.
Pl =Lower pressure.
Ro = Reaction force of pin on blade.
R1 = Reaction force of roller on blade.

INTERNAL GROOVES
VENT GASES TO THE
EXHAUST OPENING
FURTHER DECREASING
CHAMBER PRESSURES

Figure A-1: Diagram of Forces and Torques.

The second series of models used the input of the first analytical models to define the volumetric flow rates of the expander and respectively sized compressor at selected engine speeds. The variables of these models are inlet air temperature, air flow, water (steam) flow, fuel flow, combustor efficiency and heat exchanger efficiency. The internal gas temperatures are varied by changing the flow rates of fuel, air and water. The steady state design is based on constant pressure combustion (transients for fuel and steam injection are not calculated during periods of changing speed). The volume of intake air is compressed to a pressure determined by the geometry of the compressor. Potential energy is thus added to the compressed gas stream and is supplied to the combustor. Fuel is added in the combustor where leaner than stochiometric combustion occurs. Excess air is used for cooling. Some portion of inlet air contains water vapor which is used in cooling the compressor. The series of equations calculate the temperature rise of the combustion gas mixture as a function of the percent make-up of compressor water, air and fuel. The combustion gas mixture is further cooled by the steam generated by the heat of the expander housing. As the temperature decreases so does the energy contained in the combustion gas stream. The goal here is to maintain lower internal component temperatures to increase the fatigue life of the components.

A temperature limit of 593°C (1100°F) is placed on the expander inlet. By doing this the internal expanding gas temperature would drop below 288°C (550°F) at the maximum expansion position (as shown in Figure 3) while still performing work on the third blade in the loading sequence. The temperature of 288°C (550°F) was selected based on the temperature limits associated with most of the cost effective material finishes available (typically 316°C

[600°F] maximum). The model gives the pressure of combusted gas mixture at a given volume and temperature as a function of the rotative position of the expander blades. The most critical aspect of the design is to insure that the state of pressure in the positive displacement chambers (created by the rotative positions of the blades) is commensurate with the calculations for volumetric gas expansion and respective temperature. It can be more easily seen now that a temperature of 427°C (800°F) or 482°C (900°F) in the maximum expansion chamber would result in higher internal pressures during the expansion cycle. These higher pressures would yield more work and higher efficiencies, but would compound the complexity of the hardware design effort.

The following is a summary of the analytical methods used in evaluation of the ECTAM. First a series of full scale plots were generated at various blade rotation positions to obtain physical part dimensions and part orientations (similar to Figure 5). The physical volume of each expansion volume and the relationship of the blade to the inner and outer hub was input using a spread sheet format. A relationship was set up establishing the changes in internal chamber pressure as a function of the change in volume. The operating pressure is established by the configuration of the compressor blades and exit port size and location. The compression pressure is a function of temperature and volume using isothermal and adiabatic compression equations. For the current models a gas compression efficiency of 95% and a mechanical efficiency of 96% is used resulting in a compressor stage efficiency of 91%. This yields a resultant cfm at pressure and temperature supplied to the combustor. Water injection is used to lower the inlet gas temperature and help cool the combustor. The use of water has a significant impact on the efficiency of the system.

In the combustor portion heat is added using heat rates and mass flow rates for air, propane and water. Assuming a combustion efficiency of 96% and a compressed gas flow through efficiency of 97% results in a combustor stage efficiency of 93%. Steam from the expander housing is injected in the combustor using the pressure drop to reach the inlet of the expander. Heat energy is added to the combustor equations to establish the inlet temperature.

The gas is allowed to fill the chambers of the expander and, as a function of rotative volumetric change, the pressure decreases to its internal minimum at the position of maximum expansion. Here the states of temperature and pressure are evaluated as a function of volumetric supply from the water injection, steam, fuel and air sources. The expanded volumes must be filled as a function of engine speed. If the expansion volume is too large (as a function of blade width) to maintain the design pressure either the expander or compressor blade widths can be changed to either increase or decrease the volumes. Additional steam can be added with fuel and the temperatures can be altered accordingly in the expander . An expansion gas efficiency of 96% and a mechanical efficiency of 97% is used bringing the expander stage efficiency to 93%. No muffler or back

96% and a mechanical efficiency of 97% is used bringing the expander stage efficiency to 93%. No muffler or back pressure is added to the exit port. The exhaust gas flow rate and temperature is substantial enough that the feed water pre-heat coil will not have to be of substantial design under conditions of low flow as we are proposing.

Also, it has been determined that there will be a surplus of heat energy from the expander housing to heat the water to steam. Additional thermal management considerations will need to be addressed because of this.

The model for an operating pressure of 1069 kPa (155 psia) is commensurate with the hardware's ability to handle the stress, though some blade load balancing may be required. In this case a percentage of high pressure gas is intentionally bled to a lower pressure chamber to reduce extremely high blade loading. To do this small grooves are cut into the inner wall of the expander housing.

A model of a higher internal pressure ECTAM configuration has been created to establish the potential of the design. In this model a two stage compressor is used to bring the operating pressure up to 1434 kPa (208 psia). While not yet optimized, the results look very promising. Based on a 516 cfm compressor with a 9.9 cm (3.9 inch) wide expander blade, 399 cfm of flow at the point of maximum expansion and expander inlet temperature of 600°C (1,112°F) the design produces 28.2 kW (37.8 HP) at 1600 rpm and 168 N-m (124 ft-lb) of torque. The heat input is 77.6 kW (265,000 BTU/HR) with an efficiency of 36.3%. The heat rejected is 34.9% of the input (27.1 kW [92,485 BTU/HR]) leaving 28.7% for internal system losses. The maximum load of this design reaches 3,618 N (813 lb) on the blade of maximum articulation. Because this single blade contributes 293 N-m (216 ft-lb) of torque to the overall system torque, we may be spending some time finding an appropriate material to handle the fatigue stress.

APPENDIX 2: THE SEALING ELEMENTS

As with any engine the design of the sealing elements are as critical as the thermal management and lubrication challenges. The ECTAM incorporates a number of different seal types. The system has an internal sealing design which minimizes the flow of higher pressure gases to locations of lower pressure. Part of this design includes bearing seals which maintain the internal pressure of the engine as well as prevent the intrusion of contaminants into the bearings. There are also blade side seals and end seals which can be seen in Figures A-2 and A-3. The side seals are of square tooth design to minimize the flow of gases to the inner compartment of the engine (inside of the outer hub assembly). Gases that pass into this region are not available to do work and contribute to internal windage losses. These gases do however, cause the system to become internally pressurized which contributes to the ongoing sealing effectiveness of the design by decreasing the pressure differential between the individual chambers and the region defined by the inner diameter of the outer hub. The only system level entry of

Figure A-2: Photograph of Blade Seal Details.

gases is at the inlet port and exhaust gases exit only through the exhaust port.

The roller elements, as shown in Figures A-2 and A-3, contact both sides of each blade and are shrouded by the spreader elements. The rear roller is allowed to translate in a slot formed within the spreader element. This allows the rear roller to remain in contact with the blade regardless of blade

Figure A-3: Photograph of Blade Seal Details.

angle. Provisions for seals of the rear roller elements are incorporated in the spreader elements. This seal reduces the flow of high pressure gases past the rear of the roller to the inner chamber. This configuration incorporates lightly spring loaded rectangular seals which do not interfere with the functionality of the rollers.

passing from the inlet port directly to the exhaust port. The end seals also minimize the passage of gases from a high pressure chamber to a lower pressure chamber.

Other seals include the seal between the outer hub and the housing. This seal is shown in Figure 2. Currently the prototype uses a step joint to reduce the flow of gases. A production engine would incorporate a brush seal or solid seal which could accommodate the rotational speeds of the outer hub. It should be noted that the sealing methods of the compressor are the same as those of the expander.

Total Water flow: 3.63 Gal/hr

COMPRESSOR

Power:	106.05 HP	80.81 HP
Speed:	1600 RPM	-1071 BTU/min -25.24
Air Flow:	461.8 CFM	653 Efficiency:
Mass Flow air:	32.78 lbm/min	20.4 HP
T Ambient:	80 F	66.76 HP
T inlet:	303 F	30.5%
T exit:	620 F adib	52.5%heat
available		
Pressure inlet:	14.2 psia	Q eff: 100%
Pressure exit:	155 psia	93.4 model@X%eff
Work in:	4501 BTU/min	93.4 HP ACTUAL
		96%Eff gas exp
Cv air:	0.1715 BTU/lbm F	
Q compress:	4500.7 BTU/min	270,039 BTU/hr
Q housing heat:	405.1 BTU/min Heat loss 9.0%	
T'compress no water:	547.8 F isotherm	84.65 =V2

Q ph trans @180F:	990 BTU/lbm	
Cv water vapor:	0.336 BTU/lbm F	
Q rate water heat:	248 BTU/min	14,850 BTU/hr
Mass flow water:	0.25 lbm/min	1.875 Gal/hr
T' comp with water:	505.0 F	V'= 352 cfm @500F
		350 F min

COMBUSTOR

	66.76 HP	
Energy flow:	170,000 BTU/hr	2,833 BTU/min
Mass flow fuel:	8.29 lb/hr	0.138 lbm/min
Cp prop:	0.404 BTU/lbm F	

Cv Partial water:	0 BTU/lbm F	0 lb/min 0
Mass flow exp H2O:	1.75 Gal/hr	0.23 lb/min
Gal/hr		
Q Exp water:	12,418 BTU/hr	207 BTU/min
T exit comb:	1,142.5 F@.96%combustor eff	

Press compress:	155 psia	140.22 psig
Press exp inlet:	151 psia	136.22 psig

EXPANDER

Vol air @ inlet:	86.8 CFM @ 154.9	461.8 CFM
@14.2		
Vol fuel+st @ inlet:	3.08 CFM @	10.54 :1
Vol air+fuel+st:	91.70 CFM @	154.9 psia

T pre steam mix:	1,129.1 F			
Vol @ expan inlet:	125.40 CFM		121.68	3.72
T expan inlet:	1,093.7 F less Q to exp		7.7 FT^3/LBM	
T expan vol 3:	456.45 F			
Vol @ expan:	452.43 CFM	441.61	10.83	25.2
	429.81 @95%eff	430.0	22.4 FT^3/LBM	
T exp exit port:	330.27 F	10.5 psig	@450F/24psia	

FEED WATER PRE HEATER

Q to preheat water:	52.1 BTU/min	3,124 BTU/hr
T watet inlet:	80 F	
T water exit:	303.1 F	
T exhaust @ exit:	311.3 F	

EXPANDER HOUSING HEAT EXCHANGE

T Housing:	530 F	
Q liberated by exp:	313.6 BTU/min	18,815 BTU/hr
T water @ inlet:	303 F	@ 66% eff
Water flow:	0.23 lbm/min	1.75 Gal/hr
Q absorbed by water:	207.0 BTU/min	12,418
BTU/hr		
T water @ exit:	380.5 F	6,397.2 Losses

Heat rejected: 80,793 BTU/hr

ECTAM FORCE & TORQUE MODEL
SMOO1 155-psia

CFM= 430.0

VOLUMES (IN^3): Blade width = 4.2 @ 10.5 psig

		Lh	Ll	OUT	IN	RATIO
(INLET)	V1= 11.1	1.1	0.9	2.7	2.6	1.00
	V2= 15.5	1.4	1.1	3.1	2.8	1.39
	V3= 30.7	2.0	1.4	5.4	3.2	2.76
	V4= 58.1	2.9	2.8	6.3	3.4	5.22
(EXHAUST)	V5= 58.1					

Net System HP: 20.37   1600
NET SYSTEM TORQUE=   66.86 FT-LB

PRESSURES (PSIG):

(INLET)	P1=	154.9	140.2 Psig	1
	P2=	107.7	93.0 Psig	1
	P3=	50.7	36.0 Psig	1
	P4=	25.2	10.5 Psig	1
(EXHAUST)	P5=	15.1	0.4 Psig	0.6

Eff@
EXPANDER: HP: 113.8   96% 1600
BLADE FORCES AND TORQUE: 373.4 FT-LB

BLADE 1:	Lh/Ll	Ah/Al	TBh/TBl	l1/l2	LR	COS
Fbh= 588.9	1.0	4.2	2,297	3.9	3.0	30.0
Fbl= 507.9	1.3	5.5	1,854	3.7		

(roller) F=   127.9 LBS @ OUTER HUB ROLLER #1
T1=   34.2 FT-LBS @ OUTER HUB ROLLER #1

BLADE 2:	Lh/Ll	Ah/Al	Tlh/Tll	l1/l2	LR	COS
Fh= 664.1	1.7	7.1	2,424	3.7	2.1	32.0
Fl= 333.0	2.2	9.2	1,066	3.2		

(roller) F=   562.0 LBS @ OUTER HUB ROLLER #2
T2=   147.7 FT-LBS @ OUTER HUB ROLLER #2

BLADE 3:	Lh/Ll	Ah/Al	Tlh/Tll	l1/l2	LR	COS
Fh= 408.7	2.7	11.3	1,247	3.1	1.5	12.0
Fl= 123.2	2.8	11.8	370	3.0		

(roller) F=   591.6 LBS @ OUTER HUB ROLLER #2
T3=   157.4 FT-LBS @ OUTER HUB ROLLER #2

BLADE 4:	Lh/Ll	Ah/Al	Tlh/Tll	l1/l2	LR	COS
Fh= 118.8	2.7	11.3	374	3.2	2.0	13.0
Fl= 4.3	2.5	10.5	14	3.3		

(roller) F=   180.1 LBS @ OUTER HUB ROLLER #2
T4=   49.7 FT-LBS @ OUTER HUB ROLLER #2

COMPRESSOR:

VOLUMES (IN^3):   Blade width = 4.75 ******

		Lh	Ll	OUT	IN	RATIO
(INLET)	V4= 87.50	2.95	2.95	8.30	4.20	1.00
	V3= 56.63	2.60	1.70	7.00	4.10	1.55
	V2= 25.34	1.40	1.00	4.90	4.00	3.45
(EXIT)	V1= 9.97	0.80	0.25	4.20	3.80	8.78

PRESSURES (PSIG):

(INLET)	P4=	14.2	-0.5 psig
	P3=	22.9	8.2 psig
	P2=	55.5	40.8 psig
(EXIT)	P1=	154.9	140.2 psig

COMPRESSOR: W= 4.75 Eff@ 461.8 CFM
BLADE FORCES/TORQUE: -306.6 FT-LB 95% 14.2 psia
HP: -93.3925   1600

BLADE 3:	Lh/Ll	Ah/Al	Tlh/Tll	l1/l2	LR	COS
Fh= 103.3	2.65	12.6	320	3.1	1.5	12.0
Fl= (6.5)	2.75	13.1	(20)	3.0		

(roller) F= -229.3 LBS @ OUTER HUB ROLLER #3
T1=   -76.5 FT-LBS @ OUTER HUB ROLLER #3

BLADE 2:	Lh/Ll	Ah/Al	Tlh/Tll	l1/l2	LR	COS
Fh= 300.1	1.55	7.4	1,110	3.7	2.1	30.0
Fl= 79.9	2.05	9.7	256	3.2		

(roller) F= -361.0 LBS @ OUTER HUB ROLLER #2
T2=   -120.5 FT-LBS @ OUTER HUB ROLLER #2

BLADE 1:	Lh/Ll	Ah/Al	Tlh/Tll	l1/l2	LR	COS
Fh= 366.0	0.55	2.6	1,428	3.9	3.0	32.0
Fl= 183.9	0.95	4.5	681	3.7		

(roller) F= -211.2 LBS @ OUTER HUB ROLLER #1
T3=   -67.7 FT-LBS @ OUTER HUB ROLLER #1

950955

Computerized Speed Control of Electric Vehicles

Zhejun Fan,[¶] Yoram Koren, and David Wehe

The University of Michigan

ABSTRACT

This paper presents a general control module to control the speed of an electric vehicle (EV). This module consists of a microprocessor and several C-programmable micro-controllers. It uses an identification algorithm to estimate the system parameters on-line. With the estimated parameters, control gains are calculated via pole-placement. In order to compensate for the internal errors, a cross-coupling control algorithm is included. To estimate the true velocity and acceleration from measurements, a discrete-time Kalman filter was utilized. The experimental results validate the general control module for EVs.

1. INTRODUCTION

Due to the growing concern for air quality and the possible consequences of the green-house effect, major automotive manufacturers have launched aggressive programs to develop electric vehicles (EVs) for commercialization. Intense electric vehicle R&D conducted by government agencies, academic institutions, and related industries is being actively pursued [1, 5]. One essential part of this research is the improvement of electric propulsion or the powertrain. Electric propulsion technology consists of the motor and its controller. EV motors fall into three main categories: direct current (DC), alternating current (AC) induction, and AC synchronous [10]. Among these, the DC motor is the simplest and requires the least development [5]. In order to make the drivetrain more compact and reduce power transmission losses, as many motors as driving wheels may be selected and the motors are fixed to the wheel sides with reduction gears provided to drive the wheels [10]. For this kind of powertrain system, each of the electric motor for an EV generally has its own controller [2]. Since the controller for electric motors is currently more important and more costly, its cost and availability become the critical

design factors for the selection of both the type of motor and the system operating voltage [4]. To control the speed of vehicles, the motor controller generally has fixed feedback gains for each vehicle. To determine these gains, all kinds of experimental testing must be conducted. Consequently, it is impossible to control all vehicles with a single pair of fixed feedback gains [11]. However, it is possible to control them with a general control module, which is developed in our lab and is proven to be useful via experiments.

The proposed control module utilizes an adaptive identifier with unbiased parameter estimation instead of biased estimation via least square [11]. In addition, it incorporates a cross-coupling controller to handle the coupling effects and a Kalman filter to estimate the true velocities. It is primarily designed for EVs, whereas the method by [11] is designed primarily for internal combustion engine vehicles (ICEV). For an ICEV, the vehicle model is obtained through linearization about some operating points. As operating points are hard to predict due to unknown road incline and disturbances, the proposed procedure is extremely difficult for an ICEV. However, for an EV, the vehicle model is readily available without linearization and consequently the proposed control module should be applicable in all cases.

In the organization of this paper, system modeling for the speed control of EVs is introduced in Section 2. Parameter identification with an adaptive identifier is discussed in Section 3. In Section 4, pole-placement control design is implemented. Parameter estimation by Kalman filter is conducted in Section 5. In Section 6, cross-coupling control for error compensation is developed. The general control module for the speed control of EVs is presented in Section 7. Conclusions are given in Section 8.

2. SYSTEM MODELING FOR THE SPEED CONTROL OF EVs

A simple model for EV is discussed in this section. For the speed control purpose, each loop of an EV with two

[¶] Corresponding author, ATL, The University of Michigan, 1101 Beal Ave., Ann Arbor, MI 48109-2110.

independent drive loops can be modeled as a first order system with two unknown parameters such as gain and time constant.

$$G_L(s) = \frac{Y_L(s)}{R_L(s)} = \frac{K_L}{1 + \tau_L s} \qquad (1)$$

$$G_R(s) = \frac{Y_R}{R_R} = \frac{K_R}{1 + \tau_R s} \qquad (2)$$

where
R_L, Y_L, R_R, Y_R are the desired and actual velocities for the left and right drive loops respectively. K_L, K_R, τ_L, τ_R are the DC gains and time constants for the left and right drive loop respectively. $G_L(s)$ and $G_R(s)$ are the transfer functions for the left and right drive loops respectively.

Applying Z-transform to Eqs. (1) and (2) yields:

$$G_L(z) = \frac{b_L Z^{-1}}{1 - a_L Z^{-1}} \qquad (3)$$

$$G_R(z) = \frac{b_R Z^{-1}}{1 - a_R Z^{-1}} \qquad (4)$$

where $a_L = e^{\frac{-T}{\tau_L}}$, $b_L = K_L(1 - a_L)$

$a_R = e^{\frac{-T}{\tau_R}}$, $b_R = K_R(1 - a_R)$

$T =$ Sampling time

These four parameters, which are the transformed versions of those in Eqs.(1) and (2), may be unknown and time-varying due to many factors such as shifting and road incline. To identify them, an adaptive identifier will be utilized.

3. PARAMETER IDENTIFICATION WITH AN ADAPTIVE IDENTIFIER

In order to control the speed of EVs, we first need to estimate the unknown parameters. To identify the system parameters on-line, an algorithm of parallel recursive identifier is used with decreasing adaptation gain and extended adjustable parameter vector (PRIDAG). In the presence of noise, this algorithm leads to asymptotically unbiased parameter estimates, which converges with probability 1 to the right values for any initial values of the estimated parameters [9]. Since the algorithm is the same for both the left and right drive loops, only the left drive loop is discussed in detail as follows:

The integral plus proportional identification algorithm with decreasing adaptation gain and extended adjustable parameter vector can be expressed as

$$v_k^o = \theta_p(k) - [\hat{\mathbf{p}}_e^I(k-1)]^T \tilde{\mathbf{Y}}_{k-1} \qquad (5)$$

$$\hat{\mathbf{P}}_e^I(k) = \hat{\mathbf{P}}_e^I(k-1) + \frac{\tilde{\mathbf{G}}_{k-1} \tilde{\mathbf{Y}}_{k-1}}{1 + \tilde{\mathbf{Y}}_{k-1}^T (\tilde{\mathbf{G}}_{k-1} + \tilde{\mathbf{G}}_{k-1}') \tilde{\mathbf{Y}}_{k-1}} v_k^o$$

$$(6)$$

$$\hat{\mathbf{P}}_e^P(k) = \frac{\tilde{\mathbf{G}}_{k-1}' \tilde{\mathbf{Y}}_{k-1}}{1 + \tilde{\mathbf{Y}}_{k-1}^T (\tilde{\mathbf{G}}_{k-1} + \tilde{\mathbf{G}}_{k-1}') \tilde{\mathbf{Y}}_{k-1}} v_k^o \qquad (7)$$

$$\hat{\mathbf{P}}_e(k) = \hat{\mathbf{P}}_e^I(k) + \hat{\mathbf{P}}_e^P(k) \qquad (8)$$

$$\tilde{\mathbf{G}}_k = \tilde{\mathbf{G}}_{k-1} - \frac{1}{\lambda} \frac{\tilde{\mathbf{G}}_{k-1} \tilde{\mathbf{Y}}_{k-1} \tilde{\mathbf{Y}}_{k-1}^T \tilde{\mathbf{G}}_{k-1}}{1 + (1/\lambda) \tilde{\mathbf{Y}}_{k-1}^T \tilde{\mathbf{G}}_{k-1} \tilde{\mathbf{Y}}_{k-1}} \qquad (9)$$

where
$$\tilde{\mathbf{G}}_k' = \alpha \tilde{\mathbf{G}}_k; \; \alpha > 0.5$$
$$\tilde{\mathbf{G}}_o > 0; \; \lambda > 0.5$$
$$\hat{\mathbf{P}}_e^T(k) = [a_L \; b_L \; c_L]$$
$$\tilde{\mathbf{Y}}_k^T = [Y_L(k) \; R_L(k) \; e_L]$$
$$e_L(k) = \theta_p(k) - Y_L(k)$$
$$Y_L(k) = a_L Y_L(k-1) + b_L R_L(k)$$

where θ_p is the measured velocity for the left motor and Y_L is the estimated velocity for the left motor.

The coefficient λ weights the rate of decrease of the integral adaptation gain matrix G_k. As λ increases, the rate of G_k decreases more slowly. The most used value for λ is 1. α is assumed to equal -0.4. This value of α leads to the fastest convergence in the initial stage of the identification process.

Experiments were conducted to verify the effectiveness of PRIDAG. The sampling time T is 0.037 second. The experimental results are presented in Figures 1 and 2. As seen in the figures, all four parameters converge to their true values successfully. According to Figure 1, a_L converges to 0.137 and b_L converges to 0.759. Similarly, from Figure 2, a_R converges to 0.107492, b_R converges to 0.666. Both a_L and a_R converge to their true values in about 7 seconds, whereas the converges of both b_L and b_R are slower. The differences in convergence rate are mainly due to the fact that the changes in the parameters are different due to the external disturbances. Another important reason is the fact that estimated time constants are less than the sampling time.

Once these parameters are estimated, control gains can

be calculated via pole-placement on-line such that the system's closed-loop poles are at the desired locations.

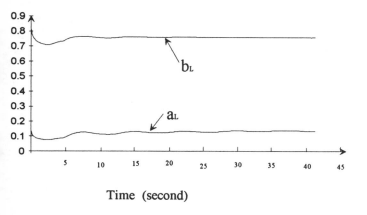

Time (second)

Figure 1. Estimated Parameters for Left Drive Loop

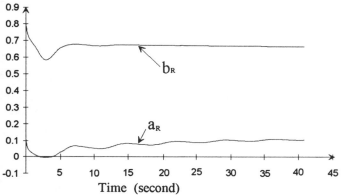

Time (second)

Figure 2. Estimated Parameters for Right Drive Loop

4. POLE-PLACEMENT CONTROL DESIGN

In order to have a zero steady state error without any overshoot, pole-placement control design was selected rather than PID design. PID controllers are generally used for the vehicle speed control. However, there is a trade-off among setting time, overshoot, and steady state error. In addition, a PID controller has to be tuned for each specific vehicle. Even with a tuned PID controller, the performance will deteriorate as the road incline changes or other external disturbances change.

Pole-placement design is a better choice for it can guarantee zero steady state error and zero overshoot with a step input. Pole-placement design begins with the selection of the desired closed-loop poles, which are usually determined from the simulation results. Then, Ackermann's formula is utilized to calculate the corresponding control gains [7]. A pole-placement diagram for the left drive loop is shown in Figure 3.

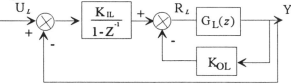

Figure 3. Pole-placement diagram for the left drive loop

where U_L is the desired velocity for the left drive loop.

Based on the simulation, the closed-loop poles were selected as:

$$z_1 = z_2 = 0.9$$

Due to the simplicity of Eq. (1), the control gains for the left drive loop can be calculated on-line with the following equations:

$$K_{OL} = \frac{-z_1 z_2 + a_L}{b_L} \quad (10)$$

$$K_{IL} = \frac{1 + z_1 z_2 - (z_1 + z_2)}{b_L} \quad (11)$$

Similarly, pole-placement control for the right drive loop can be implemented. To evaluate the performance of pole-placement design, experiments were conducted. In the experiments, the desired velocities are step inputs. As shown in Figure 4, both the right and left drive loops indeed follow the step inputs with zero overshoot and zero steady-state errors on average.

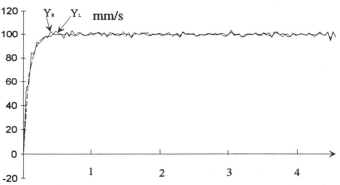

Figure 4. The Velocities for the Left and Right Drive Loops with Pole-placement control

Even though the average steady state errors are indeed zero, the vehicle actual velocities oscillate about their average values due to external disturbances such as measurement noises. In order to reduce the measurement noise, Kalman filter is implemented.

5. PARAMETER ESTIMATION BY KALMAN FILTER

To estimate the true velocities from their measurements, the application of stochastic estimation algorithms is necessary to filter the noise from the velocity measurements. For this, Kalman filter was selected because it gives an optimum estimate which minimizes the mean square estimation error [3].

Plant dynamics and the measurement equation can be expressed in a standard form as:

$$x(k+1) = \mathbf{A}x(k) + \mathbf{L}w(k) \qquad (12)$$
$$y(k) = \mathbf{c}x(k) + \varsigma(k) \qquad (13)$$

where

$$\mathbf{A} = \begin{bmatrix} 1 & T & 0 \\ 0 & 1 & T \\ 0 & 0 & 1 \end{bmatrix} \qquad \mathbf{L} = \begin{bmatrix} 1 & 0 & 0 \\ 0 & 1 & 0 \\ 0 & 0 & 1 \end{bmatrix}$$

$$\mathbf{c} = \begin{bmatrix} 1 & 0 & 0 \end{bmatrix} \quad \mathbf{x}^T = \begin{bmatrix} x_1 & x_2 & x_3 \end{bmatrix}$$

$$\mathbf{w}^T = \begin{bmatrix} w_1 & w_2 & w_3 \end{bmatrix}$$

where x_1, x_2 and x_3 represent true velocity, acceleration, and jerk respectively

$y(k)$ represents the measured velocity

$\varsigma(k)$ represents the measurement noise

$\mathbf{w}(k)$ represents the noise vector for the plant dynamics

Then, estimated states can be expressed as

$$\hat{\mathbf{x}}(k+1) = \mathbf{A}\hat{\mathbf{x}}(k) + \mathbf{H}[y(k) - \mathbf{c}\hat{\mathbf{x}}(k)] \qquad (14)$$

where H is the steady state Kalman filter gain and can be calculated via the MATLAB command *dlqe*.

To calculate H, both measurement noise and noise vector have to be specified. They are generally determined by experiments. In our experiments, they are set to the following values, which give the best parameter estimations:

$$\varsigma = 0.1$$

$$\mathbf{w} = \begin{bmatrix} 0 & 0 & 0 \\ 0 & 2 & 0 \\ 0 & 0 & 0.8 \end{bmatrix}$$

Based on these values, H can be calculated via *dlqe* to obtain:

$$\mathbf{H}^T = \begin{bmatrix} 0.4528 & 3.6222 & 2.0923 \end{bmatrix}$$

To check the effects of the Kalman filter, experiments were conducted. For purpose of comparison, the same desired inputs are specified as in Section 4. With step inputs, the measured and estimated velocities for the left drive loop only are shown in Figure 5 with the solid line and the dotted line respectively. According to this figure, the estimated velocities are indeed smoother than the measured velocities which have many sudden changes. Similar results were found for the right drive loop.

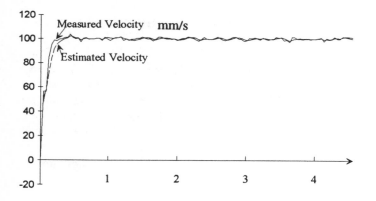

Figure 5. The Measured and Estimated Velocities for the Left Drive Loop

Even though the Kalman filter is effective in removing noise from the measurements, it can not handle the coupling effects between the right and left drive loops, which are generally due to the different parameters and disturbances on each drive loop. To remedy this problem, a cross-coupling controller was utilized.

6. CROSS-COUPLING CONTROL FOR ERROR COMPENSATION

As confirmed by experimental results, the cross-coupling controller can guarantee zero velocity differences on average between the left and right drive loops in spite of different parameters and disturbances in them. It shares the error information of both control loops, whereas a traditional controller controls each loop independently. Traditionally, for an EV with one motor on each wheel, it is assumed that all the loop parameters and disturbances are exactly the same [8]. However, they may be different. Therefore, any disturbance on one loop causes an error that is corrected only by its own control loop, while the other loop carries on as before. This lack of coordination causes errors in the resultant path. In contrast, the cross-coupling controller combines the two control loops and shares the error information; consequently the same velocities are guaranteed for the two loops [6].

The cross-coupling controller is verified by experimental results, as shown in Figure 6. According to these figures, the average velocity differences are not zero without the cross-coupling controller, whereas they are indeed zero with it. These results demonstrate that the cross-coupling controller is one of the most important components in the general control module for the speed control of EVs.

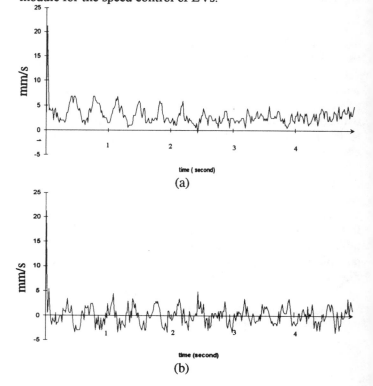

Figure 6. Velocity Differences (a) without Cross-coupling
        Controller and (b) With Cross-coupling Controller

7. GENERAL CONTROL MODULE FOR THE SPEED CONTROL OF EVs

A general control module is developed in this section. It is composed of an adaptive identifier, pole-placement design, the Kalman filter and cross-coupling controller, all of which have been discussed in the previous sections.

In the previous sections, each individual component has been proven to be effective by experiments. However, all the components need to be combined together as a single module. First an adaptive identifier is applied to identify system parameters on-line, then pole-placement is used to calculate the corresponding control gains such that each drive loop has the desired close loop poles. Next, the Kalman filter is applied to estimate the true velocities from the noise velocity measurements, and finally the cross-coupling controller is implemented to compensate for the errors due to the different parameters and disturbances between the left and right drive loops. To combine them, a computerized control structure was selected. It consists of a microprocessor (a 486 board) and several C-programmable microcontrollers (HCTL-1100 control chips). Its selection is mainly based on the fact that all its components can be implemented via discrete algorithms; as a result, each component's algorithm can be treated as a subroutine in this computerized control scheme, and the control programs have increased flexibility. The complete diagram for this general control module is shown in Figure 7. In this diagram, K_{OR} and K_{IR} are the control gains for the right drive loop via pole-placement. C_L and C_R are the compensation gains for the left and right tires respectively. In this paper, they are set to 1 for convenience. However, they can be set to specific values to compensate for the differences between the two tire diameters [6]. Another important element in this diagram is $G_L(z)$. It is the combined transfer function from R_L to Y_L, whose detailed diagram is shown in Figure 8. In this figure, the HP control chip is a C-programmable microcontroller and is commercially available.

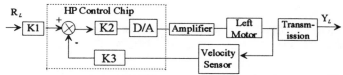

Figure 8. The Detailed Diagram for $G_L(z)$

where

$$K1 = \frac{quadrature / sample}{m / s},$$

$$K3 = \frac{rad / s}{quadrature / sample}$$

K2 = HP Control Chip Proportional Gains

To evaluate the performance of this general control module, experiments are conducted. The EV was instructed to follow a step input which results in the actual vehicle velocity shown in Figure 9. According to Figure 9, the actual vehicle velocity follows the commanding velocity without any overshoot and steady state error.

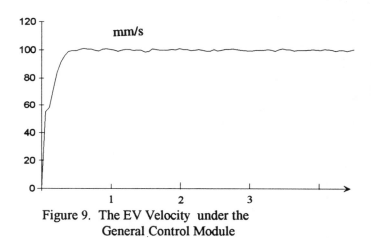

Figure 9. The EV Velocity under the
General Control Module

8. CONCLUSION

A general control module for electric vehicles with computerized speed control has been developed in our lab which should be very useful in future applications. One of its main advantages is that it can be easily applied to any kind of EV. That is, this general control module is not specific to the vehicle under consideration and can be applied to a variety of different vehicles. In experiments, it made an EV follow a user-specified speed command without any overshoot and steady-state error. In addition, each of its individual components performs very well. First the estimated parameters converge to their true values with the adaptive identifier, second the noises are effectively removed from the measured velocities via the Kalman filter, and finally the same velocities are guaranteed on average for the left and right drive loops via cross-coupling controller. The next stage is to implement this module in different EVs under different road conditions.

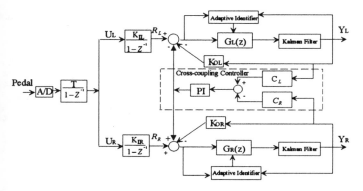

Figure 7. The diagram for the General Control
Module of an EV

Acknowledgment: This research is supported by U.S. Department of Energy grant DE-FG02-86NE37969

REFERENCES

[1] Chan, C. C., "An Overview of Electric Vehicle Technology," *Proceedings of the IEEE,* Vol. 81, No.9, September, 1993, pp. 1202-1213.

[2] Checkle, M. D., *et al.*, "Development of the University of Alberta Entry in the 1993 HEV Challenge," SAE 940339.

[3] Chui, C. K. and Chan, G., *Kalman Filtering with Real-Time Applications*, Springer-Verlag Berlin Heidelberg, 1987.

[4] Davis G.W. *et al.*, "The Development and Performance of the AMPhibian Hybrid Electric Vehicle," SAE 940337.

[5] Dvorak, Paul, "The Shock Truth about Electric Vehicles," *Machine Design,* Vol. 61, No. 18, September, 1989, pp. 86-94.

[6] Fan, Zhejun, Koren, Yoram, and Wehe, David, "Tracked Mobile Robot Control: Hybrid Approach," accepted for publication by *Control Engineering Practice*.

[7] Franklin, Gene F., Powell, J. David, and Abbas, Emami-Naeini, *Feedback Control of Dynamic Systems,* Addison-Wesley Publishing Company, Inc., 1991.

[8] Giorgetti, Alberto, *et al.*, "Design of a Lightweight Braking System for Electric Car," SAE 920649.

[9] Landau, Y. D., *Adaptive Control,* Marcel Dekker, Inc., New York ,1979.

[10] Steeg, Helga, *Electric Vehicles: Technology, Performance and Potential*, OECD/IEA, France, 1989 .

[11] Tsujii, M., Takeuchi, H., Oda, K., and Ohba, M., "Application of Self-Tuning To Automotive Cruise Control," *Proceedings of the American Control Conference*, San Diego, California, May 1990, pp. 1843-1848.

950957

The Effect of Regenerative Braking on the Performance and Range of the AMPhibian II Hybrid Electric Vehicle

Gregory W. Davis and Frank C. Madeka
United States Naval Academy

ABSTRACT

A Hybrid Electric Vehicle(HEV) has been developed for use in the intercollegiate 1993 and 1994 Hybrid Electric Vehicle Challenges. A conventionally powered vehicle was converted to a series drive hybrid electric vehicle, named AMPhibian II. The AMPhibian is designed to be an economically feasible HEV, for use in near term applications. To accomplish this, all components are based upon existing technology. Regenerative braking is used to improve the range and economy of the hybrid electric vehicle. The design and performance of the vehicle, including the relative benefits of regenerative braking are reported.

INTRODUCTION

A series Hybrid Electric Vehicle(HEV) has been developed by a team of midshipmen and faculty at the United States Naval Academy for use in the Hybrid Electric Vehicle Challenges which took place during 1993 and 1994, and is scheduled to occur during June of 1995. These competitions, involving forty two universities from North America, are jointly sponsored by SAE International, the U. S. Department of Energy, in addition to Ford Motor Company(1993), Saturn Corporation(1994), and Chrysler Corporation(1995). These competitions provide the participants with a real world design experience with a topic that is currently relevant to society. Schools competing in this challenge will aid in the development of vehicles that can meet the future emissions standards of the state of California.

To meet this challenge, a 5-door Ford Escort Wagon with a manual transmission has been converted to a series drive hybrid electric vehicle called the AMPhibian II. The propulsion system is based on a DC shunt motor which is coupled to the existing transmission. Lead-acid batteries are used to store the electrical energy. The auxiliary power unit(APU) consists of a small gasoline engine connected to a generator. To extend vehicle range, regenerative braking has been incorporated into this system. The AMPhibian is designed to be an economically feasible HEV, for use in near term applications. To accomplish this, all components are based upon existing technology. Further, this vehicle was designed to retain, to the greatest degree possible, the basic driving characteristics of a conventional gasoline powered vehicle.

VEHICLE DESIGN

The vehicle design goals involved many aspects including cost effectiveness, acceleration, range, safety, and emissions. The following discussion summarizes the design decisions, this is followed by a table of the actual vehicle components. Further information can be found in a report presented by Davis[1].

COST - Since the AMPhibian was designed to be economically feasible, minimizing cost was considered to be a major design goal. All design decisions were made only after the associated costs were analyzed. To help attain this goal, all components were based upon existing, available technology.

PERFORMANCE AND EMISSIONS - The major performance and emissions design goals for the AMPhibian included 1) the ability to travel 64 Km as a zero emissions vehicle(ZEV) using battery power alone, 2) operating in hybrid mode, the ability to travel 320 Km while meeting the transitional low emissions vehicle(TLEV) air pollution standards, 3) achieve a time of under 15 seconds when accelerating from 0 to 70 kph, and 4) climb a minimum of a 15% grade. The vehicle was also to maintain driving characteristics as similar to those of conventionally powered vehicles.

RELIABILITY AND DURABILITY - Existing, off-the-shelf components were used extensively in this design, not only helping to limit vehicle costs, but also to ensure reliable and durable operation of the vehicle. Therefore, the AMPhibian should have reliability and durability similar to that of a conventionally powered vehicle.

WEIGHT - One major disadvantage of electric vehicles has traditionally been the large weight due to the propulsion batteries which are required in order to provide sufficient energy storage capability for extended range. An advantage of the HEV concept is that it allows for a lower battery energy storage capability by replacing some of the batteries with an auxiliary power unit(APU). The APU provides the equivalent amount of energy with less weight. However, battery weight is still a major concern, requiring the team to consider all options for reducing vehicle weight. The AMPhibian was designed to weigh less than the gross vehicle weight rating(GVWR) of the 1992 Escort LX Wagon plus an additional 15%. This resulted in a maximum gross vehicle mass of 1808 kg, and curb weight of 1648 kg. The actual weights are: gross 1762 kg, and curb, at 1582 kg.

PASSENGERS AND CARGO - The HEV carries one driver and one passenger, along with a volume of cargo(50 cm by 100 cm by 25 cm). The total combined weight of people and cargo is a minimum of 180 kg.

BATTERY CHARGING - The HEV charging system was designed to recharge the battery pack in less than six hours in order to help reduce daytime charging demand on electrical utilities. Daytime charging, if necessary, could be accomplished using the APU. The charging system accepts either 110V or 220V, 60 Hz AC power.

STYLING - Vehicle styling changes were minimized to maintain continuity with existing vehicle designs. No external glass or body sheet metal was modified except to provide additional ventilation.

POWERTRAIN - The AMPhibian is propelled using a series drive configuration. That is, the only component that is mechanically connected to the drive-train of the vehicle is the electric motor. This arrangement, shown in figure 1, is considered to be superior to the parallel drive arrangement, in which both the electric motor and the APU can propel the power 2-3 times its steady state rating for short duration.

Results of simulations performed by Wyczalek[2] have shown that regenerative braking can produce potential energy savings from 6 to 20%, depending upon the driving conditions. Therefore, a controller with regenerative braking capabilities was chosen. This controller, a General Electric-Electric Vehicle Systems, microprocessor based controller is rated to provide up to 250 amps of return current when operating during regenerative braking. The vehicle's mechanical braking system has been left intact.

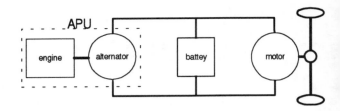

Fig. 1. Series Drive diagram for the AMPhibian II Hybrid Electric Vehicle.

vehicle. When compared with a parallel drive, the series drive requires less structural change to install, and thus is less costly. Additionally, the parallel drive system requires a more sophisticated control system to minimize driveability problems such as those associated with the transition from electric vehicle(EV) mode to hybrid electric vehicle(HEV) mode.

The conversion to a series drive system required the removal of the standard Escort engine. Since the Escort has front-wheel drive, the standard engine is coupled to the drive-train through a transaxle transmission. Thus, the transmission was retained so that a new axle would not need to be designed. The electric motor was attached directly to the existing bell-housing and flywheel. This arrangement allows full use of the existing transmission, thus providing variable gear ratios which allow the speeds of the electric motor to be maintained closer to preferred values when the vehicle is operated over varying vehicle speeds.

Prior vehicle testing and simulation indicated that the vehicle would require a power of approximately 9 kW in order to maintain a steady 80 Kph, and 10 kW when operated at highway speeds. Acceleration from a stand still to 72 Kph in less than 15 seconds would require a peak power of 32 kW(at approximately 35 Kph) for a short duration. Motor controller cost and availability became the critical design factor for the selection of both the type of motor and the system operating voltage. The use of an AC motor was investigated due to its inherently higher power density compared to a DC system. However, it was rejected due to the cost, availability, size, and weight of the associated motor controller. A General Electric DC shunt traction motor, rated at 20.1 kW(@ 96 VDC), was chosen since DC motor controllers are widely available, relatively inexpensive, and light-weight. Although the steady state rating of the motor is less than the peak incurred during acceleration, the motor can provide a peak

Regenerative braking is actuated when the brake pedal is slightly depressed. The control responds by reversing, then gradually strengthening the field on the shunt, thereby generating power in the motor. If additional braking is required, the operator simply presses harder on the brake pedal, thereby engaging the mechanical brakes. The rate at which regenerative braking is applied by the controller can be varied. This control also utilizes IGBT power transistors which are more efficient than the more commonly used MOSFETs. Finally, the control is rated for up to 144 VDC of input voltage. This determined the system operating voltage, since the controller is exposed to full charging voltage during HEV operation.

AUXILIARY POWER UNIT - The design specifications for the auxiliary power unit (APU) were derived from the mechanical power necessary to achieve the 320 km desired range while maintaining highway speeds, and allowing for reasonable accelerating and coasting time periods with the batteries at 20% of full charge at the beginning of APU operation. Calculations based on estimates of driving conditions (drag and rolling resistance) and drivetrain efficiency resulted in a minimum desired electric power availability of 10 kW required by the HEV in order to sustain highway speeds for the full range, limited only by the amount of onboard fuel. However, this power capability alone would not allow for reasonable accelerations over this distance. Therefore, the total electrical requirement was specified at 12.5 kW output from the APU. Estimating the overall efficiency of the APU to be 80%, the engine was to develop a power of 15.6 kW.

The design team chose a conventional, gasoline powered spark-ignited engine. Kawasaki donated a 16.4 kW throttle-body fuel injected engine. Speed is regulated by a mechanical governor to 3600 RPM and is adjustable. To meet TLEV emissions requirements the APU exhaust is connected to a catalytic converter which contains a ceramic monolith substrate. The outlet of the catalytic converter then leads to the existing vehicle exhaust system. An electrically driven air pump was added to provide fresh air for the catalytic converter after light-off in order to ensure complete oxidation of un-burned hydrocarbons and carbon monoxide.

To meet the electrical generation requirements, a number of alternatives involving both AC and DC generation were explored. To minimize space and weight, a custom built alternator was purchased. This alternator, rated at 13.5 kW, 150 V , 3 phase, provides 144 V DC from a three phase bridge rectifier, the maximum recommended charging voltage for the 120 V battery stack. In addition to meeting all electrical requirements, this alternator weighs only 4.6 kg, is 0.276 m in diameter and when mounted directly on the APU shaft, extends a mere 0.19 m from the engine block, making it the most feasible option.

The strategy for controlling the APU is incorporated into a digital control system with the goal of ensuring that driving the HEV would be as similar to driving a conventional vehicle as is possible. The system senses battery voltage to determine battery condition and control the APU operation. A three position switch was mounted in the passenger compartment to provide manual control capabilities if desired.

BATTERY SELECTION - The AMPhibian has two battery power systems. One system is at 12V and one at 120V. The 12V system is used to power the 12V lighting and accessories. The 120V primary battery powers the prime mover and supplies power to recharge the 12V battery.

Table 1. Summary of Components used in AMPhibian.

Chassis:	'92 5-door Escort LX
Stock GVWR/Curb:	1572 kg/1433 kg
Converted GVWR/Curb:	1762 kg/1582 kg
DC Motor:	General Electric model 5BT1346B104
Motor Controller:	General Electric IGBT based Automotive Shunt Control with Regenerative Braking Capability
Batteries (propulsion):	10 arranged in series, 12VDC Trojan 5SH(P)
Bus Voltage:	120 VDC
APU Engine:	Kawasaki , 16.4 kW @3600 RPM, two cylinder, throttle-body fuel injection
APU Alternator:	Fisher Technology, Inc., 13.5 kW, 150 Vpeak
Tires:	Goodyear Invicta GL P175/65R14, low rolling resistance
Estimated Vehicle Cost:	$26,000
Conversion Component Net Cost:	$14,000 (exc. safety items, credit for 1.9l engine)

The primary battery selection was overwhelmingly driven by cost considerations. Since the rating of the motor controller is 144V, 120V was selected as the system voltage to allow for complete charging of the batteries without damaging the controller. A cost evaluation of batteries meeting the vehicle requirements showed that a battery stack consisting of conventional lead-acid batteries would cost about $2,200, Nickel-Iron batteries would cost $36,000, and Nickel-Cadmium batteries would cost about $19,280. This analysis lead the design team to limit selection considerations to off-the-shelf lead-acid batteries.

The task of battery selection was complicated due to the general lack of published, comprehensive, technical battery performance data. Using the available information, the design team selected a Trojan 5SH(P) battery. This battery is a deep-cycle, wet-celled, 12V battery with "L" type terminals, it provides approximately 14.4 kW-h of capacity at a 3 hour discharge rate.

In order to save weight on the 12 V system, a DC/DC converter, sized to handle the sustained accessory loads of the vehicle was incorporated in parallel with a small 12V battery, sized to accommodate the APU starting loads. A 30 amp DC/DC converter was selected to accommodate not only current accessory loads, but the potential future addition of a climate control system for the passenger compartment. A lightweight GNB Incorporated Pulsar Racing Battery was used in conjunction with the converter to provide starting current for the APU engine. The AMPhibian's net 12V accessory system, occupies the same volume as the OEM 12V battery, but weighs approximately 9.5 kg less than the OEM battery alone.

SUSPENSION & HANDLING - The large increase in vehicle weight required the suspension to be altered to provide adequate jounce. Four new springs were purchased to meet these new loads. The damping coefficient of the MacPherson strut was not modified, hence the suspension characteristics have changed slightly, posing no handling problems. To maintain acceptable handling, the front to rear weight bias is 48% front axle/52% rear axle, while the side-to-side bias remains within 5% of neutral.

SAFETY - Occupant safety was a prime concern. The frontal impact zone and original vehicle bumpers were maintained to provide sufficient collision protection. The original power-assisted braking system also remained intact to ensure proper braking. Since the engine was removed, the vacuum assist was disabled, therefore an electrically powered vacuum pump and reservoir were installed to replace this loss of vacuum. A fire suppression system was added to the vehicle and battery compartments, as well as to the engine bay to minimize the chances of injury and equipment damage. Due to the additional vehicle weight, the roof structure was augmented to provide additional protection in case of a vehicle roll-over.

PERFORMANCE RESULTS

Since its inception, the AMPhibian has been tested on public roads and on a chassis dynamometer. Testing on public roads has included operation on highways, city streets, and rural roads. The terrain includes rolling hills in addition to level areas. The vehicle was also driven on a modified FUDS cycle during testing on the dynamometer. General AMPhibian II performance results are summarized in table 2.

ACCELERATION - The AMPhibian can achieve an acceleration from zero to 70 kph in less than 18 seconds when operating in either ZEV or HEV mode. This acceleration rate is somewhat lower than desired due to the motor controller ramp circuitry which does not allow large rate changes in applied motor voltage. Also, the motor controller is limited to 500 amps or less depending upon controller temperature. Finally, the stock Escort manual

transmission is not ideally suited for this DC motor. The transmission exhibits a large gear ratio increase between first and second gears. This translates into a large load torque increase which the DC motor has difficulty in overcoming. Regenerative braking has no effect on vehicle acceleration.

GRADEABILITY - Currently, the vehicle has been evaluated on a 6% grade. This level of grade posed no serious problem and, in fact, the AMPhibian was able to accelerate from a stand-still even when started in second gear. Again, regenerative braking has no effect on gradeability.

EFFICIENCY - To gain insight into the efficiency of the vehicle and the effect of regenerative braking under real world conditions, the AMPhibian was driven on a set course. This course, 11.2 km in length, covered city streets, and some highway operation. The overall terrain can be described as rolling in nature, while the nature of the traffic conditions can best be described as 'suburban'. During ZEV testing the electrical energy efficiency of the vehicle was found to be 4.8 km/kW-h without regenerative braking, this value then increased by 15% to 5.5 km/kW-h when regenerative braking was enabled. The reason for this increase is that, during regenerative braking, the motor acts as a generator, providing a charging current to the batteries. This effect can be viewed qualitatively in figure 2. In this figure, the AMPhibian is driven over a controlled test course while operating in HEV mode. Battery current will vary over the course, increasing during accelerations, and decreasing and even reversing during braking. Note that, during braking, the current decreases more dramatically when regenerative braking is used. Thus, overall, the vehicle is requiring less power from the batteries and APU, operating more efficiently. Further testing has revealed that the effect of regenerative braking is not constant, but that it varies with battery state of charge(this is discussed in greater detail during the succeeding discussion of the vehicle range). Therefore, the 15% increase in efficiency noted above requires further clarification. This value was found during

Table 2. General Performance results for the U. S. Naval Academy's Hybrid Electric Vehicle. '*' values are based upon road testing on an 11.2 km suburban driving course.

Acceleration, 0 to 70 kph:	< 18 s
Gradeability:	> 6 %
ZEV Efficiency: (with Regenerative Braking)	5.5 km/kW-h*
HEV Efficiency: (with Regenerative Braking)	1.9 km/kW-h*
Total Range Efficiency: (with Regenerative Braking)	2.7 km/kW-h*

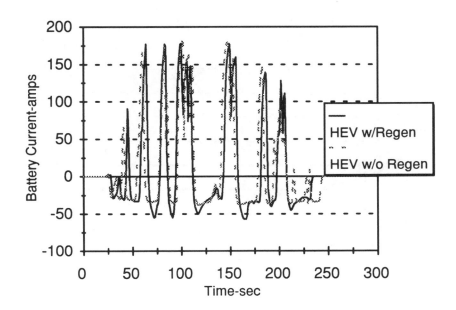

Fig. 2 . Effect of Regenerative Braking during operation on controlled driving course in HEV mode.

operation over a set course starting with a full charge. This effect will not be demonstrated until the batteries become discharged due to driving.

Assuming that, on average, the APU generator will provide all of the vehicle needs, the HEV efficiency can be determined. Using this approach, while operating in HEV mode without using regenerative braking, the vehicle efficiency was found to be 1.7 km/kW-h. This value increased by about 14% over the 11.2 km course to 1.9 km/kW-h. Again it is noted that the increase in efficiency is not constant over the entire driving course but is dependent upon the battery state of charge.

A total combined efficiency can be found through a weighted average of the two operating modes where the weighting factor is the vehicle range while operating in each mode. This yields a total range combined average of 2.4 km/kW-h with regenerative braking enabled, an increase of about 14%. Obviously, the combined efficiency will vary significantly depending upon the type and length of operation between battery charging. Further testing is underway in order to better quantify this effect.

RANGE - The total battery energy storage capability of the AMPhibian is about 19.5 kW-h at a 20 hour discharge rate. This discharge rate is much to low for practical use in a hybrid electric vehicle. A more realistic discharge rate which is currently employed by most of the electric vehicle industry is 3 hours. To convert the 20 hour energy capacity to a 3 hour capacity, an empirical relation is used. The energy capacity at a 3 hour discharge rate is determined from the 20 hour capacity by multiplying by 74%[3]. This results in an

battery capacity of 14.4 kW-h at a 3 hour discharge rate. After extensive testing, it is felt that even a 3 hour discharge rate is too slow. Under real world driving conditions, the AMPhibian performance degrades dramatically after an 8 kW-h battery drain. However, to remain consistent with the industry, the 3 hour battery capacity values will be used. During zero-emissions or ZEV mode the AMPhibian operates as a traditional electric vehicle. When operated at a steady vehicle speed of 65 kph, the vehicle has a range in ZEV mode of approximately 70 km based on a 3 hour discharge battery capacity. The vehicle has a projected range, in HEV mode, of 325 km when operated at the previous condition. Thus, the combined range between re-charging or re-fueling of the AMPhibian, when it is operated in steady state as described above, is estimated to be 395 km. Since the vehicle is operated in steady state, regenerative braking has no effect. This data is shown in figure 3. Note that the steep decline in range at vehicle speeds in excess of 80 kph is due to the power demands of the vehicle which are in excess of the capabilities of the APU alone. Thus, the vehicle is drawing power from the batteries, resulting in less vehicle range. When steady vehicle speeds are less than 80 kph, the vehicle range is only limited by the amount of fuel that can be carried on-board.

Steady state operation is not a realistic indicator of overall vehicle range, or the effect of regenerative braking. To gain insight into the range of the vehicle and the effect of regenerative braking under real world conditions, the AMPhibian was driven on 11.2 km set course, beginning with a full battery charge, as described earlier. When driven under these conditions, the AMPhibian exhibited a range of less than 70 km in ZEV mode without regenerative braking.

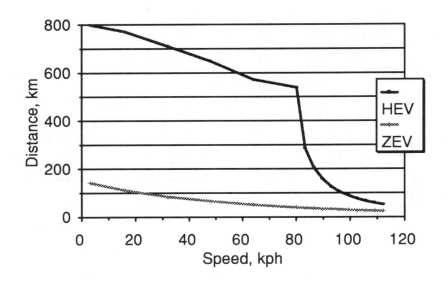

Fig. 3. AMPhibian II Steady State Range in ZEV and HEV modes for 80% depth-of-battery-discharge.

When regenerative braking is employed, the vehicle range increases by approximately 15% which is directly attributable to the increase in efficiency. The effect of regenerative braking is highly dependent upon the battery state of charge as is shown in figure 4. Regenerative braking has little impact on the energy usage of the vehicle when the batteries are near a full state of charge. Thus, the potential energy recovered by the regenerative braking system cannot be utilized by the battery. For this particular course, the effect of regenerative braking does not begin to become apparent until about 20 km into the test(1500 sec). This corresponds to a battery state of charge of about 75%(25% discharged) based upon a 3 hour discharge rate. It is apparent from this data that the effect of regenerative braking increases steadily as the batteries become further discharged. Thus, one cannot simply report a single value describing the effect of regenerative braking on the vehicle. In fact, if the vehicle were only to be used for relatively short trips between battery charging, the use of regenerative braking appears to have little impact upon the range. Further, testing is in progress to study this effect.

Regenerative braking will also assist in the HEV range and economy since it is still providing energy during braking. Looking a figure 4, the effect of regenerative braking on system performance is similar to that shown during ZEV operation. Providing roughly a 14% increase in vehicle range over the 11.2 km course. However, this effect is dependent upon both the rate at which batteries can effectively utilize the excess energy, and the battery state of charge. For example, during moderate braking, in ZEV mode all of the regenerative current may be able to be utilized by the batteries. However, had the APU also been operating, additional battery charge current would be available. If the batteries cannot effectively utilize this

energy, it will be wasted, and could also lead to premature battery failure due to excess heat generation. A significant effort is underway to determine the maximum rate of current, provided during regenerative braking, that can be effectively utilized by the battery stack.

BRAKING - The effect of the regenerative braking system on the vehicle deceleration performance has not yet been quantified. However, qualitatively the vehicle braking effort is noticeably decreased when regenerative braking is in effect. To gain maximum benefit from regenerative braking, the vehicle must be downshifted just before braking. Even when the vehicle is not downshifted, the effect is still noticeable. This is a very beneficial effect since the vehicle weight has been dramatically increased due to the additional weight of the battery stack. Without regenerative braking, the braking effort is somewhat higher than the original, unmodified, vehicle. With the addition of regenerative braking, the vehicle braking effort is closely restored to the original effort.

SUMMARY

The design of a feasible hybrid electric vehicle for use in near-term applications has been presented. Continued testing and evaluation will reveal the reliability and durability of the various system components. The total cost of components(less safety items and including a credit for the stock engine) came to about $14,000. Obviously, since the standard Escort cost about $10,000, the conversion is not yet a cost effective alternative to existing gasoline vehicles. However, the potential reduction of smog in urban areas will continue to dictate the use of these vehicles.

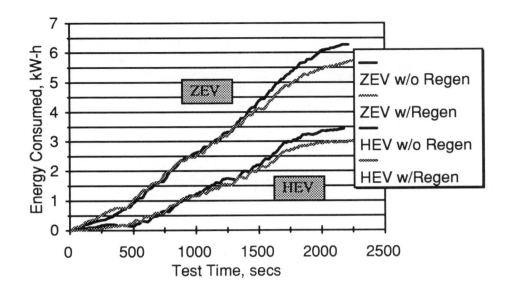

Fig. 4. Effect of Regenerative Braking on Battery Energy Consumption during operation on an 11.2 km suburban course.

Based upon preliminary testing in suburban traffic conditions, the addition of regenerative braking was found to provide approximately a 14% increase in ZEV efficiency which translates into an increase in range over a 11.2 km fixed course. This is less than the theoretical maximum of 20%, but still a significant increase in economy. It has also been determined that the effect of regenerative braking is not constant, but dependent upon the battery state of charge. When the batteries are at full charge, the effect is minimal, but as the batteries become discharged, regenerative braking becomes increasingly important. Additionally, regenerative braking will also assist in the HEV range and economy since it is still providing energy during braking. However, this effect is dependent upon both the rate at which batteries can effectively utilize the excess energy, and the battery state of charge. Additional testing is underway to determine the maximum rate of current, provided during regenerative braking, that can be effectively utilized by the battery stack, and to provide a more complete view of the relationship between battery state of charge and the effect of regenerative braking. Finally, the beneficial effect of regenerative braking on the effort required of the vehicle operator during deceleration's has been noted.

The development of this vehicle has proven to be a valuable lesson in engineering design for both the midshipmen and the faculty of the U. S. Naval Academy.

REFERENCES

[1] Davis, G. W., Hodges, G. L., and Madeka, F. C., SAE Technical Paper, 1994, 940337.

[2] Wyczalek, F. A., and Wang, T. C., SAE Tech. Paper, 1992, 920648.

[3] Brant, B., "Build Your Own electric Vehicle", TAB Books(Div. of McGraw-Hill), 1994.

950958

Fuel Economy Analysis for a Hybrid Concept Car Based on a Buffered Fuel-Engine Operating at an Optimal Point

Marc Ross and Wei Wu
University of Michigan

ABSTRACT

A hybrid car is conceptually described and analyzed which meets the goal of a factor of three improvement in fuel economy set by the government-industry collaboration, Partnership for a New Generation of Vehicles, announced Sept. 29, 1993. This car combines an internal combustion engine with a low-energy, but high-power capacity, storage unit, such as a capacitor or flywheel. The storage capacity is one-half kWh. All energy requirements are ultimately met from the fuel tank. Essentially all the performance achievements of current conventional cars are met by this hybrid.

Two versions of the hybrid are considered: one in which the vehicle loads are the same as those of the average 1993 car, but the drive train is replaced with a hybrid system, and one, where, in addition, the vehicle loads are reduced, at fixed performance and interior volume, to levels slightly beyond the best achievements in current production vehicles. The first of these vehicles has a fuel economy twice that of the average 1993 car; the second three times. Thus, the hybrid drive as such yields a factor of two; while practical load reduction yields a factor of 1.5 in fuel economy.

OVERVIEW

Hybrid vehicles involve a combination of energy storage with fuel-based operation; an aspect of most of them now being considered is storage of electrical energy from the grid [Burke 1992; Kalberlah 1991]. Consider, however, a hybrid car whose sole energy source is a fuel tank, with its fuel engine operating only at an optimal operating point. A power buffer enables the propulsion system to deliver the widely varying power required in driving. In typical driving, the engine would be on for a minute or so, and then be off for a few minutes. Vehicles of this general type, using flywheel storage, were built by Andrew Frank and Norman Beachley in the late '70s-early '80s [Frank 1976, 1979; See also Burke 1993a]. In Frank's cars the drive was mechanical. In the concept discussed here, the downstream propulsion system is electrical. In neither case is an electrochemical battery required for propulsion.

In the particular **buffered fuel-engine** configuration considered here, the engine drives a generator, which in turn is coupled to a sophisticated power controller which connects to an electrical storage device with high power capability (flywheel, capacitor, fluid under pressure, "high-power" battery...) and to motors which drive the wheels as shown in Fig. 1. (The distinction between "series" and "parallel" hybrid design is not important here. Although Fig. 1 is a series hybrid, energy can flow to the drive motor directly from the engine/generator, with a "transmission efficiency" comparable to that in conventional cars, as well as from storage.)

The required storage capacity is minimized, under the condition that the vehicle have better acceleration capabilities than today's average car. Thus the *transient performance*, of the vehicle is better than that of the average car. (This transient performance involves acceleration times much more rigorous than in the regulatory driving cycles.) The required storage is of the order of 0.5 kWh, less than that of a standard automotive battery (which stores about 1 kWh). The average efficiency of the storage device for combined input and output of energy is assumed to be about 95%, far better than that of today's lead-acid batteries. In order to enable better acceleration capabilities than today's average new car, the power capability of the power-storage device needs to be 50 to 60 kW, far higher than the capability of a conventional battery. (Since electrical energy can be made available immediately, the power output from the storage unit need not be as high as the rated power difference between the conventional and hybrid engines, in order to achieve better acceleration times than the conventional vehicle.)

For the calculations to be made here, the engine is assumed to be a gasoline-fueled internal combustion engine. There are of course other options which might be preferable, especially from an emissions standpoint, as will be discussed briefly below. For the Standard-Load and Low-Load hybrid cars considered, the engine operates at a single point, taken to be 2280 rpm and 30 or 24 kW output, respectively. The rated or maximum power of these engines is much higher, roughly 65 and 50 kW, respectively.

The engine is assumed to be a high-technology design, carefully engineered for its single-point operating speed and power, so it only requires 1.5 or 1.2 liter displacement. The 1.5 liter engine, for example, is assumed to have a torque slightly over 125 N.m at its operating speed. This is comparable to high torque to displacement engines now in production. (For example, a 1993 Honda Civic 1.5 liter engine has a wide-open-throttle torque of 124 N.m at 2000 rpm; and a Toyota Corolla 1.8 liter engine has a torque of 158 N.m at 2800 rpm, which scales to 132 N.m at 1.5 liter.)

At 30 kW, a car with average 1993 model characteristics can climb a sustained 6% grade at almost 50 mph, the steepest grade on major highways. (See Fig. 2.) With the engine operating at its optimal point, the car can sustain a speed of over 80 mph on level ground. In the unusual application of long hill climbing, the engine of the proposed hybrid could be automatically switched from its normal mode to operate at higher speeds, up to its rated power, achieving a maximum speed of about 80 mph on a 6% grade. In Fig. 2, criteria for both *sustained* and *transient* performance are illustrated. While transient performance is critical for sizing the buffer in this car, sustained performance is critical for sizing the engine. As the figure shows, transient power requirements are much higher than sustained power requirements. In sustained high-power modes the engine operates more or less continuously at its fixed point, and the buffer would play little role.

The average efficiency of the hybrid propulsion system downstream of the engine is taken to be fixed at 78% (discussed further below). With this efficiency, and with average 1993 vehicle characteristics, the engine of the hybrid propulsion system is on 14% of the time in the EPA urban driving cycle, and 36% of the time in the highway cycle. This mostly-off operation is the main source of fuel savings, since about half of the fuel use by conventional vehicles serves merely to overcome the frictions in the engine. (The frictions are rubbing friction between parts, gaseous friction in filling and exhausting the manifolds and cylinders, and operating the engine accessories, such as the pumps, fan and ignition system.) The reduction in work to overcome engine frictions associated with the on-off hybrid design almost doubles vehicle fuel economy.

Regenerative braking is also important to the overall efficiency of the hybrid vehicle, decreasing the energy required by the drive by about 14% (EPA composite fuel cycle). **Taking into account losses in the components of the hybrid drive, the buffered fuel-engine concept, at fixed vehicle characteristics like weight, provides a factor of two improvement in fuel economy.**

The energy use by three vehicles in the composite EPA driving cycle is calculated in this report: 1) AVCAR '93, the average 1993 vehicle, 2) Standard-Load Hybrid, a vehicle with vehicle loads the same as for (1), and 3) Low-Load Hybrid, a vehicle with reduced mass and other loads. (The principal reductions involved in vehicle (3) are roughly 20% in inertial weight, and 25 to 30% in drag and rolling resistance coefficients, reductions from the average that have already almost been achieved in production vehicles.) The fuel economies of these three vehicles are 28, 56, and 84 mph, respectively. The fuel economy of the third vehicle meets the factor-of-three goal of the government-industry collaboration announced last September.

The emissions likely to arise from this vehicle are uncertain, but could be extremely favorable. A major issue is the regulatory framework for evaluating the emissions of new kinds of vehicles, and we briefly digress on this point. There are two different emissions goals that one needs to consider: achievement of low emissions in actual use, and achievement of emissions below stipulated levels in regulatory tests. Many analyses seem to suggest that these goals are closely related. In fact they are essentially unrelated. In actual use of conventional cars, emissions of carbon monoxide and hydrocarbons average about ten times more than those measured in the regulatory test, because of: 1) engine and control-system malfunctions, 2) rich operations at high power, 3) evaporation, 4) frequent cold starts, and other causes. In cases (1) and (2) emissions are totally unrelated to the emissions tests [Calvert et al, Ross 1994a]. The hybrid vehicle described here avoids (2) and has strong potential for reducing the other sources of excess emissions, in part because it uses much less fuel and in part from the opportunities created by having the engine operate at only one point. For the same general reasons the vehicle has good potential for low emissions in the regulatory tests, assuming that the emissions associated with engine restart can be kept low.

Since the engine operates at only one point and fuel economy is much higher than for a conventional car, the potential for alternative fuels, and perhaps alternative energy conversion devices, is greatly enhanced. This opens up further emissions reduction options, without requiring a sacrifice of capabilities. Note, however, that the car does not have the capability of moving a substantial distance at "zero emissions", defined to be on energy from an external electrical charge. Emissions issues are discussed further below.

In the following three sections, the average 1993 car is analyzed and technical features of two hybrids are discussed. Challenges to be met by the Low-Load hybrid are discussed in a final section.

AVCAR '93

The base car has the characteristics of the sales-weighted-average 1993 model [Murrell et al, 1993]. This is a rather high-powered car at 104 kW (140 hp), 1335 kg (2943 lbs) curb weight, and 108 cubic foot interior volume. The necessary parameters are shown in Table 1b. (All the average characteristics presented in Murrell et al are used, the other parameters are estimates.) The fuel economy is initially estimated using the summary equation shown in Table 1a; the equation is derived in Ross & An and An & Ross. Some specifics of the fuel use per mile are shown in Table 2. The units are kJ/mile.

The reader is urged to turn to Figure 3 which shows the energy flows (in kJ/mile) for this vehicle in the composite driving cycle. (A slightly more sophisticated calculation than represented by the equation in Table 1a has been carried out, as noted at the bottom of the Table, to account for the decline in pumping friction with increasing engine output.) In Fig. 3, the energy sinks are given in three different accounting schemes, so readers with different perspectives can find information in the form they want. The energy flows shown in Fig. 3 are calculated on the figure starting with the four work loads taken from Table 2: kinetic energy, air drag, tire rolling resistance and vehicle accessories.

Perhaps the most important energy aspect of the vehicle shown in Fig. 3 is that 46% of the fuel use is associated with engine frictions ((1611+391)/4308). The fraction of fuel energy that reaches the drivewheels and vehicle accessories is 18%.

STANDARD-LOAD HYBRID

The first hybrid considered has the same weight, air drag and rolling resistance characteristics as the conventional car just discussed. Since the vehicle accessories are now all-electric, the accessories power requirement has been reduced. (Note that vehicle accessories are distinguished from engine accessories.) No detailed modeling of the vehicle is done, for example, to calculate a new weight. It is reasonable, however, that the hybrid drive with its added components, but its smaller engine

(1.5 for 2.8 liter), and omitting most of the transmission, would leave the weight roughly unchanged, if a low weight storage unit can be developed. Similarly, the energy efficiencies of the hybrid components are taken to be fixed, rather than calculated in detail. The generator, which operates at a single point, is assumed to be 97% efficient and the control and storage component efficiencies are taken to be 95% each, or 86% for the path control-storage-control. The motor and connections to the wheels are assumed to be 94% efficient.

A more realistic calculation is underway, for a later report, in which efficiencies are not taken to be constant. Instead, loss mechanisms, such as capacitor internal resistance, are modeled. At low levels of stored energy, and at low levels of motor output at the wheels, the efficiencies are poorer than assumed in the present analysis. Thus, it would probably be important to normally avoid deeply discharging the storage unit while the engine is off - which appears feasible with 0.5 kWh storage - and to design a motor with special windings for efficient operation at low-power.

Since the fuel engine normally only operates at a single point, it is assumed that frictional losses *at that point* are lower than for a typical engine *at the same point*. At its operating point the overall efficiency is taken to be 36.5%, corresponding to brake specific fuel consumption 224 g/kWh. In choosing a relatively small engine, we are striving to achieve low vehicle weight. Nevertheless, we are not minimizing engine size: The maximum power capability of the engine is not normally used; the modest engine speed being chosen to obtain reliable and efficient operation. For a given engine size, one designs for high torque and low frictional losses at the operating point.

The parameters and energy uses are shown in Table 1 and in an energy flow chart (Fig. 4). The most significant result shown on Fig. 4, compared to Fig. 3, is the reduction of fuel consumption devoted to overcoming engine friction from 46% to 9% of the fuel energy. This is the main focus of the buffered fuel-engine design: operation of the engine at wide-open throttle to obtain high mechanical efficiency, turning off the engine most of the time, and use of an engine designed for the purpose, thus greatly reducing the overall work against engine frictions. In addition, regeneration of braking energy enables 14% reduction in the electrical energy delivered to the control unit, from 887 to 759 kJ/mi. On the other hand, the total loss within the electrical propulsion system between the engine and drive wheels/accessories is greater than in the standard vehicle's transmission, increasing from 99 to 198 kJ/mi.

The result is a factor-of-two improvement in fuel economy, to 56 mpg (EPA composite test value). Some other characteristics of the buffered fuel-engine concept are evident in Table 2: The urban cycle fuel economy is now greater than that for the highway cycle, because the engine is on only a small fraction of the time.

Using a separate second-by-second model to analyze this car (with slighly different parameters from those shown in Table 1), we have begun a study of the size of the storage device and its management algorithm. In Figs. 5a and 5b, the time dependence of the energy stored in the device and the rate of energy storage are shown, for purposes of illustration, using the EPA urban and highway cycles, respectively. (These driving cycles are not used for evaluating vehicle components or management, since typical driving is substantially more rigorous.) For these runs, the size of storage is 0.5 kWh and the management algorithm requires that the engine be turned on if the stored energy drops below what would be needed (with the engine on) to accelerate rapidly to 85 mph, and that the engine be turned off if the capacity for further storage drops below the energy that might reach storage from regenerative braking. (The two bounds are thus velocity dependent.)

It is seen from the figures that each charging (engine on) time is about 1 minute. If the storage capacity were lower, this time would be shorter. The 85 mph criterion alone requires the minimum storage capacity to be about 0.3 kWh. With the management algorithm more energy storage is needed; 0.5 kWh provides a small cushion.

In the study still underway, the storage unit is based on commercially-available Panasonic 1500 Farad capacitors and their actual resistance [Burke 1993b]. The analysis suggests that the 95% average efficiency used in the present paper is met by this device. The Panasonic capacitor has a lower energy density than desired, at 2.1 Wh/kg and 2.7 Wh/liter, but ultracapacitor technology is still new and is moving rapidly. Another issue to be studied is whether there are driving situations which would cause the assumed energy storage to be inadequate, such as a sequence of acceleration-braking events, or acceleration on a grade.

LOW-LOAD HYBRID

Since hybrid vehicles are not being produced today, it is reasonable to consider reductions in vehicle load which could be incorporated if they came into production in 10 years or so. Keep the same interior size and vehicle performance features as for the Standard-Load hybrid, and assume a determined effort - but not a high-cost effort - to reduce loads.

Consider the following changes from the average 1993 model: 1) The curb weight is reduced 22% to 1041 kg (2295 lbs), implying a 20% reduction in inertial weight (curb weight plus 300 lbs). One justification for this large reduction is that the distribution in weight of current new cars in each of the main size classes extends some 33% about the mean for the class [DeCicco & Ross, 1993]. For example, the 1993 Escort hatchback has an interior volume of 108 cubic feet, the sales-weighted average for 1993, and a curb weight of 1075 kg (2371 lbs), fairly near the target set for Low-Load Hybrid. Moreover, considerable progress is being made in introducing lighter materials. 2) The coefficient of rolling resistance is reduced 30% to 0.007. New tires have been introduced in the market which achieve roughly this, without, it is said, any sacrifice of performance. 3) The drag coefficient is reduced 26% to 0.26, the lowest now available in a production car. Drag coefficients are coming down rapidly in conventional cars. 4) The average vehicle accessory load is reduced from 0.4 to 0.25 kW. At present this is a matter of cost; but major reductions in accessory loads, especially air conditioning, are now being made through improved design. Finally, since the vehicle's mass has been reduced, the engine displacement and operating power are correspondingly reduced to 1.2 liter and 24 kW, respectively.

With these changes and keeping the downstream hybrid propulsion characteristics the same (Table 1 and Figure 6), the fuel economy is 84 mpg in the EPA composite test, 50% higher than for the Standard-Load hybrid This meets the goal of a factor of three improvement over the regulatory standard of 27.5 mpg, announced by the Clinton Administration and US auto manufacturers.

Something interesting is revealed here which has been emphasized by Lovins: After reducing the role of engine frictions, fuel economy can be greatly increased only through reducing the vehicle load, especially the weight [Lovins et al, 1993]. The car described here is of course still quite different from the extremely-low weight 150+ mpg hybrid car advocated by Lovins.

THE COST AND EMISSIONS CHALLENGES

At this early stage, there are several technologies which have the potential to achieve a factor of three improvement in fuel economy with a relatively clean car. The purpose of this paper is to provide background on one of the more interesting possibilities, a buffered fuel-engine hybrid. What are the prospects for developing such a car? Although in important respects it would not be a major departure for the manufacturers, development of this vehicle would nevertheless certainly involve substantial engineering challenges. In two areas it is not clear whether the needed technology could be developed quickly at reasonable cost and reliability: the power buffer, and restart of the engine with very low-emissions. In addition, the overall cost of this sophisticated vehicle is at issue.

Consider the cost issue briefly. The Low-Load vehicle has a smaller engine and dispenses with much, or possibly all, of the transmission. However, it has a 24 kW generator, and a roughly 80 kW *peak* power motor, a versatile power semiconductor control, and an energy storage unit, such as a capacitor, with capacities of about 0.5 kWh and 60 kW. Some cost estimates for motor, generator and control are available [Martin 1992]. The cost of the power buffer is especially uncertain, but an estimate has been made for the DoE capacitor development effort [Burke 1993b]. We tentatively estimate a retail cost increment of 20 to 25% for the low-load hybrid vehicle with mature technology. Although this estimate is highly uncertain, it is clear that the vehicle is more complicated than a conventional vehicle, and would cost more. We believe the vehicle cost would be considerably below that of a corresponding general-purpose all-electric car and that the hybrid would have much better overall performance.

There are reasons to be optimistic about emissions control for an engine that only operates at one point, and about design of the restart of the engine with stored power available such that a little delay in engine restart would not be noticeable. There would be considerable engineering latitude.

In addition, there is great latitude as to the kind of engine and fuel chosen. Gasoline has been chosen here only to suggest the potential for the buffered fuel-engine concept in simple terms. Among other engine options are diesel and gas turbine. A gas turbine with catalytic oxidation, rather than normal combustion, to achieve extremely low emissions has been studied for hybrid application, although it might not be suitable for frequent on-off operation [Mackay 1994].

In addition, gaseous fuels would now be acceptable for a general-purpose vehicle, in terms of fuel-storage capacity and range, because of the factor of three improvement in fuel economy. For example, a well-designed compressed natural gas system would yield good range for reasonable on-vehicle storage capacity; its implementation would enable the smog problems now associated with evaporation of auto fuel to be largely eliminated. The gas industry should be interested in supporting R&D on high-fuel-economy vehicles of this kind.

As stated above, emissions are often discussed in an artificial world of standards largely unrelated to actual system emissions. We need to reform the discussion of emissions and we need to expand the research on emissions in the real world, so that differences in emissions from different kinds of vehicles, fuels, and driving can be realistically predicted. This reform would improve the prospects for hybrid vehicles.

ACKNOWLEDGMENTS

The authors thank with pleasure Feng An, John DeCicco, Mark DeLuchi, Andy Frank, Karl Hellman, Amory Lovins, Dill Murrell, Dan Santini and Kermit Schlansker for their comments. We also thank the American Council for an Energy-Efficient Economy for partial support of the work.

REFERENCES

An, Feng, and Marc Ross, A Model of Fuel Economy and Driving Patterns, SAE 930328, 1993.

Burke, A. F., Hybrid/Electric Vehicle Design Options and Evaluations, SAE 920447, 1992.

Burke, A. F., On-Off Engine Operation for Hybrid/Electric Vehicles, SAE 930042, 1993a.

Burke, A. F., Energy Storage Specification Requirements for Hybrid-Electric Vehicles, in E. Dowgiallo, organizer, Ultracapacitor Program Review Meeting, U.S. Dept. of Energy, Sept. 15-16, 1993b.

Calvert, J. G., J. B. Heywood, R. F. Sawyer and J. H. Seinfeld, Achieving Acceptable Air Quality: Some Reflections on Controlling Vehicle Emissions, *Science* **261**, 37-45, 1993.

DeCicco, John, and Marc Ross, An Updated Assessment of the Near-Term Potential for Improving Fuel Economy, American Council for an Energy-Efficient Economy, Washington DC, 1993.

Frank, Andrew, N. H. Beachley, T. C. Hausenbauer and T. Ping, The Fuel Efficiency Potential of a Flywheel Hybrid Vehicle for Urban Driving, *Proceedings of the Eleventh Intersociety Energy Conversion Engineering Conference*, September 1976.

Frank, Andrew, and N. H. Beachley, Evaluation of the Flywheel Drive Concept for Passenger Vehicles, SAE 790049, 1979.

Kalberlah, A., Electric Hybrid Drive Systems for Passenger Cars and Taxis, SAE 910247, 1991.

Lovins, A. B., J. W. Barnett and L. H. Lovins, Supercars: The Coming Light-Vehicle Revolution, Rocky Mountain Institute, Snowmass CO, 1993.

Mackay, Robin, Development of a 24 kW Gas Turbine-Driven Generator Set for Hybrid Vehicles, SAE 940510, 1994. See also SAE 930044.

Martin, Ronald, Advanced Propulsion Systems Group of General Motors, at the 1992 Solar and Electric Vehicle Conference, Boston MA.

Murrell, J. Dillard, Karl H. Hellman and Robert M. Heavenrich, Light-Duty Automotive Technology and Fuel Economy Trends Through 1993, Motor Vehicle Emissions Laboratory, U. S. Environmental Protection Agency, Ann Arbor MI, 1993.

Ross, Marc, and Feng An, The Use of Fuel by Spark Ignition Engines, SAE 930329, 1993.

Ross, Marc, Why Cars Aren't as Clean as We Think, *Technology Review*, Feb./March pp 72-73, 1994a.

Ross, Marc, Automobile Fuel Consumption and Emissions: Effects of Vehicle and Driving Characteristics, *Annual Review of Energy and Environment* **19**, pp 75-112, 1994b.

FIGURE 1. BASIC LAYOUT OF THE HYBRID PROPULSION

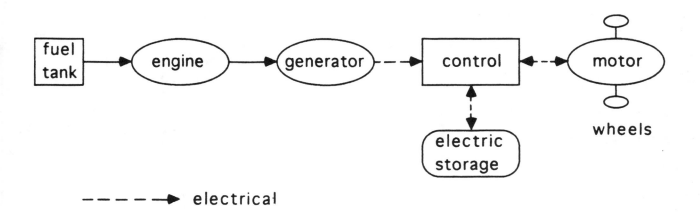

FIGURE 2. POWER REQUIREMENTS, AVCAR '93

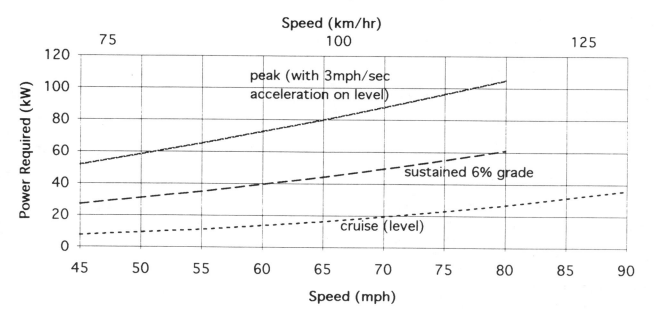

TABLE1a.   ENERGY ANALYSIS EQUATION, DRIVING CYCLE PARAMETERS,
AND HYBRID DRIVE EFFICIENCY PARAMETERS

EQUATION FOR FUEL ENERGY USE:

E (kJ/mile) =	k*V*(N/v)*v(gear)*t(pwr)/vbar	(engine friction in powered operation)
	k(idle)*V*N(idle)*t(idle)/vbar	(engine friction at idle)
	(b/eps)*CsubR*M*g	(rolling resistance)
	0.5*(b/eps)*rho*CsubD*A*lambda*vsubr^2	(air drag)
	0.5*(b/eps)*beta*M_mult*M*nsubs*vsubp^2	(braking)
	b*Pac/vbar	(vehicle accessories)

CONSTANTS:

1 gallon gasoline = 120,600 kJ

rho = 1.20kg/m^3, air density at standard conditions

g = 9.8m/s^2, gravity acceleration

DRIVING CYCLE PARAMETERS

	EPA Urban Cycle	EPA Highway Cycle	
vbar	19.6	48.2	average speed entire cycle (mph)
vsubr	10.82	21.7	average running speed (m/s)
vsubp	13.81	26.7	rms peak speed (m/s)
t(pwr)	0.56	0.89	fraction of time powered engine output
t(idle)	0.44	0.11	fraction time engine is idle (some veh. dep.)
cold_start_mult.	1.07	1.00	multiplier for a cold start
nsubs	2.41	0.10	stops per mile
lambda	1.90	1.09	ave(v^3)/(ave v)^3 (dimensionless)
beta	0.90	1.20	braking term correction factor (dim-less)

ASSUMPTIONS (for AVCAR93/Base Car):

1. Engine friction characteristic at idle is the same as that when engine is in powered operation
2. Constant idle engine speed at different operation conditions
3. Assume M5 transmission
4. No SIL(shift indicator light), which affects v(gear)
5. Assume constant vehicle accessories power, 0.75 kW

ASSUMPTIONS (for HYBRIDS):

1. Constant generator efficiency, 97%
2. Constant storage-control efficiency, 86%
3. Constant motor efficiency, 94%
4. Constant regeneration fraction, 67% (only the two drive wheels used for regeneration)

NOTE:

Because engine friction declines with increasing brake power at fixed engine speed, the above equation overstates fuel consumption for engine friction and correspondingly understates fuel consumption to provide power . Using a linear approximation, the proper allocation of fuel is :

k -> k * [1 - c * (Pb/Pb@WOT)]

b -> b + c * N * V / Pb@WOT   WOT = Wide Open Throttle

Typically for naturally aspirated engine, Pb@WOT ≈ 0.5 * N * V and c ≈ 0.35 (35% reduction in friction at WOT). Total fuel use is unaffected by this reallocation [Ross, 1994b].

TABLE1b. VEHICLE PARAMETERS

i. AVCAR 93(Base Car)

k	0.225	engine friction coeff. (hot engine) (kJ/(rev.liter))
V	2.77	engine displacement (liters)
a	0.623	engine friction characteristic: a =k * V (kJ/rev)
c	0.35	friction red. coeff: k*(1-c*Pb/Pb@WOT) (dimensionless)
b (or 1/eta)	2.5	coefficient of Pb in expression for fuel rate
indicated efficiency	urban 0.375, highway 0.377	1/(b + 2 * k * c * cold_start_mult.)
N/v	34.0	engine speed/vehicle speed in top gear (rpm/mph)
v(gear)	55	(average v in a gear)*(gear ratio/top gear ratio) (mph)
N(pwr)	1870	average engine speed in powered operation (rpm)
		N(pwr)=(N/v) * v(gear)
N(idle)	731	average idle engine speed, N(idle) = 900 - 61V, (rpm)
eps (epsilon)	urban 0.85, highway 0.90	transmission system efficiency
M	1471	vehicle inertial mass (curb weight plus 300 lbs) (kg)
M_mult	1.035	mass correction factor due to rotating parts
CsubR	0.01	coefficient of rolling resistance (dimensionless)
CsubD	0.34	coefficient of air drag (dimensionless)
A	2.00	frontal area (m^2)
Pac	0.75	average vehicle accessories power (kW)

ii: STANDARD HYBRID

engine power	30 kW	engine power output at operating point
engine efficiency	0.3653	engine efficiency at operating point, bsfc = 224 g/kWh
k	0.125	engine friction coefficient at operating point
V	1.5	small engine
a	0.1875	engine friction characteristic: a = k * V (kJ/rev)
N(pwr)	2280	constant engine rpm when engine is on
b (or 1/eta)	2.5	coefficient of Pb in expression for fuel rate
eps (epsilon)	1.00	residual transmission system losses neglected
M	1471	vehicle inertial mass (curb weight plus 300 lbs) (kg)
M_mult	1.035	mass correction factor due to rotating parts
CsubR	0.010	coefficient of rolling resistance (dimensionless)
CsubD	0.34	coefficient of air drag (dimensionless)
A	2.00	frontal area (m^2)
Pac	0.4	reduced vehicle accessories power consumption

iii: LOW-LOAD HYBRID

engine power	30 kW	engine power output at operating point
engine efficiency	0.3653	engine efficiency at operating point, bsfc = 224 g/kWh
k	0.125	engine friction coefficient at operating point
V	1.2	even smaller engine
a	0.15	engine friction characteristic: a = k * V (kJ/rev)
N(pwr)	2280	constant engine rpm when engine is on
b (or 1/eta)	2.5	coefficient of Pb in expression for fuel rate
eps (epsilon)	1.00	residual transmission system losses neglected
M	1177	reduced vehicle inertial mass
M_mult	1.035	mass correction factor due to rotating parts
CsubR	0.007	reduced tire roll resistance coefficient, better tire
CsubD	0.26	reduced air drag coefficient, improved aerodynamics
A	1.90	smaller frontal area
Pac	0.25	reduced vehicle accessories power consumption

TABLE 2. SUMMARY OF RESULTS

a. AVCAR93 (Base Car)

*lost work is the thermodynamic loss of available work in the engine

	URBAN CYCLE		HIWAY CYCLE		COMPOSITE CYCLE	
	kJ/mile		kJ/mile		kJ/mile	
Total Fuel Use	5177	100.00%	3250	100.00%	4308	100.00%
Engine friction work when engine@idle	263	5.08%	26	0.80%	147	3.41%
Engine friction work when engine@power	855	16.52%	513	15.78%	605	14.04%
Lost work associated with engine friction when engine@idle	394	7.61%	39	1.20%	244	5.66%
Lost work associated with engine when engine@power	1283	24.78%	770	23.69%	1006	23.35%
Lost work associated with power output	1429	27.60%	1141	35.11%	1441	33.45%
Transmission losses	122	2.36%	70	2.15%	99	2.29%
Tire rolling resistance	232	4.48%	232	7.14%	232	5.39%
Air drag	146	2.82%	337	10.37%	232	5.38%
Braking loss	315	6.08%	65	2.00%	203	4.70%
Vehicle accessories	138	2.67%	56	1.72%	101	2.35%
MPG	**23.3**		**37.1**		**28.0**	

b. STANDARD-LOAD HYBRID

	URBAN CYCLE		HIWAY CYCLE		COMPOSITE CYCLE	
	kJ/mile		kJ/mile		kJ/mile	
Total Fuel Use	2113	100.00%	2196	100.00%	2150	100.00%
Fraction time engine is on	0.139		0.358		0.194	
Engine friction work	78	3.69%	76	3.46%	77	3.59%
Lost work associated with engine friction	118	5.58%	114	5.19%	116	5.40%
lost work associated with power output	1151	54.47%	1203	54.78%	1174	54.61%
Losses in generator, control, motor	211	9.99%	183	8.33%	198	9.23%
Tire rolling resistance	232	10.98%	232	10.56%	232	10.79%
Air drag	146	6.91%	337	15.35%	232	10.79%
Braking loss	104	4.92%	21	0.96%	67	3.10%
Vehicle accessories	73	3.45%	30	1.37%	54	2.49%
Regeneration to storage	171	8.08%	35	1.60%	110	5.10%
MPG	**57.1**		**54.9**		**56.1**	

b. LOW-LOAD HYBRID

	URBAN CYCLE		HIWAY CYCLE		COMPOSITE CYCLE	
	kJ/mile		kJ/mile		kJ/mile	
Total Fuel Use	1415	100.00%	1459	100.00%	1435	100.00%
Fraction time engine is on	0.117		0.297		0.162	
Engine friction work	52	2.48%	51	2.31%	52	2.40%
Lost work associated with engine friction	79	3.72%	76	3.47%	78	3.60%
lost work associated with power output	770	36.46%	799	36.39%	783	36.43%
Losses in generator, control, motor	148	7.03%	122	5.54%	136	6.34%
Tire rolling resistance	130	6.15%	130	5.92%	130	6.05%
Air drag	106	5.02%	245	11.16%	169	7.84%
Braking loss	83	3.94%	17	0.78%	53	2.49%
Vehicle accessories	46	2.18%	19	0.87%	34	1.57%
Regeneration to storage	136	6.46%	28	1.28%	88	4.08%
MPG	**85.2**		**82.7**		**84.1**	

FIGURE 3. ENERGY FLOWS, AVCAR '93, EPA COMPOSITE CYCLE

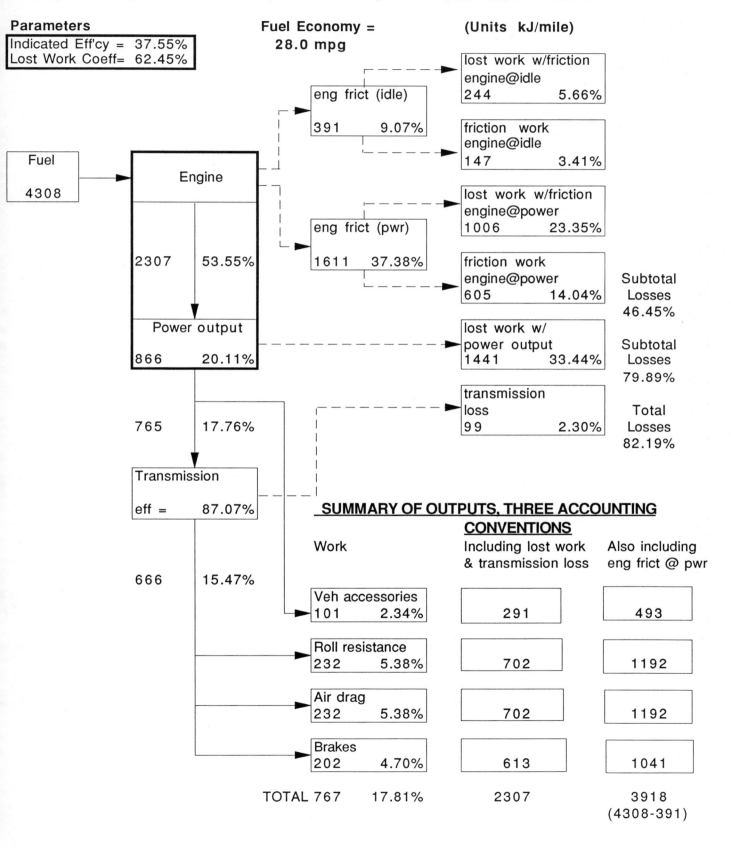

FIGURE 4. ENERGY FLOWS, STANDARD-LOAD HYBRID, EPA COMPOSITE CYCLE

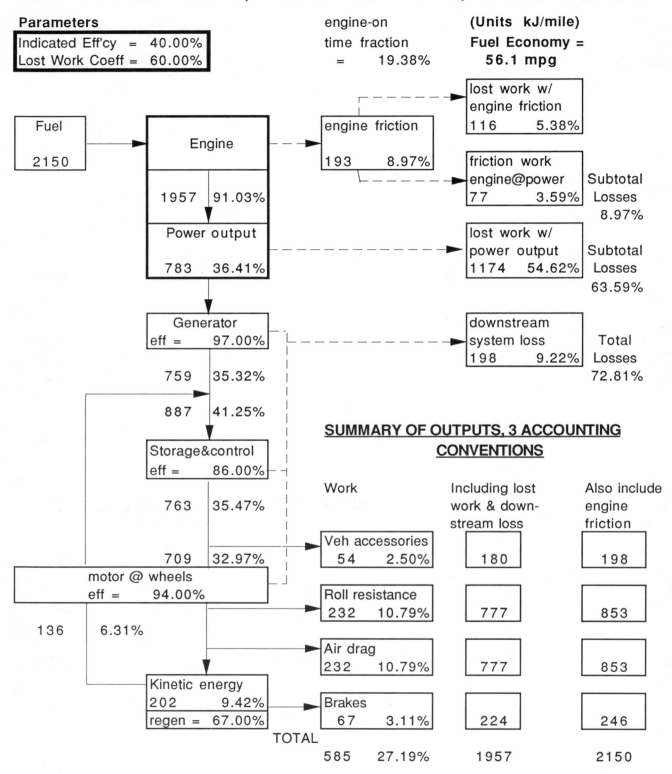

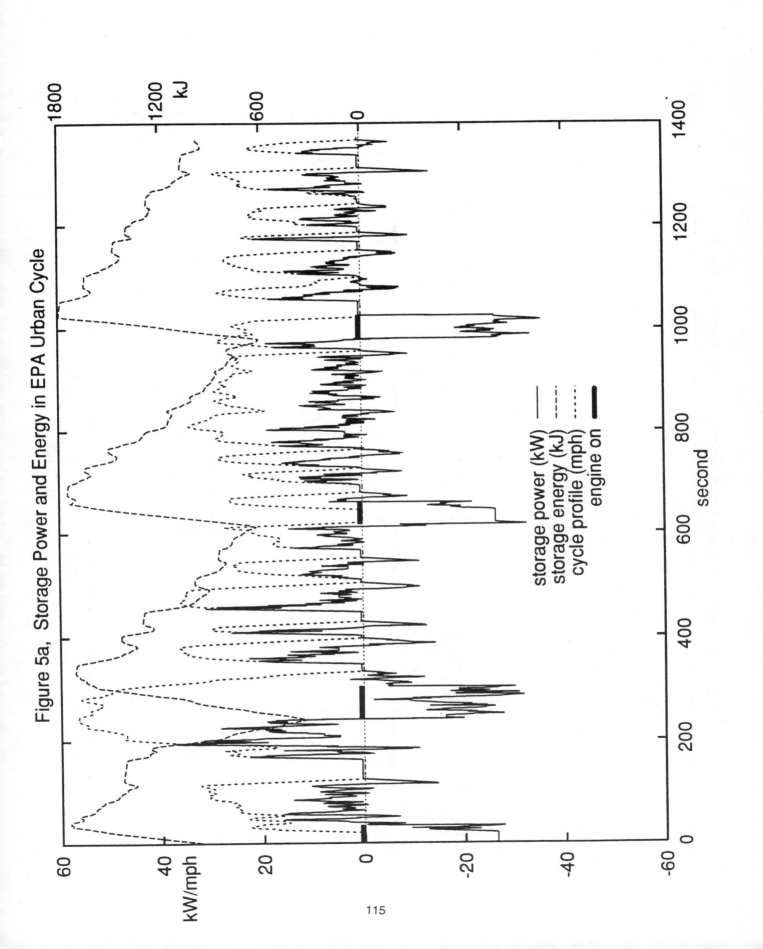

Figure 5a, Storage Power and Energy in EPA Urban Cycle

storage power (kW)
storage energy (kJ)
cycle profile (mph)
engine on

kW/mph

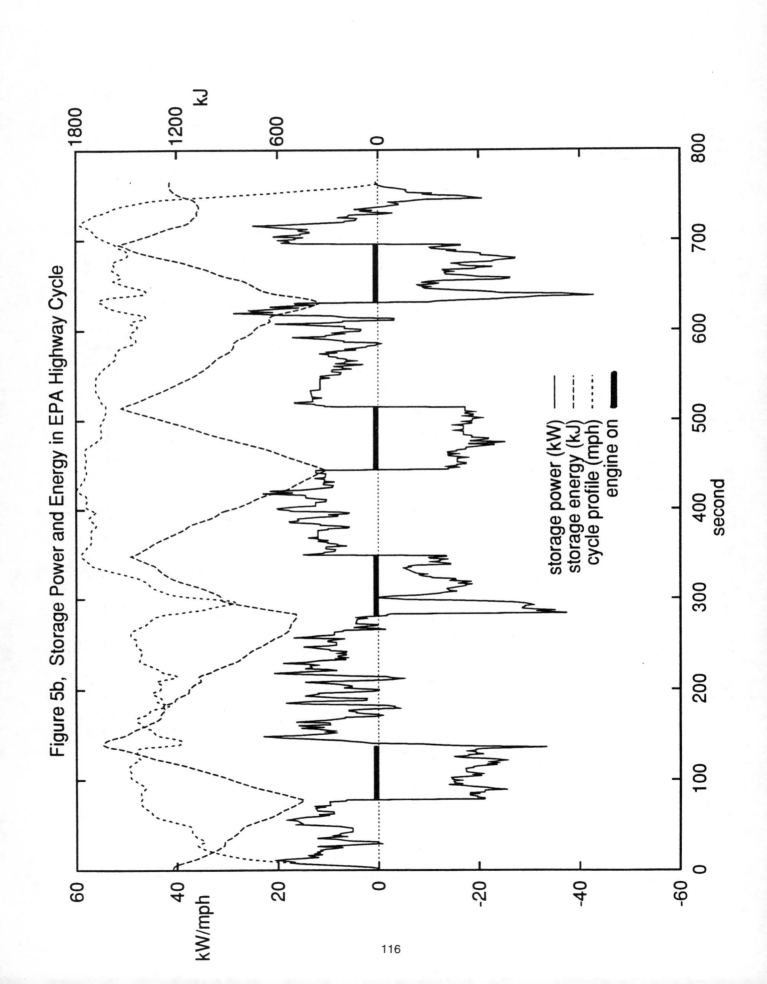

Figure 5b, Storage Power and Energy in EPA Highway Cycle

storage power (kW)
storage energy (kJ)
cycle profile (mph)
engine on

116

FIGURE 6. ENERGY FLOWS, LOW-LOAD HYBRID, EPA COMPOSITE CYCLE

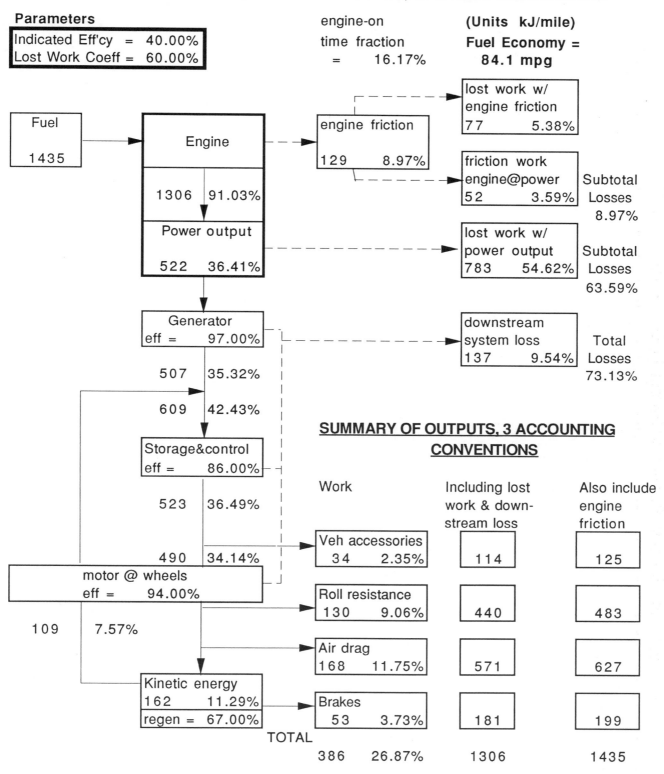

Parameters

| Indicated Eff'cy | = 40.00% |
| Lost Work Coeff | = 60.00% |

engine-on
time fraction
= 16.17%

(Units kJ/mile)
Fuel Economy =
84.1 mpg

Fuel
1435

Engine

1306 | 91.03%

Power output

522 | 36.41%

engine friction

129 | 8.97%

lost work w/
engine friction
77 | 5.38%

friction work
engine@power
52 | 3.59%

Subtotal
Losses
8.97%

lost work w/
power output
783 | 54.62%

Subtotal
Losses
63.59%

Generator
eff = 97.00%

507 | 35.32%

609 | 42.43%

Storage&control
eff = 86.00%

523 | 36.49%

490 | 34.14%

motor @ wheels
eff = 94.00%

109 | 7.57%

Kinetic energy
162 | 11.29%
regen = 67.00%

downstream
system loss
137 | 9.54%

Total
Losses
73.13%

SUMMARY OF OUTPUTS, 3 ACCOUNTING CONVENTIONS

Work	Including lost work & down-stream loss	Also include engine friction
Veh accessories 34 2.35%	114	125
Roll resistance 130 9.06%	440	483
Air drag 168 11.75%	571	627
Brakes 53 3.73%	181	199
TOTAL 386 26.87%	1306	1435

A Comparison of Modeled and Measure Energy Use in Hybrid Electric Vehicles

Matthew Cuddy
National Renewable Energy Lab.

ABSTRACT

CarSim 2.5.4, written by AeroVironment, Inc. of Monrovia, California and SIMPLEV 3.0, written by Idaho National Engineering Laboratory were used to simulate two series-configured hybrid electric vehicles that competed in the 1994 Hybrid Electric Vehicle Challenge. Vehicle speed and battery energy use were measured over a 0.2-km maximum effort acceleration and a 58-km range event. The simulations' predictions are compared to each other and to measured data. A rough uncertainty analysis of the validation is presented. The programs agree with each other to within 5% and with the measured energy data within the uncertainty of the experiment.

INTRODUCTION

The objective of this paper is to evaluate the accuracy of two hybrid electric vehicle (HEV) performance simulation programs, and to alert the reader to considerations critical to such validation efforts.

Interest and investment in HEV development continue to increase. Hybrids are seen by some as a viable, high-efficiency compromise between full-performance, conventional internal combustion engine-driven vehicles and lower-performance electric vehicles (powered by currently commercially available batteries). HEVs are an important part of the development efforts that are part of the Partnership for the New Generation of Vehicles announced by President Clinton.

As HEV development efforts grow, so does work in the computer simulation of HEVs. Computer simulation has been applied to aircraft design, structural analysis, fluid flow analysis, and conventional automobile design. It is widely recognized as a time- and cost-saving tool that helps reduce the number of actual experiments that must be performed on a system.

An engineer may <u>waste</u> time and money, however, if he uses unvalidated simulations to make time or money investment decisions. To paraphrase a friend in the chemical processing industry, all simulations are wrong, but some are useful. Computer simulations must make some simplifying assumptions that allow a mathematical description of the system being simulated. How useful the simulation is depends upon how much the assumptions affect the results. The aim of a validation effort is to determine how closely the simulation in question approximates reality.

This paper is devoted to validation of two HEV simulations and to considerations important to any HEV simulation validation. The following sections will describe the experimental data collection that took place, discuss uncertainty and a rough uncertainty analysis, compare the simulations' calculated results to measured data, and present conclusions and recommendations.

EXPERIMENTAL PROCEDURE

The general procedure followed in this validation effort measured the speed profiles and battery energy use of two HEVs competing at the 1994 Hybrid Electric Vehicle Challenge, collected data describing the components of the two HEVs, and modeled the vehicles by prescribing the speed data collected. The two HEVs are those assembled by the student teams at Pennsylvania State University (Penn State) and California State Polytechnic University-Pomona (Cal Poly-Pomona). Penn State's vehicle's zero-emission vehicle (ZEV) performance in the 58-km range event only is computed, as is Cal Poly-Pomona's performance in two 0.2-km accelerations, one as an HEV and one as a ZEV.

Two data acquisition systems (DASs) were used at the Challenge. A DAS built by Instrumental Solutions measured speed, battery current and voltage, generator current and voltage in 1-second increments. A DAS built by Cruising Equipment measured total battery energy and ampere hours.

Speed measurements were taken using magnets mounted to the drive axle half-shaft and a pickup. Speeds in the maximum effort acceleration were averaged using 3 points at time, centered in time. Speeds measured in the 58-km-long range event were averaged using 5 points, centered in time. This averaged speed profile was again averaged using 3 points centered in time. This processing was necessary to reduce noise in the data before using them as inputs for the simulations.

The simulation programs used in this study are SIMPLEV 3.0, written by Idaho National Engineering Laboratory, and

CarSim 2.5.4, written by AeroVironment Inc. SIMPLEV runs on an IBM-compatible PC while CarSim runs on an Apple Macintosh. The programs use empirical efficiency maps and other data to model series-configured HEVs.

The programs assume a vehicle layout as shown in Figure 1. The bus either accepts energy from or delivers it to the batteries and electric motor via the motor controller. The bus accepts energy only from the generator, and only when the internal combustion engine is on. The bidirectional arrows that connect the controller, motor, and transmission indicate that regenerative braking is assumed possible.

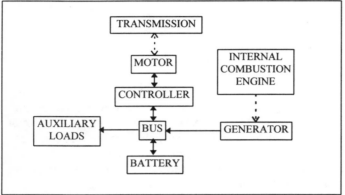

Figure 1. HEV schematic. Dotted lines indicate mechanical energy transfer, solid lines indicate electrical energy transfer (adapted from reference 1.)

The approach SIMPLEV and CarSim use is similar to that used in many other simulation programs at universities and national laboratories.[2][3][4] The programs accept input data to describe the vehicle's trip, the vehicle itself, the transmission, electric motor, motor controller, battery pack, generator, and internal combustion engine. The input data may be in the form of a scalar efficiency, for example, or a component efficiency map, with efficiency as a function of torque and rotational speed. SIMPLEV and CarSim both accept detailed component efficiency maps.

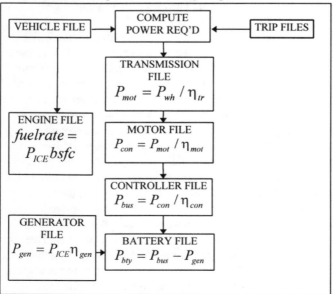

Figure 2. Block diagram of information flow in SIMPLEV

Figure 2 depicts SIMPLEV's data processing procedure. The trip files include pairs of time and speed points (at a user-specified time step) and pairs of hill grade and distance points. The vehicle file contains information such as coefficient of drag, frontal area, and curb weight. SIMPLEV uses two-dimensional look-up tables that contain component efficiency for pairs of electric motor RPM and torque for the transmission, electric motor, and electric motor controller. The battery pack is described by a table of internal resistance and open circuit voltage as a function of the battery pack's depth of discharge. See reference 1 for a more detailed description of SIMPLEV's algorithms.

ROLE OF UNCERTAINTY IN VALIDATION

The goal of validation is to determine how closely the simulation approximates reality. To know this, we must know the true value against which the simulation's output will be compared. More realistically, we must know in what range this value likely falls. And of course, a computer program is only as good as its input; therefore we must know how accurate the inputs are. The uncertainty considerations here are not believed to be an exhaustive list. They do include main sources of potential error and are meant to alert the reader to the significance of uncertainty analysis in validation.

Input data such as component efficiencies and operating limits are measured quantities, and as such have some measurement uncertainty associated with them. Consider an electric motor, for example. The particular motor used in the vehicle may not have been tested, rather it may be one of a manufacturer's lot of motors, some fraction of which have been tested. In this case, some variation between the tested motors and the motor in question should be expected. Even if the motor used in the vehicle were tested, both bias and random uncertainty will exist in the test. Furthermore, the motor will likely be operated in an environment (temperature) dissimilar to that in which it was tested, introducing more uncertainty.

Significant uncertainty may also be introduced in applying the input data to the simulation program. The simulation user must fully understand how the program uses supplied data. For example, electric motor torque limits as a function of RPM are accepted by both SIMPLEV and CarSim, and to use the torque limits, the program user must interpret the manufacturer's data. It may be unclear whether the maximum torque is that maintainable for 1 minute, indefinitely, or for 5 seconds. The user may also introduce error by inputting or processing the data incorrectly.

Energy use data measured for comparison to the simulation predictions are also subject to measurement uncertainty. The data may be imprecise because of insufficient resolution, an inappropriate sampling rate, or random measuring equipment fluctuations. Inaccuracy may be caused by inappropriate calibration of the measurement equipment or by environmental effects. Interference is particularly significant in on-board vehicle data collection systems. Error may also be introduced by post-processing techniques.

UNCERTAINTY ANALYSIS

Where possible, bias uncertainty is separated from random uncertainty in the analysis described below. Bias and random uncertainties are propagated using Taylor series:

$$S_r^2 = (\frac{\partial r}{\partial x} S_x)^2 + (\frac{\partial r}{\partial y} S_y)^2 \qquad (1)$$

where S_x is the uncertainty in x, and r=f (x,y)[5]. Bias limits are simply added where appropriate, however. Special note is made of these instances. Bias limits, B, and random uncertainty limits, R, are combined into the total uncertainty U by

$$= \sqrt{B^2 + R^2} . \qquad (2)$$

INPUT DATA-Uncertainty in component specifications, in speed measurements, and those introduced by the user are considered.

Component Specifications-The sources of component data and estimated uncertainties are listed in Table 1. The effect of these uncertainties was estimated by modeling "best" and "worst" case vehicles. The best case vehicle was the most efficient possible given the uncertainty intervals in Table 1, and the worst case was the least efficient.

Table 1. Component Data: Sources of Information and Uncertainty Estimates

Component	Data Source	Estimated Uncertainty
Cal Poly-Pomona:		
generator output	student measurement	± 35%
motor η	Advanced DC*	±5%
controller η	estimate	+2/-4%
transmission η	estimate	+2/-4%
mass	measured at Challenge	±1%
inertial mass	estimate	±1%
coeff. of roll. resist.	estimate	±20%
coeff. of aero. drag	student measurement	±10%
frontal area	student measurement	±10%
Penn State:		
motor η	Solectria*	±8%
controller η	Solectria*	±8%
transmission η	estimate	+2/-4%
mass	measured at Challenge	±1%
inertial mass	estimate	±1%
coeff. of roll. resist.	estimate	±20%
coeff. of aero. drag	Ford*	neglected
frontal area	Ford*	neglected
regenerative braking fraction	student estimate	±50%

* indicates manufacturer of the component

The generator set output (for Cal Poly-Pomona) has a relatively high uncertainty associated with it. Both programs were used with a constant power output generator set model, but tests completed at Cal Poly-Pomona indicate that power varied with generator current and voltage. The means by which the internal combustion engine's output was regulated is unknown.

Measured Speed- Random error in vehicle speed includes the contribution by limited resolution above as well as observed scatter in a repeated distance measurement. The speed measurement equipment's resolution is one, where one pulse (caused by the axle-mounted magnet passing the vehicle-chassis-mounted pickup) per second corresponds to 1.50 and 0.926 km/h on the Cal Poly-Pomona and Penn State vehicles, respectively.

Bias error was introduced by uncertainty in the calibration.

The effect of this speed uncertainty on the programs' battery power calculations is calculated as follows:

$$P_{bty} = \frac{1}{\eta_d}(m_i \frac{\partial v}{\partial t} + mgC_{rr} + \frac{1}{2}\rho C_D A v^2)v \qquad (3)$$

where $\eta_d = \eta_{motor}\eta_{controller}\eta_{transmission}$ is the average efficiency at which electrical energy at the battery is converted to mechanical work at the tires, m_i is the inertial mass of the vehicle, greater than the actual mass of the vehicle because it includes the inertia of spinning components, mg is the weight of the vehicle, C_{rr} is the tires' coefficient of rolling resistance, ρ is air density, C_D is the coefficient of aerodynamic drag, A is the vehicle's frontal area, and v is the vehicle speed. This equation assumes component efficiency independent of torque and speed.

The equation is dicretized, with the speed derivative approximated as $(v-v_{prev})/\Delta t \equiv v_{diff}/\Delta t$. V_{diff} is defined by this equation while v_{prev} is the vehicle speed at the previous time step. V and v_{diff} are treated as independent variables with estimated random and bias uncertainties (the bias uncertainty in v_{diff} is zero), and EQ (1) is applied.

This results in a random and bias uncertainty in the battery power that the codes compute. To compute the uncertainty in energy use for the entire trip, the random uncertainties in each time step are added in quadrature, as in EQ (1), and the bias limits are simply added.

User Error-The author has used SIMPLEV and CarSim for roughly nine months and has frequent communications with SIMPLEV's developer and other engineers who use CarSim. User error is assumed to be zero.

MEASURED ENERGY USE DATA-Measurement uncertainty is introduced by interference, random fluctuations in the measurement equipment, limited resolution, inappropriate sampling rates, and failures in calibration. The following discussion applies to the Instrumental Solutions DAS only. Uncertainty in the Cruising Equipment meter's measurements is estimated from readings taken on other vehicles at the 1994 Hybrid Electric Vehicle Challenge to be 10%.

Random Error-Interference is a significant consideration for on-board vehicle DASs such as those used in this study. The effect of interference on the Instrumental Solutions system is estimated by considering the magnitude and frequency of readings far from expected values. Note that these outliers are not discarded. There are seven instances where the battery voltage jumps by a factor of two between 1-s readings without a corresponding change in current or the battery current reading is negative when there is no regenerative braking or other battery charging. These apparent errors occurred in 6%

121

of the measurements considered. The random uncertainty in voltage and current readings was estimated at 20 V and 20 A.

Random fluctuations in voltage and current readings were noted during constant voltage and constant current bench tests of the Instrumental Solutions DAS at the National Renewable Energy Laboratory (NREL). These fluctuations were roughly 1-3% over the course of 30 s, and are considered to be lumped with the above uncertainty for this analysis.

The Instrumental Solutions DAS measures voltage with 2.0 V resolution and current with 3.9 A resolution. These resolutions contributed to the random error in power measurement .

Voltage and current are sampled at a rate of roughly 2500 Hz. These readings were averaged every second by the DAS. During the hard accelerations for which the DAS was used, current can be expected to change significantly in less than a second. Also, interference patterns may perhaps be discerned by inspecting the data at a greater than 1 Hz rate. The 1 Hz output rate is believed to contribute error in interpreting the data. This error is not estimated.

Bias Error-The DASs were bench calibrated using an NREL-owned voltage source with an uncertainty, traceable to National Institute of Standards and Technology (NIST) standards, of less than 0.001%. This uncertainty is neglected. Calibration took place in an air-conditioned environment, however, and resistors in the DAS are temperature dependent. Engineers at Instrumental Solutions estimate the higher operating temperature caused overpredictions of 4.0 V and 7.8 A. These uncertainties are included in the analysis.

RESULTS

0.2-km ACCELERATIONS-CarSim and SIMPLEV use similar approaches and levels of detail in modeling series HEVs, so we would expect that they agree very closely. One significant difference between the programs is the way they compute the power required at the wheels. Recall EQ (3), which computes power required at the battery from the road load. SIMPLEV takes the speed at the current time step as v in this equation, while AeroVironment takes the average of the speed at the previous time step and the current time step as v. This causes AeroVironment to predict lower battery power requirements than SIMPLEV in cases where the previous speed is less than the current speed, as in positive accelerations. CarSim's implementation assumes that speeds corresponding to given time steps are known instantaneously; that is, at time t=1 s, the vehicle speed is as is prescribed. This is equivalent to assuming that the speeds entered for given times are centered-in-time averages. SIMPLEV's implementation assumes that the speed corresponding to a given time step is the average speed over the time step preceding that instant. That is, the speed prescribed at time t=1 s is the average speed from the times t=0 to t=1 s. See Figure 3

Figure 4 shows the battery power computed by SIMPLEV and CarSim for Cal Poly-Pomona's vehicle over the acceleration run it completed in zero emission vehicle (ZEV) mode. The simulation programs use at these speeds at each time step. From time t=0 to 23 seconds, SIMPLEV predicts higher powers than does CarSim. This is explained by the way SIMPLEV and CarSim use the speed inputs described above.

As the difference between the speeds used by the programs at a given time step decreases, so does the difference between the calculated power use.

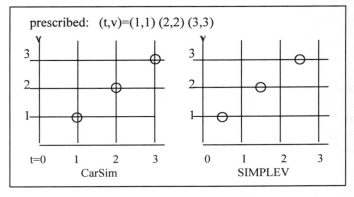

Figure 3. CarSim and SIMPLEV assume different speeds

Figure 5 compares the battery power computed by SIMPLEV and CarSim for Cal Poly-Pomona's HEV acceleration run, where the internal combustion engine and generator are producing electric power. We again see CarSim predicting lower powers than SIMPLEV, and that the difference decreases as the rate of acceleration decreases. The roughly 10 kW discrepancy at 8 seconds is caused by the way the two simulations treat gear shifts. Both simulations predict a gear change between 7 and 8 seconds. CarSim uses the torque and RPM state before the gear shift to compute the time step's component efficiencies, while SIMPLEV uses torques and RPMs after the gear shift. The motor/controller efficiency before the shift (used in CarSim) was 0.95, while after the gear shift (as in SIMPLEV), the efficiency was 0.69. The lower efficiency in SIMPLEV at this point causes more power to be required of the battery.

Table 2 summarizes the energies computed and measured for Cal Poly-Pomona over acceleration runs and short return trips, which are not presented in Figures 4-7. The total trip time averaged about 53 s. The data in the table indicate that SIMPLEV and CarSim agree to within 0.034 kWh for a runs that require roughly 0.2 kWh electrical energy. The table contains battery energies, equal to the electrical energy required by the motor, less the energy supplied by the generator. In the ZEV run, there is no energy supplied by the generator, and the battery energy is equal to the total electrical energy required. The total energy required by the motor depends on the trip and vehicle. Because the trips are very similar, (0.2-km maximum effort accelerations,) and the vehicle is unchanged, 0.2 kWh-electric is characteristic of both runs. The difference between CarSim and SIMPLEV is therefore 0.01/0.2*100=5%.

Table 2. Battery Energy Use Computed and Measured for Cal Poly-Pomona

	Measured (kWh)	CarSim (kWh)	SIMPLEV (kWh)
ZEV	.198 +.005/ -.018	.208 +.044/ -.047	.218 +.044/ -.047
HEV	.030 +.003/ -.016	.048 +.080/ -.068	.060 +.080/ -.068

Modeled Versus Measured-The data in Table 2 show that the energy predictions of the two simulation programs agree with the measured energy use to within the error bounds on the data. The error bounds are large relative to the measured energy use, however, roughly 10% on measurements on the ZEV run, and 20% on simulation results for the same run. As mentioned above, the battery energy use for the HEV run does not represent the total electrical energy used; it is therefore not appropriate here for computing percent uncertainty. Uncertainties on the calculated energy use are larger for the HEV run than for the ZEV run because of the significant uncertainty assumed in the internal combustion engine/generator output.

Figure 6 shows the upper and lower bounds on measured and computed battery power for the ZEV acceleration run. The bounds are computed from measurement uncertainty for the measured data and from the estimated effects of uncertainty in measured speed (which is used as an input to the program) and input parameters. For readability, only CarSim's results are shown. The shape of SIMPLEV's results curve is as shown in Figure 4, while the uncertainty at each point in SIMPLEV's results is similar to that uncertainty shown in CarSim's.

We see generally good agreement between the simulation and the measured data; in many sections CarSim's predictions fall within the uncertainty bounds on the measured power. Significant disagreement is seen at times t=1 second, 7 and 8 s, and at 11 s.

The spike in the measured power at 1 s is believed to be an error. The measured voltage at this point is 215 V, 71 V greater than the nominal pack voltage. We would expect the pack voltage to decrease from the no-load pack voltage as current is drawn from the batteries. Measured current at this time is 156 A.

The downward spike at 7 and 8 s is believed to be accurate. Pack voltage at 7 s is measured at 122 V, very close to what is measured during the deceleration at the end of this run, when the motor is off. This spike is caused by a gear shift, where the accelerator pedal is released for the shift. This downward spike occurs at roughly the same time and speed and for the same duration in two other Cal Poly-Pomona acceleration runs, including the HEV run considered. The downward spikes occur at roughly 45 km/h, which corresponds to a motor speed of 4500 RPM in Cal Poly-Pomona's first gear.

Neither CarSim nor SIMPLEV predicts this drop because the measured speed does not decrease at this point. Previously mentioned uncertainty in the speed measurement is believed to be responsible. In particular, better resolution may have allowed the speed meter to measure a dip or lull.

Measured power dips below zero at 8 s. Because the vehicle is not equipped with regenerative braking and its generator is not running, negative power must be an error.

The spike at 11 seconds is also believed to be an error. The measured pack voltage at this point is 250 V, 106 V greater than the nominal pack voltage. Measured current is 254 A. 1 s before this point and 1 s after it, the measured pack voltage is roughly 110 V while the measured current varies by less than 6% among the three measurements.

Figure 5 shows the upper and lower bounds on measured and computed battery power for the HEV acceleration run. Again, only CarSim's results are shown.

The measured data jumps around at time t=3, 4, and 5 seconds because the measured voltage jumps from 265.6 to 125.1 to 162.1 V while the current increases consistently from second to second. The 265.6 and 162.1 V measurements are taken to be erroneous as argued above.

The downward spike at 9 seconds is again believed to be caused by a shift, as the driver takes his foot off the accelerator. No lull in speed is measured, however, and therefore CarSim and SIMPLEV do not predict this spike.

CarSim does not predict the drop to negative power, which corresponds to charging the batteries by the generator set during deceleration following the run, at the same time as it is measured (t=17 s) because of inconsistency in the data. From 16 to 17 s, the measured battery power becomes negative but the measured speed increases. Therefore, CarSim and SIMPLEV calculate that power is drawn from the battery during this second.

58-KM TRIP- Instrumental Solutions' voltage and current measurements were not believable for this trip (presumably because of interference from Penn State's AC motor and controller), it was used only to measure speed. The Cruising Equipment kWh-meter was less sensitive to AC motor/controller interference on Penn State's and other vehicles, and its results are presented here.

Simulation Comparison-The difference between CarSim's and SIMPLEV's predicted energy use in Figures 4 and 5 was seen to decrease as the difference in their assumed speeds decreased. The 58-km range event contains only moderate accelerations, and as a result, the CarSim and SIMPLEV agree more closely. See Table 3.

Table 3 indicates battery energy computed by the programs for the measured speed profile on a flat surface. There are hills on the measured trip, but SIMPLEV is difficult to use for extended trips with elevation changes. SIMPLEV predicts higher energy use than CarSim by 2.6%.

Table 3. SIMPLEV's and CarSim's Calculated Energy Use for the 58-km Event (no hills)

SIMPLEV (kWh)	CarSim (kWh)
7.55	7.36

Measured Versus Modeled-Table 4 compares the measured energy use to CarSim's prediction when the measured speeds and known hills are input. CarSim's prediction is 10.0% greater than the measured energy. The large uncertainty in CarSim's result is likely due to the uncertainty in the effectiveness of the regenerative braking system The uncertainty in Cal Poly-Pomona's calculated energy due to the uncertainty in parameters is roughly 10% for the ZEV run, and Penn State's is roughly 20%. Penn State's vehicle includes regenerative braking and Cal Poly-Pomona's does not.

Table 4. Measured and Calculated Energy Use for the 58-km Event (hills included in model)

Measured (kWh)	CarSim (kWh)
7.36±0.74	8.18 +2.09/-1.70

CONCLUSIONS

SIMPLEV 3.0 and CarSim 2.5.4 were used to simulate the performance of two student-assembled HEVs; one run on two 0.2-km maximum effort accelerations, and the other on a 58-km trip that includes hills. Speed and battery power and energy were measured. Input component parameters were estimated, and measured speed was input to the simulations to calculate second-by-second power, which was compared to measurement. Also, measurement uncertainties were estimated and propagated, and their effects on this comparison were estimated.

Careful uncertainty analysis is particularly important to a validation effort, whose goal is to determine how closely a computer simulation approximates actual experimentation. There are many uncertainty sources in an HEV simulation validation because of the complexity of an HEV. Propagating and analyzing these uncertainty is difficult; the work here is quite rough and involved many approximations.

Given the same inputs, SIMPLEV and CarSim make nearly identical power and energy use predictions. Because they use prescribed speeds differently in the basic vehicle dynamics equations, the difference between their power predictions depends on both acceleration and speed. As acceleration or speed (or both) decrease, so does the difference between the programs' predictions.

The programs considered predict ZEV and series-configured HEV energy use to within the significant uncertainties (±50%) of this experiment.

RECOMMENDATIONS

HEV simulation codes must be carefully validated before being trusted. A careful validation includes accurate characterization of each HEV component, using NIST-traceable instruments. Accurate knowledge of the strategy for generator set output control is absolutely critical to an HEV simulation validation. Generator output is generally on the order of vehicle energy use and uncertainties in generator output may dominate the uncertainty of the experiment. The temperature and sensitivies of each component and the DAS must be understood. The DAS must be well insulated from electromagnetic interference, and should ideally be pre-tested in an environment with noisy electromagnetic interference (EMI) sources to determine its sensitivity to EMI.

The validation should include repeated runs on a precisely and accurately measured speed profile probably on a dynamometer, as well as road testing.

REFERENCES

1. Cole, G.H.,"SIMPLEV: A Simple Electric Vehicle Simulation Program Version 2.0", DOE/ID-10293-2, Idaho National Engineering Laboratory, Idaho Falls, Idaho, 1993.5.
2. Marr, W.W., W.J. Walsh, "An Electric/Hybrid Vehicle Model for Establishing Optimal Battery Requirements," Argonne National Labs, Argonne, Illinois, 1985.
3. Slusser, Ron, "ELVEC-An Electric/Hybrid Vehicle Performance Simulation Computer Program," EVC No. 8053, Electric Vehicle Council, Washington, D.C., 1980
4. Wimmer, Robert, "Hybrid 30 Computer Simulation Program for a Fuel Cell/Battery Powered Vehicle Operations Manual," Georgetown University, Washington DC, 1992
5. ANSI/ASME, "Measurement Uncertainty," PTC 19.1-1985, The American Society of Mechanical Engineers, New York, New York, 1985
6. "The AeroVironment Electric/Hybrid Vehicle Simulator CarSim 2.5.4," AeroVironment, Inc., Monrovia, California, 1994
7. Wells, Chester V., "Measurement Uncertainty Analysis: What It Is and How to Do It, with Examples," National Renewable Energy Laboratory, Seminar Presented to the Central Colorado Section of the Precision Measurements Association, Golden, Colorado

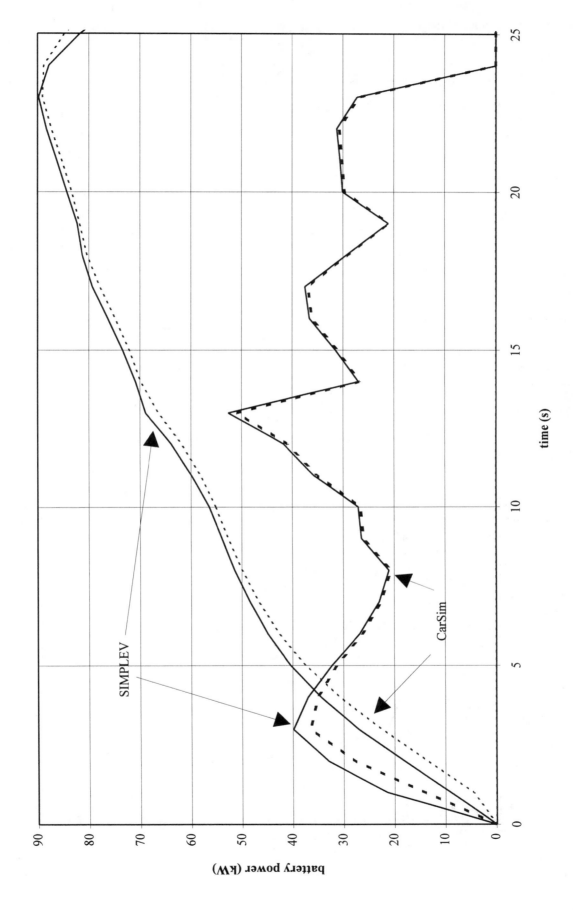

Figure 4. Simulated battery power for Cal Poly-Pomona's 0.2-km maximum effort acceleration, ZEV mode

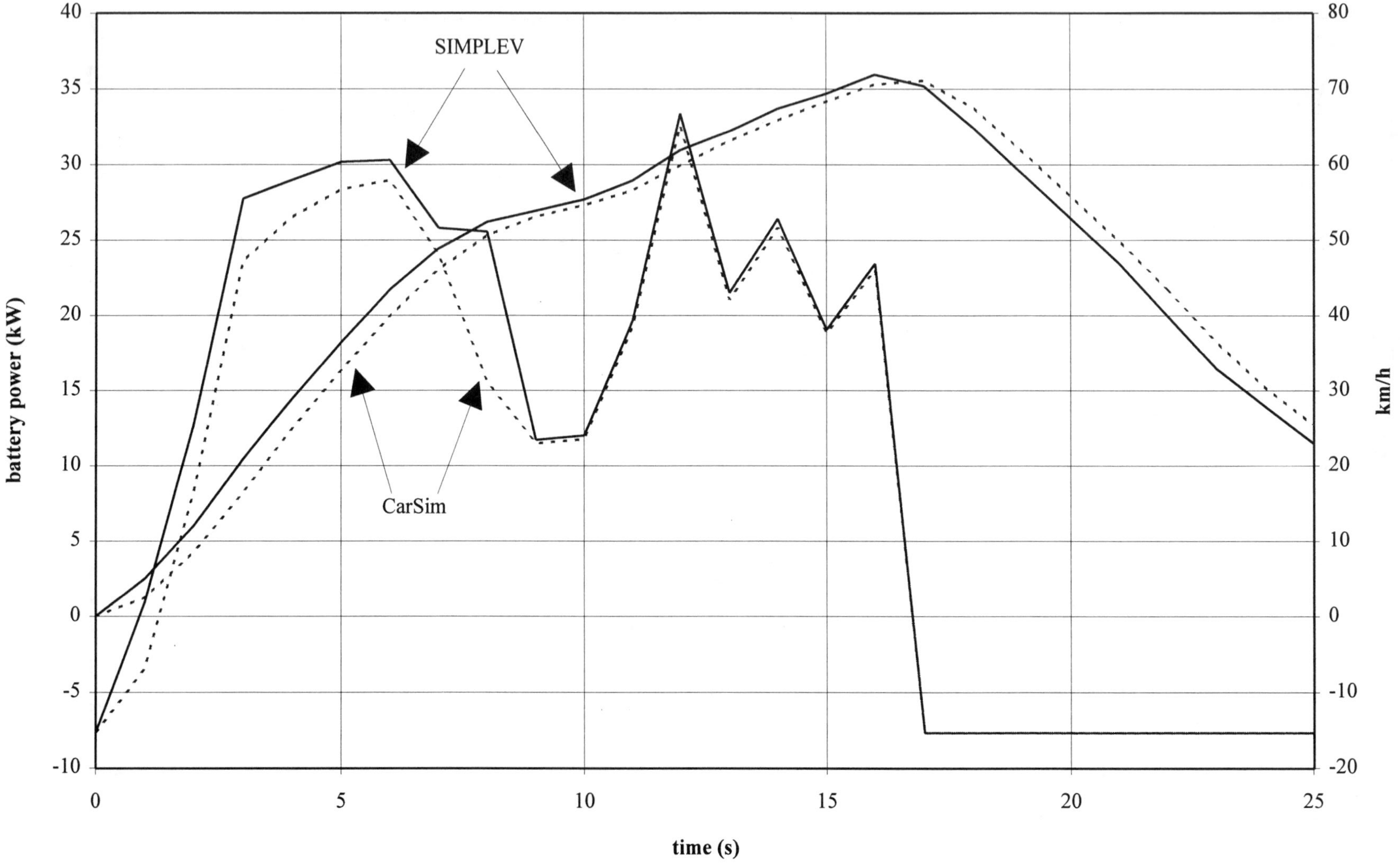

Figure 5. Simulated battery power for Cal Poly-Pomona's 0.2-km maximum effort acceleration, HEV mode

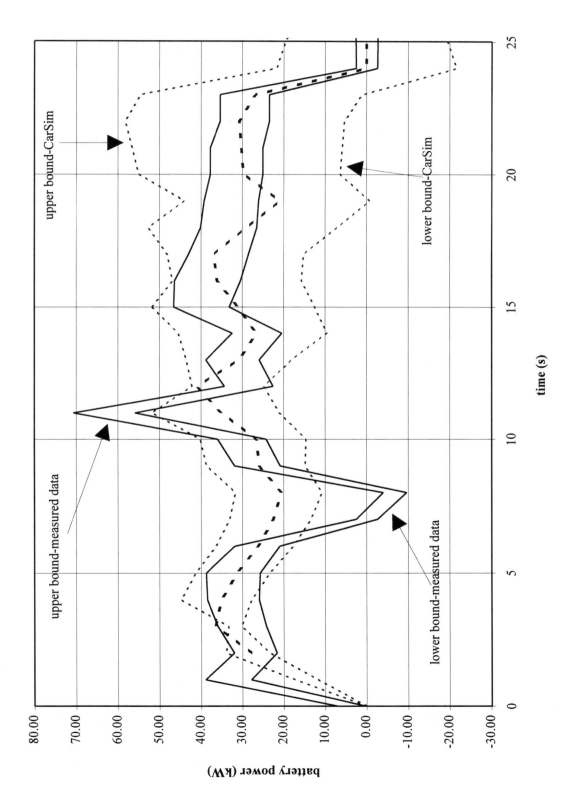

Figure 6. Measured and simulated battery power for Cal Poly-Pomona on 0.2-km maximum effort acceleration, ZEV mode

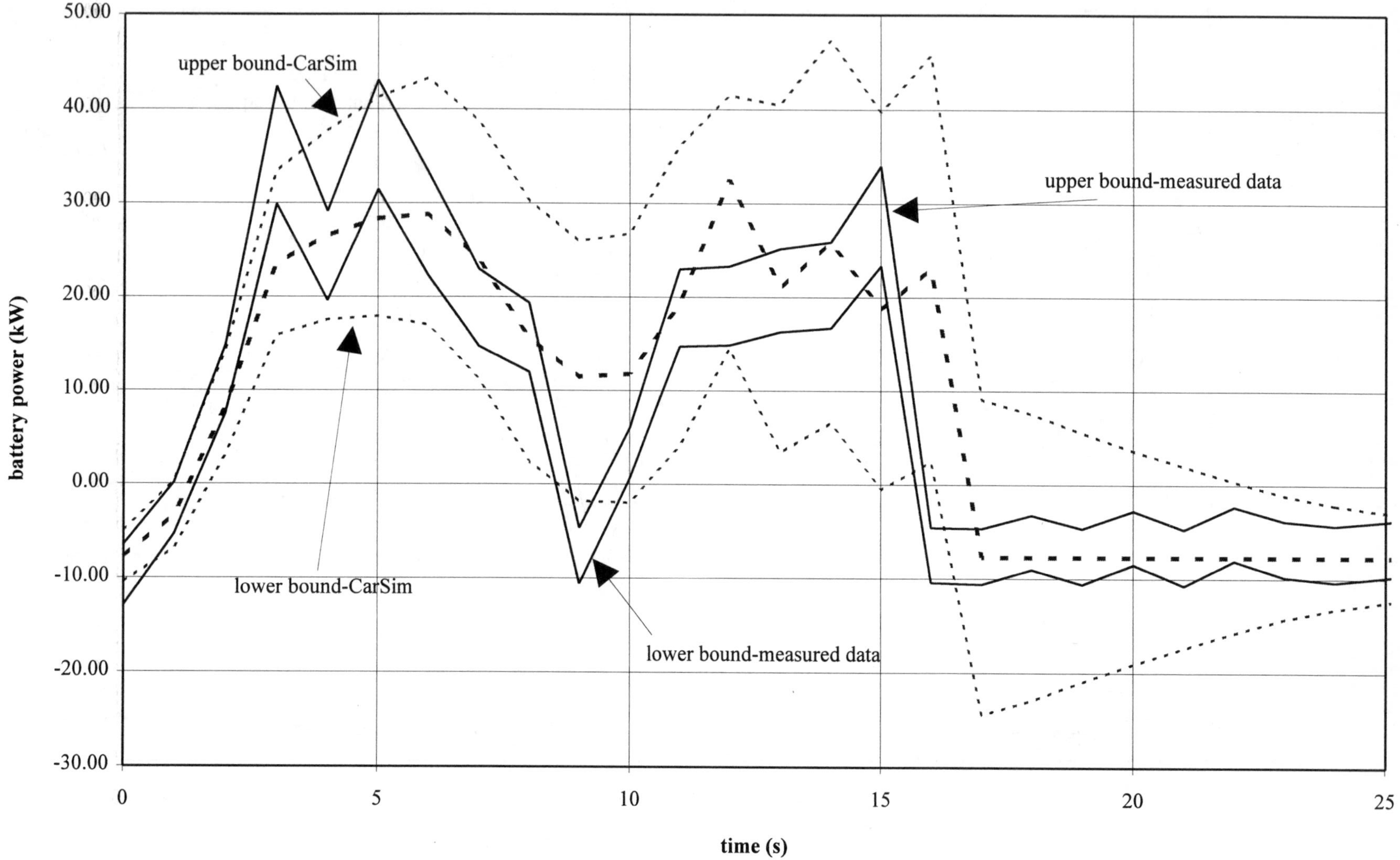

Figure 7. Measured and calculated battery power for Cal Poly-Pomona on 0.2-km maximum effort acceleration, HEV mode

Comparison Between On-Road and Simulated Performance of the KEV Electric Vehicle

C.H. Kim, S. B. Koh, and E. NamGoong
Kia Motors Corp.

ABSTRACT

Vehicle simulation for performance will help develop an electric vehicle that meets goals before making a decision of the type of propulsion system. In this research, performance simulation program has been developed and applied in developing an prototype electric vehicle, KEV. In order to compare the simulation results with that of on-road tests, the KEV was evaluated on the proving ground in terms of driving range at steady speed and on SAE J227a "D" cycle, accelerability, maximum speed, as well as vehicle road energy consumption. The simulation results are in good agreement with on-road test results except vehicle road energy consumption. The factors affecting the performance of the vehicle significantly has been discussed in this paper.

INTRODUCTION

A lot of consideration should be given in selecting a propulsion system for traction motor, controller and battery at the beginning stage of the electric vehicle developments because vehicle performance depends significantly on propulsion system. Electric vehicle simulation is widely used for evaluation of propulsion system before vehicle developments, but the results are usually not in good agreement with on-road test results. The performance predicted by a well-designed simulation would give a guide for the type and performance of the required propulsion system.

In this research, we developed a performance simulation program and applied in developing a converted type of electric vehicle, KEV. Various propulsion systems were evaluated by the performance simulation program at a given vehicle performance goal. A propulsion system showing the nearest performance to the goals was chosen and integrated into the KEV along with other subsystems such as cooling system and DC/DC converter. The on-road test of the KEV was also performed on both the proving ground and the vehicle dynamometer for comparison with the simulated results. The comparison results showed good agreement between both evaluations, and significant factors for more advanced simulation has been discussed.

DEVELOPMENT OF KEV

PERFORMANCE GOALS OF THE KEV – To establish the performance goals for the KEV, considerable efforts were made to acquire the actual vehicle requirements such as the conditions of practical usage, driving condition, present technology and so on. The performance goals of the KEV are as follows:

(1) Driving range of 130km at a speed of 40km/h.
(2) Driving range of 60km at D-Cycle.
(3) Maximum speed of 120km/h.
(4) Acceleration from 0 to 60km/h at 9 seconds.
(5) Percent gradability limit of 30%.
(6) Energy consumption rate of 120wh/km at a speed of 40km/h.

PROPULSION SYSTEM – The performance of a motor for the KEV was found to be about 50kw and 12000rpm as a result of simulations with candidate propulsion system. In order to drive the vehicle with the range of 130 km at 40 km/h, the required capacity of traction battery is about 15.6 kWh. The battery system consists of two parallel connected set of twenty-six lead acid battery (12V, 26Ah) modules in series for a nominal 312V.

INTEGRATING SUBSYSTEMS INTO THE KEV – The KEV was converted with the SEPHIA manufactured by KIA Motors and subsystems like cooling system was designed on the basis of the required cooling power of propulsion and auxiliary system. The capacity of the cooling system was determined from the amount of heat generated from motor and controller as well as DC/DC converter from amount of auxiliary electrical loads imposed by control logic devices, lamps, heater, air conditioner, power window and so on.

FIELD PERFORMANCE TEST OF KEV

The test and evaluation of the KEV for driving range, maximum speed, accelerability and vehicle road energy consumption were conducted on the proving ground. SAE J227a "D" cycle test was also performed on the vehicle dynamometer. Data logger, portable computer, non-contact velocity and other necessary sensors were placed on the vehicle. These measuring instruments were powered by an additional battery. The test vehicle weight was 1,781kg including one driver, one passenger and measuring instruments.

RANGE AT STEADY SPEED – The purpose of this test is to determine the maximum range of an electric vehicle on a level road at steady speeds. The test was conducted at the speeds of 40 and 80 km/h. Driving range is calculated separately from the distance driven at the speeds within ±5% compared to that of initially programmed. Full charge of traction battery was used and the tests were done until the terminal voltage of the battery indicates that below 5% of nominal voltage.

Figure 1 shows the KEV driving on the proving ground for on-road performance test. The tested driving range is 136km at 40km/h and 61km at 80km/h. Less driving range at 80km/h compared to that at 40km/h originates from the fact that road-load losses are larger at higher speed and less capacity of battery is available at higher discharge rate.

SAE J227a "D" CYCLE – This test aims at determining the maximum range traveled and energy consumption of the vehicle when operated

Figure 1. The KEV driving on the proving ground for performance test.

on a level surface in the definite repeatable driving cycle(1). This test provides more actual driving condition so that the result may indicate driving range in urban driving situations. This test was also conducted on the chassis dynamometer. The actuator was installed on the accelerator to follow the speed schedule. The wind generator was placed in front of the vehicle and realizes the wind with the progress of the speed schedule. Figure 2 shows the KEV under testing on the chassis dynamometer.

The test results indicate a driving range of 51km and 10kwh energy consumed from the battery over a total of 30 driving cycles.

MAXIMUM SPEED – This test is for measuring maximum vehicle speed on a level road. In general the maximum speed is determined at the speed corresponding to the maximum wheel propulsion power, which is equal to the road-load power. However, if the maximum wheel power is over the road-load power at all range of vehicle speed, then the maximum speed is determined by the maximum rotation speed of the motor and the specific power of the battery.

This test was performed repeatedly at the full charge of traction battery on the proving ground and resulted in 123km/h. The speed limit was

Figure 2. The KEV under SAE J227a "D" cycle test on chassis dynamometer.

proved to be constrainted by the maximum rotation speed of the motor, 12000rpm.

ACCELERABILITY - This test provides the maximum acceleration the vehicle can achieve on a level road. Accelerability is governed mainly by the power of motor and battery. Tests for 40km/h, 60km/h, 80km/h and 100km/h were conducted 5 times each on the proving ground. The results are 5.23sec for 40km/h, 8.55sec for 60km/h, 13.61sec for 80km/h and 21.32sec for 100km/h.

ROAD ENERGY CONSUMPTION - The purpose of this test is to determine the power and energy consumed at varying vehicle speed to overcome aerodynamic drag and rolling resistance. The test provides the most economic speed for the vehicle. The test was performed at speeds stepped by 10km/h from 20km/h to 100km/h on the proving ground to measure driving range and energy discharged from battery. The discharged energy divided by the range results in road energy consumption as indicated in Table 1. The most economic energy consumption is 118wh/km at 60km/h, which indicates the most economic speed for the KEV. The results are mostly related to the motor

efficiency at a given revolution and road-load losses.

The summarization of on-road testing results of the KEV is indicated in Table 2.

Table 1 - Vehicle Road Energy Consumption

Speed (km/h)	Discharged Energy (kwh)	Energy Consumption (wh/km)
20	0.25	150
30	0.32	133
40	0.44	133
50	0.52	129
60	0.58	118
70	0.84	145
80	1.10	167
90	1.30	193
100	1.60	215

Table 2 - Summary of On-Road Testing Results

	On-Road Test	Remarks
Range at Steady Speed	136km @40km/h 61km @80km/h	PG
D-Cycle Range	51km @10kwh	CD
Maximum Speed	123km/h	PG
Accelerability	5.23sec to 40km/h 8.55sec to 60km/h 13.6sec to 80km/h 21.3sec to 100km/h	PG
Energy Consumption Rate	Most Economic 118wh/km@60km/h	PG

PG : Proving Ground
CD : Chassis Dynamometer

COMPARISON BETWEEN FIELD PERFORMANCE AND SIMULATED PERFORMANCE

To verify usefulness of performance simulation program for propulsion system in designing stage, it is required that the simulated performance is in good agreement with the on-road tested performance. A series of comparison between on-road performance and simulated performance was made.

The specifications of the KEV such as rolling resistance coefficient, aerodynamic resistance coefficient, tire radius, gear ratio, projected frontal area as well as transmission efficiency were employed in this simulation. Maximum torque versus revolution and efficiency map were considered for motor. In addition maximum power and available capacity as a function of discharge for battery were also considered. Power consumed by auxiliary components through DC/DC converter was assumed to be constant.

DRIVING RANGE – Driving range is dominantly influenced by the capacity of battery which varies with load condition. Figure 3 revealed the available capacity of the tested battery with discharging power, which decreased exponentially with increased discharging power. The higher the vehicle speed, the larger power was required and the available energy from the battery with the power was reduced. Bench tests for the variation of battery capacity were conducted under a given load condition and the results were interpolated through the power required ranging from 0kw to 45kw with the speed as shown Figure 3. The driving ranges simulated with vehicle speed are shown in Figure 4. It was assumed that steady power of 700 watts was being consumed by auxiliary components. The difference between the simulated and the tested driving range were revealed to be about 9%. It may be considered that the capacity of battery and the direction of wind are major effects on the driving range.

SAE J227a "D" CYCLE – In the driving schedule of this test, a cycle consists of five regions of acclereration, cruise, coast, brake, and idle. To achieve the simulated driving range, the energy consumed during driving at each region per cycle was firstly calculated. The number of driving cycles was obtained from dividing the available energy of the battery by the sum of energy consumed during a cycle. The available capacity has been approximated by using the battery characteristics in Figure 3, supposing that the average power is consumed during a cycle as a steady load. The available capacity of the battery is approximated to be about 11.3kwh. The number of driving cycles is 35 and the driving range is 54.6km. The results revealed that the simulated driving range is in good agreement

with that tested, 51km. More accurate simulation can be obtained after consideration of energy flowing to the auxiliary components and characteristics of the battery.

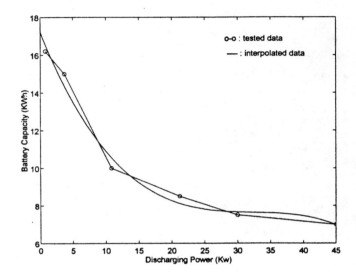

Figure 3. The characteristics of the battery capacity versus steady discharged power

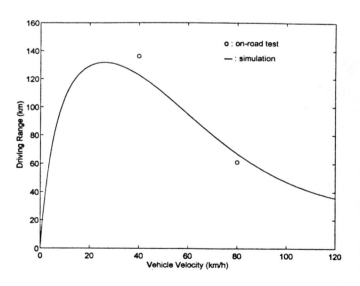

Figure 4. Comparison of driving range at steady speed.

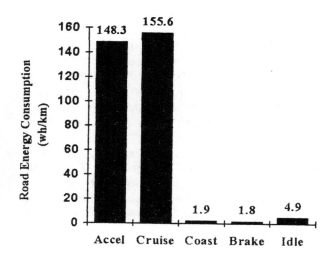

Figure 5. Energy consumed during each region per cycle

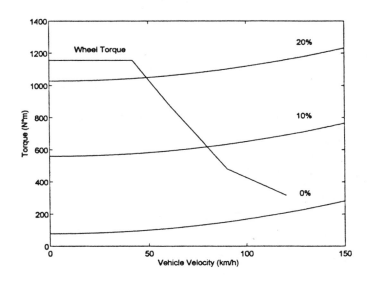

Figure 6. The maximum torque of motor and road-load curves versus speed.

MAXIMUM SPEED - The wheel torque of motor is greater than that of the road-load required on the 0% grade at the whole range of speed as shown in Figure 6. This indicates that the maximum speed of vehicle is determined by the maximum rotation speed of the motor which in this case is 12000rpm. The maximum speed simulated is 120km/h and in good agreement with on-road tested results of 123km/h. The difference may be originated from the road conditions such as wind and rolling resistance.

ACCELERABILITY - The vehicle is accelerated by the motor power remaining after road-load losses are taken into account. Therefore accelerability is governed dominantly by the capability of the motor. A series of comparison between the simulated and the on-road tested results was made. As can be seen in Figure 7, the simulation of elapsed time to given speed is good agreement with results of on-road test.

ROAD ENERGY CONSUMPTION - The simulated road energy consumption of vehicle is obtained from dividing the power consumed for the periods of driving by vehicle speed. That is related with total efficiency of the vehicle and power consumed by auxiliary components. As indicated in Figure 8, the simulated results show differences as compared with that of on-road test, but the similar trend has been shown. More precise definition of road condition would reduce the difference between the results. It may be thought that the lowest road energy consumption was revealed at the speeds between 40km/h and 60km/h.

Table 3. shows the summary of the results from simulation and on-road tests.

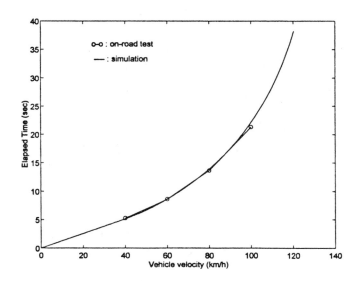

Figure 7. Comparison of accelerability

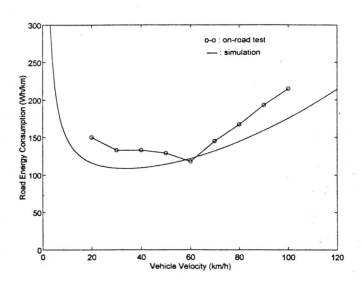

Figure 8. Comparison of vehicle road energy

CONCLUSION

Performance simulation program developed and applied in the propulsion system was employed for developing a prototype electric vehicle. The performance goals have been simulated and a set of propulsion system is found to meet our goals with the help of simulation program.

A series of comparison between simulated performance and on-road performance indicated that the program can be employed for on-road performance and it can be used as a tool to design a electric vehicle. Moreover it was discovered that the differences resulted from comparison are mainly caused by the poor-defined characteristics of battery and slightly by the road-load conditions and auxiliary consumed energy.

Well-defined characteristics of battery and analysis of energy flow from battery to each components will make it possible to design better simulation program.

REFERENCES

1. Electric Vehicle Test Procedure - SAE J227a, SAE Recommended Practice.

Table 3 - Correlation of Simulation and On-Road Performance

		KEV Goal	Simulation	On-Road test
Range at Steady Speed (km)	40km/h	130	122	136
	80km/h		67	61
D-Cycle Range (km)		60	55	51
Maximum Speed (km/h)		120	120	123
Accelerability (sec)	40km/h		5.1	5.2
	60km/h	9	8.6	8.6
	80km/h		13.9	13.6
	100km/h		22.3	21.3
Energy Consumption Rate (wh/km)	40km/h	120	110	133
	60km/h		122	118
	80km/h		145	167
	100km/h		176	215